GILLIAN TINDALL

The Tunnel Through Time

A New Route for an Old London Journey

VINTAGE

3 5 7 9 10 8 6 4 2

Vintage
20 Vauxhall Bridge Road,
London SW1V 2SA

Vintage is part of the Penguin Random House group of companies
whose addresses can be found at global.penguinrandomhouse.com.

Penguin
Random House
UK

First published in Vintage in 2017
First published in hardback by Chatto & Windus in 2016

penguin.co.uk/vintage

A CIP catalogue record for this book is available from the British Library

ISBN 9780099587798

Printed and bound by Clays Ltd, St Ives plc

Penguin Random House is committed to a sustainable future
for our business, our readers and our planet. This book is made
from Forest Stewardship Council® certified paper.

MIX
Paper from
responsible sources
FSC
www.fsc.org   FSC® C018179

We have not an abiding city, but we seek after the city that is to come.
From Paul's Epistle to the Hebrews, chapter 13, verse 14

Remembering how generations of men and women come and go, and how swiftly the lingering memories of their lives follow them, one cannot help looking with some degree of interest upon the old houses in which they were born, lived, and died. We fancy that the walls which echoed their first wailing cry, and caught, in the hushed, awful silence, the sound of their last breath, deaf, dumb and blind though they are, must cherish remembrance of such daily doings; of loving, hating, rejoicing and grieving, hoping and fearing; of hard struggles and terrible failures, or glorious victories.
From an editorial in *The Builder*, 11 September 1875

Yerkes, the projector of the new Charing Cross, Euston and Hampstead electric underground, said to me that in spite of the opposition which he meets at every turn he proposes to go through with it . . . He predicted to me that a generation hence London will be completely transformed; that people will think nothing of living twenty or more miles from town, owing to electrified trains. He also thinks that the horse omnibus is doomed. Twenty years hence, he says, there will be no horse omnibuses in London. Although he is a very shrewd man, I think he is a good deal of a dreamer.
From R. D. Blumenfeld's *R.D.B.'s Diary*, 6 October 1900

These works, like all alterations and repairs, will give employment to many, and be a nuisance to others, as long as they are being constructed; but when the mess is cleared up, and the new channels are thrown open, a sense of comfort and relief will be felt throughout the vast general traffic of London.
The concluding words of John Hollingshead's
Underground London, 1862

Contents

Contents

List of Maps

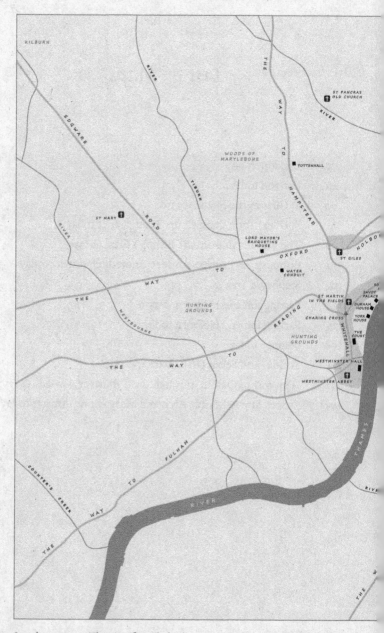

KILBURN

RIVER

THE WAY TO HAMPSTEAD

ST PANCRAS OLD CHURCH

RIVER

EDGWARE

WOODS OF MARYLEBONE

TOTTENHALL

TIBURN

ST MARY

ROAD

LORD MAYOR'S BANQUETING HOUSE

OXFORD

HOLBORN

ST GILES

RIVER

WATER CONDUIT

SAVOY PALACE

WAY

TO

ST MARTIN IN THE FIELDS

DURHAM HOUSE

THE

READING

CHARING CROSS

YORK HOUSE

HUNTING GROUNDS

WESTBOURNE

HUNTING GROUNDS

WHITEHALL

THE COURT

THE

WAY

TO

WESTMINSTER HALL

WESTMINSTER ABBEY

FULHAM

TO

THE

COUNTER'S CREEK

RIVER

THAMES

RIVER

THE WAY

THE W

London, *c.* 1550. The significantly built-up area is shown in darker grey

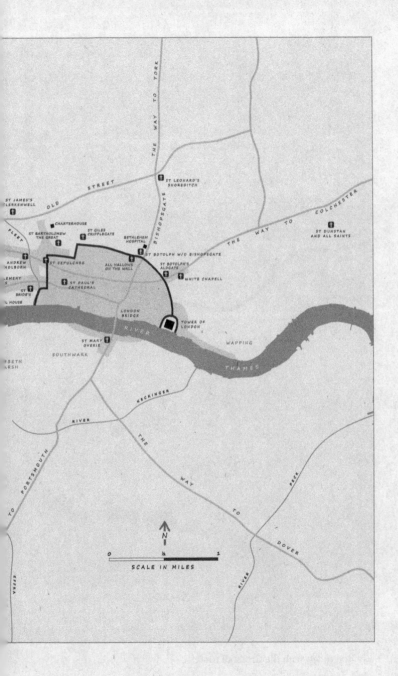

THE WAY TO YORK

OLD STREET

THE WAY TO COLCHESTER

ST JAMES'S CLERKENWELL

CHARTERHOUSE

ST BARTHOLOMEW THE GREAT

ST GILES CRIPPLEGATE

ST LEONARD'S SHOREDITCH

BETHLEHEM HOSPITAL

ST DUNSTAN AND ALL SAINTS

FLEET

ANDREW HOLBORN

ST SEPULCHRE

BISHOPSGATE

ST BOTOLPH W/O BISHOPSGATE

ALL HALLOWS ON THE WALL

ST BOTOLPH'S ALDGATE

EMENT

ST PAUL'S CATHEDRAL

WHITE CHAPELL

ST BRIDE'S

L HOUSE

LONDON BRIDGE

TOWER OF LONDON

RIVER

WAPPING

ST MARY OVERIE

THAMES

SOUTHWARK

BETH RSH

NECKINGER

RIVER

THE WAY TO PORTSMOUTH

PECK

THE WAY TO DOVER

EFFRA

RIVER

N

0   ½   1

SCALE IN MILES

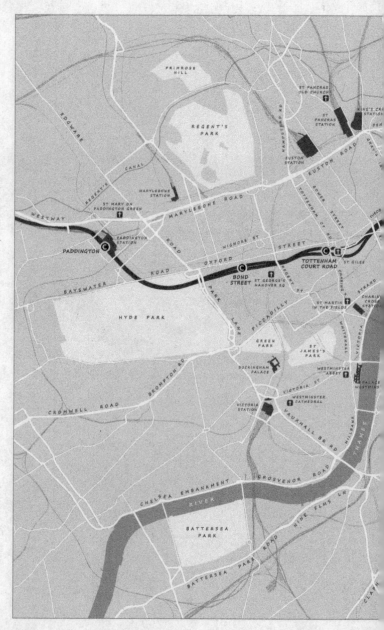

London today, with the Crossrail route

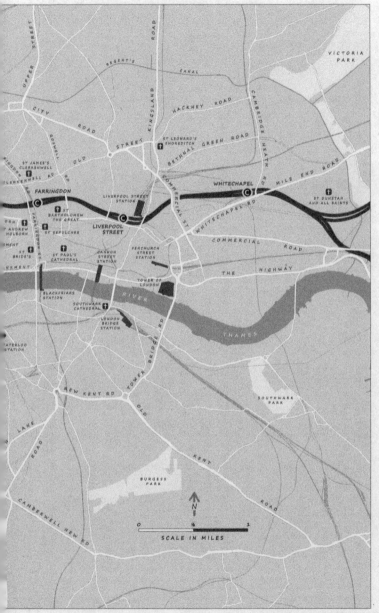

VICTORIA PARK

REGENT'S CANAL

UPPER STREET

CITY ROAD

ROSWELL

KINGSLAND ROAD

HACKNEY ROAD

OLD STREET

ST LEONARD'S SHOREDITCH

BETHNAL GREEN ROAD

CAMBRIDGE HEATH RD

MILE END ROAD

ST JAMES'S CLERKENWELL

CLERKENWELL RD

FARRINGDON

LIVERPOOL STREET STATION

WHITECHAPEL

COMMERCIAL ST

ST DUNSTAN AND ALL SAINTS

ORN

ANDREW HOLBORN

ST BARTHOLOMEW THE GREAT

ST SEPULCHRE

LIVERPOOL STREET

WHITECHAPEL RD

MENT

ST BRIDE'S

ST PAUL'S CATHEDRAL

CANNON STREET STATION

FENCHURCH STREET STATION

COMMERCIAL ROAD

NEMENT

THE HIGHWAY

BLACKFRIARS STATION

RIVER

TOWER OF LONDON

SOUTHWARK CATHEDRAL

LONDON BRIDGE STATION

THAMES

WATERLOO STATION

NEW KENT RD

TOWER BRIDGE RD

OLD

SOUTHWARK PARK

LANE

ROAD

KENT

BURGESS PARK

ROAD

CAMBERWELL NEW RD

N

0   ½   1

SCALE IN MILES

INTRODUCTION

The new Crossrail underground line, which has been built across central London even as I have been writing this account, is, for the greater part, invisible. It is the biggest building project in Europe today, yet surface evidence for it is limited to a small number of deeply excavated sites that have opened up in the heart of London like bubbling geyser holes in a volcanic region. When completed, the new long-distance line, re-baptised the Elizabeth line, is designed to carry passengers from areas outside London to key points in the City and the West End, bypassing intermediate inner-London stops. The great scheme has been on planners' desks for several decades, through propitious and unpropitious seasons, but by 2012 construction was well under way and on time, with tunnelling and earth-shifting machines moving very slowly but inexorably, like mythic underground monsters, from separate directions to their final meeting point beneath Farringdon on the western edge of the City.

Yet as a route tunnelled out by machines boring deep under central London, Crossrail is not essentially different in kind from the other tube lines, which began to be constructed in the final years of the nineteenth century. In the Edwardian era, when money for public works was easily found, the popular journalist George R. Simms wrote:

> To the engineer of the tube railway, as to the passengers who travel through it, the buildings overhead are a matter of supreme indifference. Eighty or a hundred feet beneath the surface, under the foundations of the houses, the bed of the river, the gas and water pipes, and the older underground railways, he worms his way through the earth, leaving a section of iron tube behind him at every yard of his advance.[1]

That remains as true today, and the photograph that accompanied this article, of a great, round tunnelling shield attended by workmen with moustaches and pickaxes, depicts essentially the same technology that is being used for Crossrail.

It was the development of electric traction which made the Tube as we know it possible. Before that, the trains were steam-powered, so their underground course could only be a series of relatively short and shallow tunnels punctuated with openings through which the sulphurous smoke could excitingly escape – evoking shocked speculations about the Underworld from impressionable Londoners. Because of this, for the Metropolitan line and also for the District line which grew from it, the cut-and-cover method of construction was used. The whole surface of the route over which the line would run was dug up, usually following an existing roadway to keep demolition of buildings to a minimum, the line was laid in the bottom of the cutting and then an arch was built over the top with the roadway restored above. But in the 1890s the possibility of letting electric trains run for miles in deep-down tunnels without obvious communication with the upper air changed all this, and finally severed subterranean trains' connection with the surface railways.

Contrary to various myths and expectations that have attended its construction, Crossrail does not run significantly deeper than the existing tube lines, nor much faster – except in that it will stop at fewer stations. Paddington, Bond Street, Tottenham Court Road, Farringdon, Liverpool Street and Whitechapel are its core central route. Beyond Whitechapel, at Stepney Green in the East End, it divides into two, one branch going to the new docklands development at Canary Wharf and eventually to Woolwich, and the other via Stratford out to Ilford and finally to Shenfield. Most of this latter branch runs in the open air over pre-existing tracks.

The same is true of the westward extension from Paddington, which runs over established lines through suburbs such as Ealing and Southall, with a spur line to Heathrow airport, and then on to Slough and Maidenhead. There has been, as I write, an announcement that it will be carried on as far as Reading. Although it has always been understood that Crossrail must link the City with Heathrow (indeed, some people seem to be under the illusion that this alone is what it is for), the western part of the line has been the most volatile and uncertain in the planning.

The Crossrail stations, most of which will be alongside the hundred-year-old tube stations or amalgamated with them, are designed to be lighter and far more spacious than the traditional rabbit-warren tube stop. However, they will not have the above-ground walk-in grandeur of some of these. Instead, the new ticket halls are being inserted as 'boxes' not far below the surface of the ground, and it is the excavation for these, rather than the tunnelling itself, that is giving archaeologists extraordinary and probably unrepeatable opportunities for careful examination of what lies there before it is finally displaced, opportunities eagerly taken up by the team of the Museum of London.

Such digs call up once again a question that is always there, both in waking life and in our dreams, concerning the nature and identity of place itself. What do we mean by 'a place'? To what extent can a location still be said to 'be' the place that it was long ago, when a boggy field has been replaced by a Georgian square or by Victorian warehouses and then again by glass towers, and when even the earth of the original field has been dispersed to other sites as landfill? Yet how can it *not* be the same place when we uncover, beneath the sewers, gas pipes, water mains and electricity and telephone lines, the remains of the conduits our ancestors built to contain London's streams and the clay pipes of men who worked in holes in the earth, just as several thousand orange-jacketed men have been doing today? Much of what lies beneath is the buried detritus of what, once, was human life in the light of the day and in all its varied busyness.

This book makes figurative historical excavations on several of the oldest and most significant sites through which the brand-new Elizabeth–Crossrail is passing. Rather, I should say, under which it is passing, for though the stations break through to the surface the line itself runs at a depth of thirty metres and thus below the accreted two thousand years' residue of what has been there before. Archaeology disinters layers of actual matter; one may also disinter the layers of different human life that walked where many of our streets, however altered in appearance, still run today. These people spoke the names of ancient places that now belong to our squares and our tube stations. They suffered the cycle of the seasons as we do; they ate, drank, laughed, worked, prayed, hoped, dreamed and despaired in what are essentially, despite enormous physical and social changes, the same spaces we occupy now. They also made some of the same regular journeys.

To follow these journeys and their staging points over many centuries is to move chronologically as well as through physical space. A true account cannot always run across London in one direction, nor yet tell one continuous story from the Norman Conquest to the twenty-first century. Each of my chapters has its own central subject, whether that subject is a past traveller, the gradual unfolding of transport, the presence everywhere of dead Londoners or the transformation over hundreds of years of what are now key places along the Crossrail journey. A handful of these places have such long and changeful histories that I have devoted more than one chapter to each. In this way, the journey in space across London also becomes a series of journeys through time.

CHAPTER I

Coming into London

People were travelling in and out of London long before there was any question of railways, long before horse-buses, stagecoaches or the earliest bumpy hackney coaches made their appearance. Five hundred years ago the rich, or moderately well-to-do, rode in and out on horseback, or drove a horse with a laden cart behind if that was part of their trade. Everyone else walked.

Some of the main routes in and out of London are extremely old. Watling Street, which is thought to be prehistoric, is followed by the present-day Edgware Road. The way eastwards from Aldgate in the direction of Colchester, which is today a major artery through the East End, was an important Roman road, and so was Ermin Street which ran north from the City through the Bishop's gate and up to Shoreditch, destined for Lincoln (where a Roman arch across it still survives) and eventually York. York Way itself, running north from King's Cross, is another ancient route to the same destination. The 'way to Oxford', leading west from St Giles-in-the-Fields, was also the Roman road to Silchester on the route to the south-west, and equally old is the way south from London Bridge in the direction of the English Channel.

It is a measure of the persistence of geographical habits, through time and urban change, that the route chosen for Crossrail follows some of the same ancient paths, coming into central London from the west and leaving it again east of the City, or the same journey in the opposite direction.

* * *

One day in 1826, eleven years after the end of the Napoleonic Wars and another eleven before Victoria would start her long reign as Queen, a boy decided to keep a diary of his daily comings and goings across London.

Comings and goings was what his days often amounted to, for John Thomas Pocock, who was then not quite twelve years old, was acting much of the time as his father's messenger boy. Mr Pocock was a builder and he and his wife, with several children younger than John, lived in a house that he had himself designed and built, along with others, in Kilburn, north-west of Paddington. The pretty fields of Kilburn were not yet part of London, and they must have seemed an excellent prospect for property development in the building boom that followed the wars, but that boom had collapsed by the mid-1820s with disastrous results for a number of banks and for the optimistic Pocock and his kind. The building of a station at Paddington lay ten years in the future, for railways had not yet come. The Bristol-to-London line that became the Great Western was only a dream in the mind of Isambard Kingdom Brunel, and when it did arrive the hilly land to the north of it was only gradually developed.

When his son's diary¹ begins, Pocock had rented out his previous offices in the City and was working from home. He was being helped out financially by a prosperous coal-merchant brother, dealing in coal then being a lucrative and continually expanding trade; but because of unpaid loans raised on land he had bought but which now lay fallow, Pocock was at several moments in imminent danger of being consigned to a debtors' prison. (This alarming fact is only referred to in the diary in code, as 'Banco Regis' – the King's Bench – and by manly references to 'blackguards' who wished Father ill.)

John Thomas seems to have been temporarily removed from school during the family's financial crisis, and left entirely at fourteen, unable (he said later) 'to dictate a letter or spell with any accuracy'. As the eldest boy still living at home it was his job to come and go between Kilburn, Fenchurch Street where there was rent to be collected, St Bride's Wharf off Fleet Street² where the uncle had his coal business, and various other places in the City, Southwark, Ratcliffe Highway in the east, and elsewhere. Huge numbers of men employed in the City then walked to work every day, but few of them would have lived anywhere as far off as Kilburn. John also made frequent trips for his mother, walking the one and a half miles to Paddington village, the nearest place where there were a few shops and sometimes a market. In the past the Pococks had kept a horse and gig, but that had now been given up. Money for the Kilburn-to-City coach could not often be spared either, unless Mrs Pocock was visiting one of her London relations, nor yet would it be for the new omnibus, the very first one, that was started by Shillibeer in 1829 to run from a large inn not far from Paddington as far as the Bank in the heart of the City. So it was on foot that young John made his expeditions, apparently cheerfully, since he enjoyed playing a remarkably grown-up role for his age much more than he enjoyed school at Regent's Park during the periods he was sent back there.

A typical set of entries runs:

Ap.9 [1829]. To the City for my father. Took an advertisement concerning our bricks to the 'Morning Advertiser' office, Strand, and then went to the Wharf and to Bouverie Street.

Ap.11. In the afternoon I went to Walham Green calling upon Marshall concerning our bricks. It rained on my return from Notting Hill home.[3]

Ap.14. To Liverpool Street. Mr Wright and myself went to Wesley's, who was from home. I am 'to call again to-morrow'. Went to Price's and to Fred Gurney on my road to Ratcliffe Highway, saw Mr Holmes and walked home.

To this last entry he added, unusually, 'very fatigued', which is not surprising considering that he had quite recently had a feverish cold and a 'troublesome cough' bad enough to elicit a bottle of medicine from a friendly doctor neighbour. In general, he evidently enjoyed walking for its own sake. He took trips out beyond the built-up area for pleasure as well as duty, and must sometimes have walked ten or fifteen miles a day.

Feb 3, Sunday [1828]. From after breakfast Josiah [the teenage son of Mr Wright of Liverpool Street] and I took a walk, and, passing Shoreditch Church (where my 2 poor sisters are buried who died in one day of Hooping Cough shortly before my birth) we took the Tottenham Road and reached Lower Edmonton before we turned homewards. Here, near the Cross, Josiah went to School. The only part of the road which took my fancy was Stamford Hill, which is very picturesque.

Another time he and Josiah went on an expedition east of London to Bow, and then across by ferry at Greenwich into Kent: 'It must have been easily thirty miles. Josiah, like myself, is a rare pedestrian'.

John Thomas once made a two-day march to Hastings, where his father was currently 'ill and lonely', surprising even his family who had not imagined he could do the seventy miles in so short a time. It is as if he simply set Shanks's pony going and continued without thoughts of effort or boredom, though he did admit to his diary on this occasion that at the end of the marathon first day his right foot was hurting.

Although so many of his journeys took him into the narrow lanes and wharves of a City that was still a packed trading and manufacturing hub, his initial trek from Kilburn down south-eastwards to arrive in Holborn, the Fleet valley and thence to London's heart, began in unmade country lanes. The Grand Union and the brand-new Regent's Canal branching off it still ran through fields north of Paddington. When John was sent to order some potatoes at Shepherd's Bush he 'crossed a winding brook 6 times . . . much splashed'. In the winter of 1829 'a beautiful stag, hunted by His Majesty's hounds and about 60 riders of distinction', swam across the Grand Union and was finally taken at bay inside the open doors of Paddington church. Sheep and cattle in huge quantities were still driven through London streets en route to Smithfield market not far from St Paul's. Chickens and geese were sold alive on street corners. But this was the final era of these customs. By the mid-century, the seven-hundred-year-old habit of slaughter right on the edge of the City was due to be moved to a

purpose-built enclosure up the Caledonian Road. At the same period
rows and rows of stuccoed villas, such as Pocock senior had hoped to
build in the fields off the Edgware Road, were, after all, beginning to
go up at a relentless rate there, and all round what had been London's
country rim.

John Thomas Pocock did not remain in London to see this sooty
transformation. In 1830, when his father had died and he himself
was not yet sixteen, he was apprenticed to a surgeon who, like many
other British subjects at the time, was setting out for a new life in the
New World. He and the surgeon were initially aiming at Australia,
but the route in those days was round the Cape. They made landfall
in South Africa, and this turned out to be the permanent destination.
John was not to see his homeland again for over forty years, by
which time the centuries during which the roads and paths of
England were perpetually sprinkled with trudging figures had
finally come to an end. The hugely expanded mass of London was
now ringed by mainline railways and criss-crossed by horse-bus
routes. In the 1860s the first Underground line, the Metropolitan,
had been constructed.

The arrival of this Underground, Crossrail's first and most momentous
predecessor, made a huge difference to the lives of ordinary Londoners.
Had it been there in John's boyhood, it would have transformed his
childhood experiences – though possibly his knowledge of London
would have been less intimate and less passionately experienced. For it
was decided that the line should run from the Great Western Railway's
new terminus at Bishop's Bridge, Paddington, which had opened in
1838,[4] cross beneath the Edgware Road, and then follow the line of
the mid-eighteenth-century New Road (Marylebone and Euston Road)
past Euston and King's Cross stations (opened respectively in 1837 and
1854) before turning southwards down the valley of the Fleet to what
became Farringdon station on the edge of the City. In other words, the
line followed by the Metropolitan was an updated version of the very
old route coming from the north-west down to London proper, the

The new Metropolitan Railway near Farringdon, 1860s

route linking Watling Street with the one-time Roman city – our City of today.

Before the New Road attempted – not entirely successfully – to create a bypass for London and thus to get the herds of animals on the hoof out of the older streets, the traditional route ran a little further south. It is this very ancient route, 'the old path, where the good way is', that John Pocock, going to and from his home and his various places of business, would usually have taken. Making its way from Paddington down to Tyburn, the western extremity of St Marylebone parish, last outpost of anything that in the sixteenth or seventeenth centuries could have been regarded as London and the last place before their eyes for many felons executed there, the route then turned eastwards along the 'way to and from Oxford', present-day Oxford Street. On reaching the present junction of Charing Cross and Tottenham Court Roads – where a road took off north to Hampstead – the 'way from Paddington' then launched into a curve and became the High Street of St Giles-in-the-Fields, a settlement established from the early Middle Ages. For hundreds of years, much of the traffic of all kinds entering London from the west made its tumultuous way through this village street, past what became the parish church.

After St Giles the name of the road changed to High Holborn, where it curved its way south-east between fields and where, by 1600, a few runs of houses had begun to ribbon-develop it. It finally arrived at Holborn bars, where London's jurisdiction began,[5] and hence to St Andrew's and Holborn Hill.

Since 1868 – the same decade in which the Metropolitan began to transform the lives of Londoners in other ways – the valley has been bridged by Holborn Viaduct. Until then, all travellers, whether on foot, in cart or coach or driving an intransigent herd of beasts, had to descend into the steep gorge of the Fleet river, the 'Town Ditch', and up the other side. From here, narrow Holborn Bridge led to Snow Hill and Newgate on the right, and Cowcross and Smithfield on the left. There were two other equally slim bridges over the valley, one further upstream and another nearer to the Thames, leading to Ludgate Hill and St Paul's (see maps pp. 124–125).

Farringdon Metropolitan station, being established at Cowcross – very near to Smithfield, near to St Bartholomew's and the Charterhouse too, and just outside the line of the one-time walls of the medieval square-mile City – was thus placed on a very ancient site. The ward of Farringdon[6] was already, by then, and remained for centuries, a place of marginal and equivocal activity. It was a venue for markets and riotous assemblies, for fairs and bloody uprisings, for the slaughter of both men and beasts. It was also the district of arrivals and departures. Several of London's most substantial galleried inns there saw huge numbers of coaches in and out each day in John Pocock's time, the high noon of the coaching era before its sudden eclipse by the railways. These same inns under the same venerable names had also received travellers passing in and out of the City for hundreds of years before.

Today, a century and a half since the Metropolitan Railway first adopted a version of the old route into London from the north-west as its own, London's newest tube line is following the same groove. The Metropolitan ran under the New Road, because Euston and King's Cross stations were there already and because the roadway could be used for cut-and-cover. However, the central and most significant section of Crossrail follows instead the time-honoured footprint from Paddington down to Tyburn. Then it runs along the Oxford road to where a remnant of St Giles High Street still survives behind the dominating bulk of the Centre Point skyscraper. After that, it weaves a little through the old Holborn district to avoid a few other deeply rooted modern buildings, passing under the northern part of what we now know as the Covent Garden area, curving under Drury Lane (a very old artery), then a little northwards under Red Lion Square, then slightly southwards again under Gray's Inn gardens that are still green and open, Hatton Garden that is not, and so to its destination not far from the one-time Holborn Bridge.

Thus Crossrail arrives, like the first-ever Underground, at Farringdon. But this station, which spent most of the twentieth century as an antiquated and little-regarded stop on the ageing Metropolitan line, has been substantially enlarged and rebuilt. Its finely

graded mid-nineteenth-century brick arches now shelter a key Crossrail exchange station, where this newest Underground line, the oldest
one, and the overground railway line that now runs from Bedford to
Brighton, all meet. It is also the station designed to serve the Barbican
complex, with a new Farringdon East ticket hall near the fourteenth-
century foundation of the Charterhouse.

The first section of the Metropolitan line, opened in 1863, was so
successful that Farringdon did not remain its terminus for long. Within
a year or two the line had been extended to Moorgate, and that is the
same route that Crossrail is now taking. Crossrail continues on to
Liverpool Street station (which did not yet exist when the Metropolitan
began rolling), thence across Spitalfields to Whitechapel – the City of
London's oldest suburbs – across the Mile End Road and on to Stepney.
This too is an ancient pedestrian route, for people, cattle and goods
coming into London from the east – from Essex and Mersea, from
the Roman town of Colchester and from Harwich, the port at which
ships from the Low Countries traditionally docked. 'Mile End' gets
its name from being one mile from Aldgate, the City's eastern entry.

One may reasonably assume that a long-ago traveller, a medieval
John Pocock, walking eastwards to the far side of the City, or one
coming back west out of the town, did not make his way through the
crowded, close-packed lanes of the City. Unless he had business there,
or wanted to buy a drink of ale or a pie, he would have chosen a circuit just outside the confining walls.[7] Here lay the Moorfields, with
Spitalfields to the east and Finsbury to the west – London's oldest 'green
lung'. By circling in either direction just outside London's high wall,
our medieval traveller, or even an Elizabethan one, could go most of
the way over grass and small footpaths, past trees and 'garden houses',
orchards, drying grounds for washerwomen and grounds where dyers
spread their cloth. There were also burial places, acknowledged or forgotten, including the site of the oldest Jewish cemetery in England,
just north-west of St Giles Cripplegate church, where London Wall
turned a corner at a bastion and the Barbican High Walk turns a corner
today. Jews from the original ghetto outside the walled City had been

laid there from soon after the Norman Conquest to the end of the thirteenth century, when Edward I expelled the community from his kingdom. Part of the site is currently occupied by the City of London Girls School (see maps pp. 80–81).

It is this edge-of-the-City route that Crossrail is taking today, unlike the hundred-year-old Central line, which bores through from St Paul's to the Bank right beneath the City's heart before reaching Liverpool Street. Today, when the City's jurisdiction has long been expanded northwards, well beyond the old Bishop's Gate, up Bishopsgate Without almost to Shoreditch, and when London Wall is principally the name of a thoroughfare dominated by ever-higher glass towers and by the modern fortress of the Barbican Centre, it is not immediately obvious that we are here on an old frontier. But the fact is that Moorgate and Liverpool Street, Crossrail's next stop after Farringdon, both lie significantly over the edge of London's original northern limit. They are on one-time marginal land that was liable to flood, a place of reed beds and wild ducks and of London's longest-buried stream, the Walbrook. We shall return to the Walbrook, for so long nothing but a name attached to a City lane nearer to the Thames, but originally a shaping force of this whole patch of earth beyond the northern wall.

Recent excavations for the new Crossrail ticket hall at Liverpool Street have uncovered traces of a Roman crossing point over the Walbrook along with the seeds of water plants that grew alongside. Not far off have come to light a Roman dagger, with its wood or bone handle rotted away, a sharp brooch-pin for holding a robe or a cloak in place, several Roman coins, Roman hairpins and gaming counters, the remains of iron 'hipposandals' that preceded horseshoes, a medieval key, slightly more recent workshop offcuts of animal bone and ivory, and of course bits of broken pottery. Two Roman burial urns complete with ashes have also appeared, one falling pat into the hands, not of an archaeologist, but of a workman engaged upon the roof of a new sewer – fortunately his reaction was swift and effective.

There are also, as in many other places that were once on the margins of the City, a great many human bones both fragmented and whole, the remains of the innumerable Londoners who trod this way before us. We shall revisit these hosts, for they are all about London, in graveyards both known and utterly vanished, under our busy, careless feet.

Further west in Crossrail's trajectory, out in the one-time fields round Paddington, the human occupation is relatively recent. Dig down deep in most streets or gardens there and you will soon reach unturned London gravel or clay.[8] Whatever long-ago country buildings were scattered in those fields, their foundations did not go very deep, and when the classic London terraced houses began marching over the landscape in the nineteenth century the wholesale digging-out of their semi-basements and the building-up of the roads in front tended to destroy all traces of earlier occupancy down to the Palaeolithic era. But in the City, the old heart of London, and in other long-inhabited places such as St Giles-in-the-Fields, the present-day buildings sit on twenty or more feet of the compacted, churned, reused debris of past habitation. Under soaring modern glass and metal constructions lie figuratively, and sometimes actually, the fragmented bricks of Victorian office blocks and warehouses, eighteenth-century stuccoed terraces, the stones or timbers of earlier houses on the site whether modest cottages or substantial manor houses, below that the compost of Saxon wattle-and-daub dwellings and below that again perhaps a Roman watercourse, shards of a sarcophagus or of a tessellated pavement. Matter can be smashed, burnt, pounded to dust, subsumed into other walls, other floors, used as backfilling for new edifices, but it does not disappear utterly.

CHAPTER II

The Engines of Progress

Over the course of centuries, the endlessly trodden paths were broadened, gouged out into deep troughs and sloughs by the feet of men and horses, made up again with stones and rubble, given some paved sections where they passed through towns, much later improved with sand and gravel, with drainage ditches alongside, and finally with macadam. But before that happened another new element had been introduced into travel. From the beginning of the eighteenth century, in the last years of the last Stuart monarch, Queen Anne, new turnpike roads (toll roads) began to appear. Built on the initiative either of landowners or of special local boards of shareholders set up for the purpose, they were aimed both at making money and at improving life, and they were roads laid out for the first time for wheeled vehicles as much as for travellers on horseback. At the same period the clumsy, jolting, unsprung coaches of the seventeenth century began to be replaced by better-designed ones, which could go faster over the new gravelled turnpike surfaces. The age of the swift stagecoach was born.

The mid-eighteenth-century New Road, running in the fields from Marylebone, past Bloomsbury, to coincide with the top of Gray's Inn Lane at Battle Bridge (our King's Cross) and so on to Islington, where it became the City road leading to Old Street, was originally a turnpike. Two pairs of toll houses still stand on it today at each end of Park Crescent. The plan for the road was opposed by the Duke of Bedford who owned much of Bloomsbury, although it was intended to take London's traffic out of the old lanes of Marylebone and therefore also out of the exclusive new estate he was gradually laying out. Parliament ignored the Duke and approved the road. It achieved its aim to some extent (though many carters and drovers preferred the old route via St Giles for which they did not have to pay) but it also created something which the old, twisting high streets never did: a barrier. The areas immediately north of the New Road, what were to become Camden Town, Somers Town and Pentonville, came to be perceived as separated off from London proper. This was one reason among several why, when these districts began to be developed towards the end of the century, they were not on the whole designed with people of means in mind, but were built up with modest terraced houses on only sixty-year building leases. The New Road thus created a social divide which still persisted a hundred years after its opening. (In Trollope's mid-nineteenth-century political novels to live 'north of the New Road' is felt to lead to social oblivion.) Still today, the sheer busyness of the road, with an urban motorway leading in at one end and a daunting 1970s underpass at the junction with Tottenham Court Road, creates a perceptible step-change between what we look on as central London and the beginning of the vast rest-of-London. It is, logically, where today's Congestion Charge area begins and ends.

In our own time, a main road as a divider of one district from another, a roaring river of noise and ceaselessly moving vehicles, has become so common that we do not usually realise the nature of the townscape that has been destroyed. Many of inner London's older streets, which were for hundreds of years places of meeting, markets, public forums onto which houses happily faced, have become dividers, perilous and discouraging to cross. Other, newer arteries, constructed as nineteenth-century improvements, such as Farringdon Road, Clerkenwell Road, Charing Cross Road, Shaftesbury Avenue and Kingsway, create the same problem and have also bisected traditional districts, alienating one part from the other so that their original geographical coherence is obscured. Who, today, perceives Lincoln's Inn as a neighbour to Drury Lane, part of St Giles's one-time parish, or understands the intricate wholeness of old Clerkenwell in the days of Oliver Twist, Fagin and the early Italian immigrants?

Old roads grew incrementally. Not till the coming of the turn-pikes did people see wholesale road creation, involving men with maps and strings, great piles of hard core, and one long-familiar cow pasture being separated from another. But soon after the prolifer-ation of turnpikes there came a more major place-changing under-taking: the first piece of real Industrial Revolution engineering – the canals.

The cost of transporting goods overland, especially heavy things like timber, coal, iron and stone, had always been enormous, in terms of labour, horsepower and the sheer time it took ponderous, jolting carts to get their loads to another part of the country. Traditionally, easier and smoother transport by river had been used for some materials where fortunate geography made this possible. Since the thirteenth century, Cotswold stone had been carried down the Windrush to the Isis at Oxford (where the earliest colleges were built of it) and thence down the Thames to London. Similarly, London's coal had long been supplied from opencast mines in faraway Northumberland and Durham and shipped from Newcastle all the way down the east coast and round into the Thames estuary. Hence the many coal wharves along the river in the heart of London, including that of John Pocock's uncle. But better-quality coal brought laboriously overland from deep mines in the north-west and from Wales was inevitably expensive. Until, that is, late in the year 1761: that was when the Duke of Bridgewater, who owned mines in Lancashire, completed a section of canal, locks and all, which would allow him to send his coal by water into Manchester and thence to the river Mersey and the sea. This almost halved the price of transport. As a researcher who has studied the subject extensively has put it:

Every bank, every entrepreneur, every developer in England suddenly seemed to believe that the canal was the highway of the future. The owners of turnpike roads howled their dismay. Farmers, angry that their land would be torn up, raised all man-ner of objections.[1]

But canals had arrived. Soon, great plans were laid for connecting the whole country by water. The big rivers already used for trading, the Mersey, the Severn, the Thames and the Trent, were all to be linked.

By the last decade of the eighteenth century, when the mill towns of the north were expanding rapidly, producing more and more goods to be transported to other places including London and out of London's great port to the world, a fair network of canals covered the land. But the only water route to London from Oxford southwards was still down the Thames. Finally, after much negotiation, the Paddington and Grand Junction Canal (which became the Grand Union Canal), linking the west side of London with the Midlands and hence with the rest of England, was opened in 1801. This was the canal that the hunted stag swam across in 1829, to be cornered in Paddington church. A few months before, John Pocock had been on a fishing expedition:

> along the Harrow Road to the River Brent, a very shallow stream . . . and continued along the river till we came up to the Grand Junction Canal. Here, the Brent runs 'under' the canal and I do not remember seeing anything so dark and terrible as the water just here.

The winding brook in which he was used to getting splashed, 'clear and cool, clear and cool' as in Charles Kingsley's poem,[2] was already showing signs of becoming 'foul and dank, foul and dank / By wharf and sewer and slimy bank'. The transformation of landscape had begun, and would continue apace. Certainly the general effect of the new canals, at many points along their route, was awe-inspiring and a little frightening. Now, we tend to see the ageing remnants of this once-dynamic industrial system as pastoral, a breath of the country in London's immensity and a haven for waterbirds. But when new and in full commercial use, the canals were seen as denaturing England's green and pleasant land. The intimidating conjunctions they created, like the one with the Brent; the huge lock gates with their heavy iron machinery; the enormous volume and weight of the waters poured in and out and the sheer depth of the locks; seemed alarming to a population used to wells, springs and meandering streams. The ordinary bed of a British canal is mud and not many feet deep, but if you enter a lock that is completely drained – on the rare occasions that this happens for maintenance – you find yourself in something that feels like an urban railway cutting. The floor is lined with bricks and slightly concave, like the shallow arch of a railway tunnel upside down. The relationship between the canals, the first invaders, and the railways that soon overtook them becomes apparent.

Despite their appearance of being disciplined rivers, canals do not flow. They are, in effect, vast reservoirs of water, taken often from old, depleted streams, and used to move great barges of merchandise about. And there is no jumping across a canal. People found they had to go where the canal company had built a bridge. Canals divided one old farm from another, or a country property from its fields and orchards, far more than the turnpikes had done.

When John Pocock was a small child in Kilburn, what became the Regent's Canal was being carved out from Paddington Basin and the Grand Junction Canal across the innocent fields to the north of London. The chief promoter was a man of vision but rather dubious probity called Thomas Homer, who owned several barges on the Grand Junction Canal and had the inspired idea of a branch leading from Little Venice, by Paddington, to Limehouse in the east, where a channel had already been cut from the meandering river Lea to the Thames. The new waterway was at first referred to as the 'London Canal', since it was designed to form an arc around the capital, ending up at the new docks far to the east of the traditional Pool of London.

The scheme languished for some years, till Homer heard of John Nash's plan for the new Regent's Park, which would lie on the canal's route, and approached him. Nash, who had influence in high places, took to Homer. He agreed to incorporate an arc of the canal into his design, and got Homer appointed as superintendent of the whole project. As was – and is – frequently the case with grand plans, the canal ran wildly overbudget, not helped by the fact that Homer began quietly embezzling some of the funds. (He was found out, tried, imprisoned, and then transported to Australia, that classic nineteenth-century repository of both disgrace and hope.)

The canal works continued unabated. Yet even as its bed was being hacked out of the virgin earth by shoals of navvies with shovels and baskets, mile after laborious mile, London was reaching out to meet and absorb it. On a map of 1820 it is shown completed round the top of Regent's Park, with a basin down to the planned Cumberland market off Hampstead Road. The rest of the route eastwards and southwards is in place, but is marked 'intended line of Regent's Canal'. In fact, most of it was opened that same year. But very soon Camden Town, Pentonville, Islington, Hoxton and Hackney spread north towards it.

The docks increased in number; so did wharves, basins and factories alongside the canal, which flourished financially. But less than twenty years later the London–Birmingham railway reached its terminus on the stretch of the New Road that would come to be called the Euston Road. The railway age had fully begun, and was to take developers and speculators by storm still more than the passion for canals had done the century before. The canals were abruptly felt to be out of date – though in practice they were still extremely useful, especially for bringing coal to the new railways.

The year of railway mania was 1845, when lines were proposed to go anywhere and everywhere. *Punch* was full of jokes about exploding engines, collapsing bridges and viaducts being built across cottage vegetable patches. In the spring an editorial commented:

Every man who has got a 10-pound-note is rushing into the market to purchase an interest in something or other which he don't understand, but he is satisfied with the fact that an advertisement has appeared calling the concern a railway.

One of the many plans put forward that year was to convert the Regent's Canal to a railway line. The plan failed (the shareholders' company, like many others, went bankrupt) but there were, for decades afterwards, a series of projects to run a line alongside the canal. All of these came to nothing, in part because those in charge of Regent's Park objected. Canals, though industrial, were, with their horse-pulled barges, relatively quiet and clean. Railways, it had now been realised after the first rush of enthusiasm, were invariably noisy and dirty.

Now the shape-changing effects on London really began. Far more than the turnpike roads or the canals, railways cut brutally through the fabric of already-built townscape. They carved great chasms, deeper and wider than canals, between one set of roads and another, cuttings that disappeared into the black mouths of tunnels like entrances to doom. They erected viaducts past the upper windows and roofs of houses that had stood for decades in peace and dignity; they turned ancient country-style footpaths into mini-tunnels between brick walls, dank and echoing. Railway promoters liked to claim that a desirable side effect of their activity was the demolition of slums lying in their route; in practice, the noise and dirt that the lines brought in time created new slums out of hitherto respectable districts, and sterilised acres of land for shunting and coaling areas. Thackeray, who was born in 1811, wrote towards the end of his life in the 1860s of the railways creating barriers; neatly he turned this into a metaphor of a barrier between past and present, between one generation and another:

> Your railroad starts a new era, and we of a certain age belong to the new time and to the old one . . . They have raised those railroad embankments up, and shut off the old world that was behind them. Climb up that bank on which the irons are laid, and look to the other side – it is gone.[3]

Dickens, born the year after Thackeray, famously described the coming of the railway in *Dombey and Son*, which came out in monthly parts just after the height of railway mania, between 1846 and 1848. In the more sombre parts of the novel the passage of the train and everything that it ignores or crushes in its wake becomes a metaphor for the nemesis that will eventually overcome Dombey:

Away, with a shriek and a roar, and a rattle, from the town, bur-
rowing among the dwellings of men and making the streets hum,
flashing out into the meadows for a moment, mining in through
the damp earth, booming on in darkness and heavy air, bursting out again into the sunny day so bright and wide; away, with
a shriek and a roar and a rattle, through the chalk, through the
mould, through the clay, through the rock, among objects close
at hand and almost in the grasp, ever flying from the traveller, and
a deceitful distance ever moving slowly within him – like as in the
track of the remorseless monster, Death.

But in lighter and more positive mood in the same novel, there is the
equally famous passage on Staggs Gardens, a little semi-rural semi-slum
in Camden Town, and the transformation the railway has wrought:

There was no such place as Staggs Gardens. It had vanished from
the earth. Where the old rotten summer-houses once had stood,
palaces now reared their heads, and granite columns of gigantic
girth opened a vista to the railway world beyond . . . The old
by-streets now swarmed with passengers and vehicles of every
kind . . . Bridges that had led to nothing, led to villas, gardens,
churches, healthy public walks. The carcasses of houses, and
beginnings of new thoroughfares, had started off upon the line
at steam's own speed, and shot away into the country in a monster train . . . there were railway patterns in its drapers' shops,
and railway journals in the windows of its newsmen. There
were railway hotels, office-houses, lodging-houses, boarding-
houses, railway plans, maps, views, wrappers, sandwich boxes
and time-tables . . . The very houses seemed disposed to pack up
and take trips.

But note that all this frenetic change and expansion is going on in
Camden Town, well north of the New Road, not in inner London. The
same might have been written of Southwark and Lambeth, similarly
outside the bounds of London proper. The first railway line of all had

arrived on a viaduct from Greenwich to London Bridge in 1836. It was followed shortly after by a terminus at Nine Elms, Battersea, for a line coming in from Southampton, and a decade later by another long viaduct, this one straddling Lambeth marsh, to bring the line from Nine Elms to a new station at Waterloo – again, kept to the south side of the river. Not till the 1860s would lines be allowed to cross the Thames and then only as far as Victoria, Charing Cross and Blackfriars. In other words, although the railway had become crucial to London's growth, wealth, power and prestige, all the stations were kept on the edge of the central area, encircling it but not penetrating it. Similarly the Eastern Counties Railway which made its way as far as Shoreditch in the 1840s was not allowed to approach towards the City down Bishopsgate till the 1870s, and even then it had to settle for a terminus at Liverpool Street, firmly to the north of London Wall.

Why was this? It was a combination of the power of the City and of wealthy estate-owners such as the Bedford or Grosvenor families to exclude railways, and the related fact that demolishing less valuable housing for railway lines cost less in compensation to the ground landlords. (Tenants did not, for many decades, get compensated at all for the loss of their homes.) Railway companies were interested first and foremost in profit for their shareholders rather than in town planning or the best interests of the public they served. It was, for example, the existence of three competing companies that led eventually to three huge stations, Euston, King's Cross and then St Pancras, all drawn up in a line, ignoring each other along a half-mile strip of main road. But the London street traffic generated by people arriving at one station and making their way to another, or simply to a central location, was increasing year on year. Might it not be more convenient and sensible, people began to say, to have a central terminus?

Among those who thought so was Charles Pearson, a man of modest background who rose to be Solicitor to the City of London, Liberal MP for a while, reformer and campaigner. He was a man of very advanced ideas for his time, being in favour of universal suffrage and of the disestablishment of the Church of England, and opposed to capital punishment. He was also not immune to the passion of the time for creative but unworkable schemes for new transport through London. He himself produced a plan as early as 1845 for an 'atmospheric railway' that was somehow to consume its own smoke, running down the Fleet valley under a glass arcade. Other glassy schemes in the following decade, inspired by Paxton's Crystal Palace, included an arcaded line twelve feet below ground level between St Paul's and Oxford Circus – the route that would be followed at a much deeper level half a century later by the Central line. But this and many other proposals were considered impossibly destructive of existing townscape by the newly formed Royal Commission on Metropolitan Railway Termini. This body had been set up in the wake of the mania of 1845 to make sense of the chaotic, competing proposals of lines and stations that were by then on countless drawing boards and optimistic share-raising brochures.

Essentially, Pearson had understood that what was needed was a central meeting point, a way of linking one mainline terminus to another without whole trainloads of people and goods having to be decanted into carts, wagons, cabs and omnibuses or taking to London's overcrowded pavements. It was this, rather than a passion for an underground railway as such, that drove his idea of the Metropolitan. In its early incarnation, as a steam railway like all the others, it was constructed to carry not just its own designated trains, but also regular trains, including goods trains, that arrived from Paddington and from King's Cross as well. As a leading railway historian of our own time[4] has written:

> To understand the role of the Metropolitan in these early days, it is best to visualise the railway as a part of the mainline network which happened to go underground when it reached London.

In other words, it was about much more than relieving traffic jams, though much of the publicity about it concentrated on these. John Hollingshead, a prolific journalist and defender of the common man, writing at the beginning of the 1860s while the line was being built, noted astutely that the newspaper-reading public tended to concentrate on high-profile stories about 'Indian rebellions or Parisian riots', rather than reading their way through the detail of dull-looking blocks of legal print regarding 'projects more revolutionary in their effects' that were happening, literally, under their feet. He observed:

it is widely supposed that [the Metropolitan's] sole 'mission' is to relieve the over-charged road-traffic of the City. General observers peep through the long walls of thin boards which inclose its labourers, its shafts and its engines, and, as they see men descending and ascending[5] to and from the bowels of the earth, they conclude that some wonderful suburb is being constructed that will draw off the meat 'blocks' of Newgate Street, the carriage 'blocks' of Ludgate Hill, and transform London Bridge from a bridge of curses into an agreeable lounge . . . at present, it is merely to be a connecting link between the Great Western and Great Northern Railways, which, when constructed and opened about the middle of 1862, will begin at Paddington and end in Finsbury Circus. (Published in 1862 in *Underground London*)

Hollingshead had grasped Charles Pearson's core vision of a central exchange station, which indeed was shared by the railway companies themselves. He described them, drawn up with their termini in a ring around the capital, 'looking wistfully toward that coveted spot within the shadow of St Paul's'. For a while their hopes had been set on:

the open space at Farringdon Street, where formerly stood the famous Fleet prison.[6] That area seems now to be given up, and every eye is turned to Finsbury Circus. This neighbourhood of Greek merchants, institutions and chapels . . . may become the home of a great central railway station. The project involves connecting lines of railway above and below ground, the appropriation of many existing streets and alleys, and the construction of new thoroughfares . . . It is not many months since the public shook its head and laughed at the idea of a railway among the sewers.

Punch jokes were now about the tenants of cellars, who were traditionally the least respectable of the poor, planning to make a fortune by letting out their back kitchens to the Metropolitan Company. But, as Hollingshead added, people should remember how the stagecoachmen of a generation before had jeered at the very idea of a railroad.

The site where Farringdon station came to be placed had indeed been Pearson's favoured spot for the central terminus, complete with a visionary scheme for trains carrying workers to and from the City, past King's Cross and onward on the Great Northern rails to new 'cottage settlements' in Hornsey and Tottenham. His innocent dream of endlessly expanding suburbs was eventually to come about, all too much so, but, as we know, the central terminus at Farringdon did not happen. Nor did one materialise at Finsbury Circus either, though the building of Liverpool Street station on the extended Metropolitan line a decade later was geographically not far removed from Hollingshead's prediction.

Invited guests on the inaugral trip, January 1863

By the time the Metropolitan was triumphantly opened, with a banquet for the great and good in the newly completed Farringdon tunnel in January 1863, Pearson himself had died the previous September. Perhaps this was one reason among others why his concept of a central terminus was never realised. In 1865, two years after its opening, the line was already so successful that it was extended from Farringdon, not just to Moorgate but also directly south, with a tunnel under Snow Hill, to join up with the London, Chatham and Dover line coming from the far side of the river. Unfortunately the viaduct on which it had to be carried over the lower slope of the Fleet valley was to interfere with the view of St Paul's from Ludgate Circus for the next hundred and thirty years. Both the Royal Commission on Metropolitan Railway Termini and the City fathers seemed to have had their attention too far distracted at that point by the new subterranean wonder to realise that, even if they were not allowing a station 'in the shadow of St Paul's' they were allowing a metaphorical shadow to blight London's most famous monument.

The early 1860s were, in London – as in other cities around the world – a time of particularly intense activity. Rail bridges were at last thrown across the Thames, Holborn Viaduct was planned across the precipitous valley of the Fleet. The Embankment, complete with Bazalgette's sewer system, was being laid out: schemes for new roads, parks and acres and acres of housing were on drawing boards or under way all over the expanding area of the metropolis, many of them under the aegis of the Metropolitan Board of Works that had been founded a few years earlier. The London immortalised in Dickens's famous early novels – *The Pickwick Papers, Nicholas Nickelby, Oliver Twist, A Christmas Carol* – was disappearing piecemeal before the eyes of its overwhelmed inhabitants, who were told to admire such Progress. This was particularly true in ancient Clerkenwell, that historic hinterland between the City and the westward rest of London. In August 1863 the *Illustrated Times* wrote:

In no part of the metropolis have greater changes been made than in this quarter. Houses which sheltered a population of more than 13,000 people have been demolished; and, considering the condition of these dwellings, their destruction cannot be a matter for regret. The rotting and filthy Fleet river has been hidden from view . . . Sharps-alley, once of such unsavoury notoriety, with its catgut manufactury and other noisome trades, will, in the course of a few days, be numbered amongst the matters of the past.

But naturally not everyone took the same view of the destruction that Progress wrought, and Hollingshead was among those perturbed by it. Here he is on the Clerkenwell section of the Metropolitan line, where the most substantial transformation was taking place as he wrote:

Whole parishes are threatened with demolition, venerable churches and landmarks are to be elbowed aside, half buried monuments of antiquity are to be ploughed up, like the decayed stump of an old tooth, ground into powder, and scattered to the four winds; the ancient ways upon which our forefathers stood, made bargains, drank, feasted and trained their children are to be deserted, closed, built upon, transformed or utterly destroyed . . . plastered over with the bills of some authorised auctioneer to be sold as 'old rubbish' . . . carted off in a hundred wagons leaving not a trace behind.

Putting the new line down the Fleet valley was indeed the biggest and most hazardous part of the Metropolitan works. From one point of view it was the obvious route down to a site on the fringe of the City near the Charterhouse and Smithfield: railways have always tended to follow valleys. But the Fleet ditch, the ancient river that traditionally demarcated the City of London on the west and had, long ago, been navigable right up to St Pancras Old Church and beyond, had had a chequered history. By the mid-nineteenth century, it had declined 'from a river to a brook, from a brook to a ditch, and from a ditch to a drain'[7] and had been covered over for most of its course. But the insalubrious trades such as tanning and butchery that used water and had once been strung along the open stream, fouling it, had remained.

So too had much ramshackle housing and small alehouses of dubious repute. This was some of the ancient material that Hollingshead complained was being 'ploughed up . . . and scattered to the four winds', but with it too went venerable street names, churches, a workhouse and its graveyard that were in the direct route of the lines, and also the humble tenement homes of a large number of people (see map p. 124).

Officially, it was claimed that only 307 people were displaced in this area by the new railway, but in such an overcrowded and lawless district the actual numbers (as the *Illustrated Times* seemed aware) were probably much higher. Certainly various well-informed observers thought so, and the lack of any compensation or provision for these disinherited inhabitants was vigorously pointed out by the self-appointed champions of the poor – of which, by the 1860s, there were quite a few.

The Fleet slums, mid-nineteenth century

Meanwhile, the more middle-class inhabitants along other parts of the Metropolitan route were busy with lawyers, seeing if they had claims for subsidence.

In the end, very few genuine claims were registered, and the general feeling, once everyone got used to the idea and stopped wondering if it might incur the wrath of Almighty God, was that the new subterranean railway would be an elegant and modern blessing. In February 1862, the year in which the blessing was at that point supposed to open, the *Illustrated London News* wrote:

> This line has a width of nearly 30 feet, and its tunnelled arch along the line of what is known as the New-road forms a graceful curve, the majestic sweep of which can be seen at any point, as the whole is well lighted by gas.

It then moved, geographically, along to King's Cross, showing an engraving of the complex workings there, what with the need to incorporate a link with the main line and to deal adequately with the Fleet and with other sewers:

> Fleet ditch is turned and its bed laid bare, a tunnel having been made under it for the rapid removal of the rubbish which comes from the destruction of the houses cityward . . . [at Frederick Street] the Fleet ditch is temporarily diverted from its course, previously [*sic*] to its being boxed up, as it is at King's-cross, in an iron tube; and hence we may catch what may possibly be a last glimpse of the Fleet, now a sewer, but once a crystal stream running its short but pleasant career from smiling uplands through orchards, gardens and meadows to slide at last 'babbling o'green fields' into what was then the 'silver Thames'.

That was not, however, to be quite the last appearance of the Fleet, and the opening of the line turned out to be delayed till the beginning of the following year because of it. Watercourses, when imprisoned in brick or even in iron, are notoriously difficult to abolish utterly. The surrounding earth holds a memory of when it formed the banks of a stream, and tiny capillaries still make their way through it. Even today, where the trains run down to Farringdon, the cutting's high walls are festooned with dank greenery wherever a gap lets the light in, and it feels like the bed of a stream. Indeed, there has long been a story current that the Metropolitan Railway Company simply bought up the Fleet at this stretch, buried it deeper, and laid iron rails on top to keep the ancient waters in their place.

It is true that the brick drain that the Fleet had by then become had to be sunk more deeply in the earth, but in reality the old waterway, encased in pipes, curves round just to the west of the railway cutting. It runs where old maps and the lie of the land both indicate – under the lowest-lying streets in that hilly quarter, such as Phoenix Street, Warner Street where it passes under the Rosebury Avenue viaduct, Ray Street, and then down Saffron Hill and under Holborn Viaduct. The claim, made in a brochure put out by the Company two years later, that in building the line they had had 'to cross the Fleet three times', has been repeated in accounts ever since, but it does not seem to be true once they had navigated the buried river at King's Cross.[8] Confusion has also been caused by the often-repeated 'fact' that Turnmill Street, just to the east of the railway line, preserves the memory of mills along the Fleet in the Middle Ages. Mills there must have been, but it seems more likely that their wheels were turned here by a smaller tributary running westwards down from Clerkenwell which met the Fleet just below this point. No doubt the Railway Company had to deal with this buried stream too.

I think that when they wrote their brochure (designed to appeal to investors for further extensions) the Company were still busy excusing themselves for the near disaster that occurred in June 1862, four months after the *Illustrated London News* had confidently predicted that the Fleet was supressed for good. Already, earlier that year, it had been discovered that effluent was leaking out of the Fleet sewer in Saffron Hill. In late June, after a big rainstorm, a section of it collapsed near Ray Street, the location of an ancient hollow formerly known as Hockley-in-the-Hole. Filthy water crossed under Farringdon Road and backed up against the western retaining wall of the railway cutting. For two days the railway contractors and the Metropolitan Board of Works

Fleet Tunnel works by Frederick Street

(who were by then responsible for sewers) made desperate efforts to shore up the wall, but it collapsed, 'in a cracking, heaving mass', with a surge of water so violent that it broke up the network of scaffolding and beams being used to build the tunnel walls. It flooded the workings to a depth of ten feet, and also swept into the cutting some bodies that had been walled up in a vault after their removal from the pauper burial ground that had been in the way of the railway. This aspect of the collapse created much bad publicity and a number of rather overwrought artists' impressions of the scene. Amazingly, no living man was drowned, and repairing the damage only set the completion date back by a few weeks, but it put up costs very much: a further £300,000 had to be raised from shareholders, a huge sum for that time.

The new Metropolitan Railway was soon a big success with all classes of people, even though they rode variously in carriages marked First, Second and Third. It was undeniably rather smoky, but so was a great deal of London by then and the *Illustrated London News* continued to stress its salubriousness:

> the tunnels, instead of being close, dark, damp and offensive, are wide, spacious, clean and luminous, and more like a well-kept street at night than a subterranean passage.

This wonder was, in addition, the first really reasonably priced town transport: most white-collar workers could afford it, and the year after it opened the Company became the first in the world to introduce extra-cheap workmen's return fares on trains running before 6 a.m. You could use the return half to go home at any hour, which made the deal both attractive and logical. Charles Pearson's dream of a London workforce dwelling not in nearby garrets and basements but in clean 'cottages' beyond the smoke of town was beginning to gather weight – with the not entirely foreseen result that a lot of rather cheap little terraced houses began to be built north-west of Paddington, at the western end of the line, driving down the social 'tone' of that still-countrified district.

Mr Pocock senior, had he still been alive, might not have been entirely pleased. John Thomas Pocock, when he finally returned to England as an elderly man, ten years after the Metropolitan Railway opened, found the landscape of his boyhood changed beyond recognition. It was in the 1860s that the concept of commuting was born, though it took another hundred years for the word, imported from the United States, to enter British speech. But the Metropolitan Railway, and its soon-to-be-built extensions into a Circle and then a District line,[9] were not the only new projects effecting a substantial change in how and where Londoners lived.

The attempt in the 1840s to turn the Regent's Canal into a railway line running west to east round London was, we know, seen off, but the essential idea of a peripheral circuit took root. By the late 1840s a 'Birmingham Junction Railway' was being built to link the Euston goods yards at Chalk Farm with the docks in east London, where there was already a short line between the docks and the City, the Blackwall

Railway. This one ended in Fenchurch Street, near the Tower, in the south-east corner of the City, the only terminus that managed to insert itself so far in. By 1850 the two companies got together, and the Blackwall line was extended north-east to Bow, to meet what was soon to be rechristened the North London Railway coming down from Hackney Wick. Although this had originally been envisaged as a goods line carrying freight onwards from the Birmingham–Euston main line towards the shipping lanes of the world, it was soon realised that there was a potential for passenger traffic. The line, which already passed through part of Islington, Highbury, Dalston and Hackney, acquired a station at Camden Town, where it linked up with another new railway, the Hampstead Junction Railway, that continued westwards to Kentish Town, Hampstead Heath, Finchley Road and eventually to points further south, thus neatly forming an arc round London's then extent, even as the Regent's Canal had done a generation before.

City businessmen and clerks living near to country air in the then-select outer suburbs of Hackney, Highbury, Canonbury and Camden Square eagerly took advantage of this new way of getting to and from their place of work – even though the route in the 1850s and early '60s was, to our way of thinking, extraordinarily circuitous. A gentleman travelling, say, from his nice detached villa somewhere near Hackney Downs, having joined the train at Kingsland or Hackney stations, due north of the City, then made an excursion in apparently the wrong direction into the distant east. He was carried all the way round, beyond where Victoria Park was being laid out on fields, then on an iron bridge over a canal cut and some marshy, uninhabited land to still-rural Bow, then southwards through market gardens, before finally curving back westwards past a new cemetery and a big gasworks, to the old East End of Stepney, Ratcliffe, past Wapping and at last to Fenchurch Street. The same journey, of course, had to be retraced each evening. It was surprisingly quick, considering how much ground was covered, the whole detour being achieved in about half an hour – which is presumably why, against geographical logic, it became popular.

The lonely stretch of the line between Hackney Wick and Bow, however, briefly became notorious when it was the scene of the first 'railway murder' – a sign, some people said, of the dangers of mixing all classes and conditions of people in one vehicle of conveyance, even if they were in separate carriages. A Mr Thomas Briggs, aged sixty-nine, who was chief clerk to a prestigious City bank, lived in a large house with some of his family and a number of servants in Lower Clapton. He was typical of the kind of person who, late in life, had taken to this modern form of travel, and it was his habit to go to and fro between Hackney station, near his home, and Fenchurch Street. One July evening in 1864, he was found, mortally injured, near the canal bridge between Bow and Hackney Wick, while the first-class carriage in which he had been travelling alone, and where he had apparently been surprised by his murderer, rattled empty on its way to the terminus at Chalk Farm with blood spattered all over the buttoned cushions of its interior. The motive did not seem to be robbery. A German immigrant was arrested because he had subsequently pawned Mr Briggs's watch, and he was eventually hanged for the crime of murder; but the evidence pointing to him was weak and somewhat contradictory. To this day, no one knows what really happened.[10]

If the extremely unfortunate Mr Briggs had survived another year, he would not have ended up in such a wasteland and would have found his journey made much shorter and more logical. For in 1865 a spur line was built, running down from Dalston, through Haggerston and Shoreditch, to a new station at Broad Street.[11] Now the citizens of London's respectable northern residential districts could reach the heart of the City much more quickly. The station at Broad Street was no distance, either, from the new Metropolitan line station at Moorgate.

Because of the station now at Broad Street, in the following decade the owners of the Eastern Counties Railway, who till then had not been able to get any nearer the City than Shoreditch, were finally allowed to build their own grand terminus at Liverpool Street. Very soon, the Metropolitan was extended further to serve it, and then on to Aldgate, Whitechapel, Stepney Green, Mile End and Bow. Once again, we are back with the ancient eastward route out of London. We are also back with the line of Crossrail.

CHAPTER III

The Underground in the Mind

It is a little-known fact that the first version of *Alice's Adventures in Wonderland* was called by its author, Lewis Carroll, *Alice's Adventures Under Ground*. It is also worth noting that the date on which the story was narrated to young Alice Liddell, the 'golden afternoon' of 4 July 1862, was exactly the time that London's first Underground was battling its way to Farringdon, and that the story was enlarged and finally written down at the beginning of the following year, just as the new line had its ceremonial opening, top-hatted banquet and all. The Revd Charles Lutwidge Dodgson (alias Carroll) might have been cocooned in Christ Church, Oxford, but the jokes, puzzles, parodies and intellectual references in the story show that he was well aware of the world outside.

The next year saw the publication of Jules Verne's *Voyage au Centre de la Terre*, rapidly translated into English as *Journey to the Centre of the Earth*. The prehistoric wonders that an uncle and his nephew find there probably derive from Darwin's *On the Origin of Species* (published five years before) and from the rapidly evolving study of geology; but the whole idea of roaming around in caverns beneath the earth's surface seems to owe something to the concrete reality created by the new Metropolitan's hidden territory of tunnels 'wide, spacious, clean and luminous'.

There was a significant French population in London in the 1860s, many of them refugees from the Empire of Louis-Napoleon, under which they were regarded as dangerous subversives and potential revolutionaries. When the Emperor was forced to resign in 1870 (and took refuge in England himself) his compatriots went joyfully back to

France. One of them, who had been a *député*, a Member of Parliament, before the Emperor had dismissed the whole administration in 1852, and was to become one again on his return, was particularly taken with the Metropolitan Railway. He was a skilled mason by trade; he recognised good structural engineering when he saw it.[1] Once back in France, he devoted much of the twenty-five years of public life that remained to him to lobbying the Paris municipality regarding the need for Paris, too, to have underground lines. For a long time the municipality were unimpressed. Surely, it was said, the Parisian spirit, unlike the traditionally fog-bound London one, was too airy to submit to the 'Stygian gloom' of an underground railway? When the need for a new public-transport system became obvious, it was suggested that, rather than an underground *métro*, an overhead one would fit the bill? There would be elevated tracks in tasteful wrought iron running down the centre of the principal boulevards and avenues, including the Champs-Élysées . . .

Fortunately, the inconvenience and blight of such a scheme was realised just in time, possibly because New York and Philadelphia had made that mistake. The Parisian *Métro* began to be built, on the established cut-and-cover method, in 1898, just as, in London, the first deep tube lines were being tunnelled in a quite different and more modern way.

There had been legends concerning tunnels under cities for centuries, usually identified with smugglers, spies, eccentric noblemen or concealed deaths. Most of these tales probably derived from abandoned water conduits, including Roman ones, medieval sewers leading into rivers, and from former quarries. From the 1860s, the popular imagination in London had something more solidly present to work upon. The Jeremiahs who predicted that passengers on the Metropolitan would be asphyxiated wholesale by the smoky, crowded conditions were mainly wrong, but not entirely. There were a few early casualties of this new form of travel including Henry Stephens, the very successful inventor of 'Stephens' Blue-Black Ink'. Feeling unwell, he let his son go on ahead at Farringdon, the year after the station opened.

Unable to see his father through the crowd on the platform, Stephens junior ('Inky') got on the train thinking that his father must have done so too, but the older man was found dead hours later, slumped on a bench. There were other occasional shocking news stories of a Person Under a Train, usually because he had tried to jump on or off while it was moving, or because he had missed his station and had attempted to walk back through the tunnel. By and by these led to more elaborate invented tales.

In a story published in 1886 in a fashionable magazine[2] a man is murdered in the short distance between King's Cross and Gower Street, which is today's Euston Square station. The killer then gets out, but in again into another compartment where he travels on apparently blamelessly to Edgware Road. In a better-known story of 1891 by Baroness Orczy',[3] written just at the time when the first deep tube was also opening, the same fate befalls a woman going eastbound between Gower Street and Aldgate. The killer, who plays the same trick of getting off at an intermediate station, turns out to be her husband.

It is worth noting that both these grisly tales are based on the anonymity of mass Underground travel, in those days long before CCTV, and also on the possibility of isolation if you chose to travel in First Class – as in the case of Mr Briggs on the North London Railway. These were new features of journeying round London: on the old, small horse-buses and horse-trams travel was quite a sociable, public activity. New and daringly modern, too, was the freedom that the Metropolitan and District lines brought to women to travel much further than before on their own. Not everyone accommodated well to this. In George Gissing's *The Odd Women* (1893) Monica, the youngest and prettiest of three hard-up, genteel sisters, marries the only man available to her, the socially isolated, middle-aged Widdowson. He lives occupationless on a small private income, in a villa in Herne Hill, then the last southern outpost of suburban London:

Monica soon found that his idea of wedded happiness was that they should always be together. Most reluctantly he consented to her going any distance alone, for whatever purpose.

He becomes obsessively jealous, and Monica's blameless excursions on the District Railway to see a female friend eventually give him cause to explode. He has her followed and watched and finds proof for his paranoia when it is reported to him that she has been sitting on the Underground conversing with A Man – in fact, the brother of her friend, who happens to get into the first-class carriage where she is travelling.

Gissing, who was born in 1857, only arrived in London in 1878, when the 'Dickensian London' he passionately sought was vanishing and the Metropolitan and District lines were an established feature of life. He was once, in his 1894 novel *In the Year of Jubilee*, tempted to portray the Underground as the infernal underworld, but the real Gissing complaint in this scene, which is set in King's Cross, concerns the advertisements that by then were plastering the stations:

> They descended and stood together upon the platform, among hurrying crowds, in black fumes that poisoned the palate with sulphur. This way and that sped the demon engines, whirling lighted wagons full of people. Shrill whistles, the hiss and roar of steam, the bang, clap, bang of carriage doors, the clatter of feet on wood and stone – all echoed and reverberated from a huge, cloudy vault above them. High and low, on every available yard of wall, advertisements clamoured to the eye . . . A battle-ground of advertisements, fitly chosen amid subterranean din and reek; a symbol to the gaze of that relentless warfare which ceases not night and day, in the world above.

Alas for the 'wide, spacious, clean and luminous [tunnels] like a well-kept street' that the *Illustrated London News* had praised thirty years before. The very success of the Underground had degraded it as a physical setting; and in any case London stretched many miles further in all directions than it had in the 1860s and sheltered a far bigger population.

Gissing's friend and fellow novelist H. G. Wells also made use of the classic image of a subterranean city which is a sinister alternative to the

A Metropolitan line steam train in Farringdon station on the 150th anniversary of its opening, by Richard Lansdown

city on the surface. Most notably, in Wells's *The Time Machine* (1895) a troglodite and evil race called the Morlocks live in the nether regions and prey upon the Eloi, who live above and are superficially more attractive but actually weak and effete. Wells returned to his underground fantasies in *The War of the Worlds* (1898) and to some extent in *The Sleeper Awakes* (1910), though the futuristic London depicted in the latter book is so dominated by extraordinary galleried structures that concepts of above or below seem hardly relevant. Later in his long life Wells's intuitive visions were to provide fertile material for the rising film industry. Both *The Time Machine* and *The War of the Worlds* have been filmed more than once, and have been mined as well for ideas for other films. A 1972 horror movie called *Death Line*, starring Donald Pleasence, is set in the London Underground and features cannibals descended from Victorian railway workers, who are clearly another version of the Morlocks. The most famous film to be inspired by London Transport's subterranean domain is, however, Anthony Asquith's 1928 classic, simply called *Underground*. Here there are no supernormal beings, but the entire plot of the film is driven by the coincidental meetings of underground travel, now complete with moving staircases, and by the manners and customs of tube travel that were by then established. The climax of the film is a classic chase-to-the-death round the frightening, heavyweight machinery of the Lots Road power station, which had been built largely to service the expanding tube system.

Wells's most famous tales tend to take off into whole other worlds of limitless possibilities: he is often more effective and thought-provoking when his invention is more closely based on reality. Clearly rooted in the excavations and upheavals London had actually gone through in the preceeding fifty years is his 1910 short story 'The Door in the Wall', even though its connection with the Underground only becomes apparent at the end. In this story, a small and lonely boy out on his own in Kensington finds a green door in a wall that lets him for one afternoon into a huge garden. It is full of flowers, tame wild animals, friendly playmates and a kind and lovely young woman. For his entire life he remembers the place as 'a secret and peculiar passage of escape into another and altogether more beautiful world'. He grows up and into a career of increasing success and prosperity, eventually becoming a cabinet minister, but he never quite manages to find his other world again. At long intervals he catches sight, unexpectedly, of the green door, but each time he is in a hurry for an exam or a meeting, or going to see a woman he cares about, or in deep conversation with a colleague. Then, late one night, two days after he has confided in an old friend (the Wellsian narrator) about his lifelong, frustrated quest, he apparently comes upon the door again and at last goes through it:

> They found his body very early yesterday morning in a deep excavation near East Kensington Station. It is one of two shafts that have been made in connection with an extension of the railway southwards. It is protected from the intrusion of the public by a hoarding upon the high road, in which a small doorway has been cut for the convenience of some of the workmen who live in that direction. The doorway was left unfastened through a misunderstanding between two gangers, and through it he made his way . . .
>
> By our daylight standard, he walked out of security into darkness, danger and death. But did he see it like that?

There, in a sentence, you have the paradox of the modern era which underground railways embody. From one point of view they are all part of the ever-increasing convenience, protection and estrangement from nature that constitutes life in a modern urban setting. No longer do we, as our ancestors did for so many centuries, tramp long distances over muddy, unlit roadways, subject to all the vagaries of time, chance and weather, ready prey to assault and disease, aware of death as an ever-present possibility. Instead, warm trains beneath the earth carry great crowds of us efficiently, quickly and safely to our distant home destinations. What could be more reassuring, humdrum and less of a memento mori than a familiar Tube journey? And yet these heedless trains are, of course, carriers of death: every year, about fifty people successfully commit suicide by jumping in front of them, and a rather larger number make botched attempts. The unfortunate driver who happens to be in the cabin usually sees what is about to happen but cannot brake in time. Moreover, there are railway cuttings all over London which, though carefully walled off, form caverns in the texture of the city, classic openings into the underworld that, by long tradition and legend, lies beneath our careless feet. Wells's central figure walks 'out of security, into darkness, danger and death'. But what he was seeking was something more like the *'joyous land, / Joining the town and just at hand'* to which the Pied Piper of Hamelin leads the children in the fable of death that Browning turned into a poem,[4] a land:

> *Where waters gushed, and fruit-trees grew,*
> *And flowers put forth a fairer hue,*
> *And everything was strange and new.*

A 'wondrous portal' opens in the hillside, and the children disappear into it and are gone for ever. So too is Wells's successful and apparently fortunate man, the surface of his life abruptly broken by the chasm of a profound buried emotion.

Some people have a visceral dislike of underground travel, even when they are accustomed to it. For them, as for many plane travellers, a half-suppressed fear is always present, the claustrophobia of being imprisoned in an unnatural situation over which they have no control. T. S. Eliot captures this moment 'when an underground train, in the tube, stops too long between stations'.[5] At first conversation rises; then an uneasy silence supervenes with, beneath it, 'growing terror'.

Mr Basil Green climbing the lift-shaft.

One of the best evocations of being lost, helpless and indeed trapped in an underground world he cannot recognise occurs in John Betjeman's tale about Mr Basil Green, who gets off the tube train by mistake when the door opens momentarily at the disused South Kentish Town station.[6] There is a peculiar horror attached to a derelict Underground station, as to an abandoned swimming bath, frozen in time with old tiling and notices still intact. Finding himself alone on the entirely dark platform, Mr Green first tries in vain to hail passing trains, but eventually resorts to feeling his way to one of the disused lift-shafts. He climbs up its iron ledges, hand-over-hand, only to hit his head at the top on the floor of the shop that now occupies the space above:

> I will not pain you with a description of how Mr Green climbed very slowly down the lift-shaft again . . . All I will tell you is that when he eventually arrived at the bottom, two hours later, he was wet with sweat and he had been sweating as much with fright as with exertion.

Mr Green fumbles his way back to a platform, lies down and cries a little:

> he almost welcomed the oncoming rumble of those cruel trains which still always passed him. They were, at any rate, kinder than the dreadful silence in the station when they had gone away and when he could easily imagine huge, hairy spiders or wet reptiles padding down those dark passages by which he had so vainly tried to make his escape.

There you have the quintessential fear of the Underground. Poor Mr Green is, happily, rescued in the small hours of the morning by a posse of workmen with lamps coming down the tunnel to check the track.

On a personal note, I will add that this story fascinated me as a young, country-dwelling child, when I had hardly ever been on the London Underground and could not possibly foresee that much of my adult life would be lived half a mile from the old oxblood-red station of South Kentish Town. So I kept the bulky Christmas annual containing the story, through decades of change and dispersal, and have passed my enthusiasm for it to younger generations. Like, I suspect, a number of other people, I also have intermittent dreams featuring underground railways, usually in a benign form. Sometimes in such dreams it is essential that I cling on to the handrail as I reach the bottom of an escalator, in order to get rolled round to another and unfamiliar level. Usually the train, when I finally reach a profoundly deep platform, is a strange, decorated, open-truck affair, like some narrow-gauge railway on a country-house estate, only swifter. Often it turns out to serve improbably distant destinations for a Tube. Brighton, say. Or even Berlin. I wonder, in a distracted, dreamlike way, how I will actually get back . . . Such night-time excursions leave a pleasant if frustrated sense that there is indeed a world elsewhere, if only I were able to access it more completely.

It is evidently not an uncommon feeling. The French writer André Maurois exploited it for his much-loved 1930 children's book *Patapoufs et Filifers*.[7] The twin kingdoms of the enormously obese and the skeletally thin, which seem to owe something of their inspiration to Swift's Lilliputians and Brobdingnagians, are found by two small brothers out rock-climbing, one of whom slips down a cleft:

'There's a huge cave, and it's all lit up with electric lights, just like a railway station.'
  'Are there any trains?'
  . . . 'No, but it's awfully interesting. Come on down.'

The brother does so, and at the end of 'an enormous grotto filled with blueish light' they discover:

A moving staircase, so long that one could not see its end, rumbling down into the centre of the earth . . . Down and down they went for more than half an hour; down and down, though a half-darkness occasionally broken by red and green electric lights.
  'It's just like the signals in the Underground,' said Edmund. 'But what a long way we've come!'

So they finally reach the Other World, complete with open air, sea breezes and opposing towns that are filled either with spiky Gothic pinnacles or with bulbous baroque, and become involved, like Gulliver, in the two factions' preposterous battles.

Incidentally, what we have here, writ enormous, is the experience undergone today by strangers of any nationality confronted with alien city life. One sees them embarking with suitcases, trepidation and nervous exclamations at the tops of escalators, clearly feeling that they are no longer in charge of their own destiny.

Conversely, not a few office workers who are habituated tube users and who daily leave remote suburban homes for their known destination near, say, the Bank or Holborn, have not the vaguest general idea of inner London's overall geography. This becomes apparent when there is an Underground strike and they are forced to find their way on foot or on unfamiliar buses. They are at a complete loss, appealing to others on the pavements as to the direction in which they should set out. For them, the artificial, sealed-off underground world has become the reality of travel, and the complex texture and extent of the urban world above ground is largely unknown.

Maurois' book, beneath its fun about fatties and thinnies, their architecture, furnishings, diets and prejudices, is a satire on the folly of war between neighbouring countries. Some ten years after he published it France was indeed at war once again with her nearest neighbour and Paris was occupied by German forces. Another fantasy inspired by underground travel was published in 1943 during the Occupation, *L'Enfant du Métro*. Its co-authors, one the writer and the other the illustrator, were two Franco-Peruvian sisters, Madeleine and Lucha Truel, who were involved in making fake identity papers for Jews and members of the Resistance. Lucha survived the war; Madeleine was arrested and died while she was being marched between two concentration camps. *L'Enfant du Métro* is an allegory of a search for safety and for a solution to a complex problem, a graphic metaphor therefore for the workings of the 'underground' or secret service. I did not of course understand this when, as a young child, I seized on the book: I was simply delighted by the fantasy Paris it presents, based on the evocative names of the *métro* stations. In the Truel sisters' world, Chambre des Députés is an elegant room in which moustachioed gentlemen of a certain age are neatly tucked up in iron beds; Campo Formio is a sinister desert landscape at sunset on which large ants disport themselves; while Denfert-Rochereau features an ineffectual, be-hatted devil surrounded by rocks and flames. Other stations are transfigured accordingly.

It is said that this now-obscure and rare book provided some part of the inspiration for Raymond Queneau's over-praised 1959 novel *Zazie dans le Métro*. But what it essentially embodies is, once again, the idea of an alternative world lying just beneath the surface of the known one, and in a complex way linked with it: Alice's Wonderland perennially reappearing.

The science of archaeology has developed out of all recognition since the antiquarians of the early eighteenth century fantasised about druids. Near the end of the nineteenth century the governmental Board of Works, aided by various newly formed bodies for the Protection of Ancient Monuments, began to take some interest in buried remains as well as in what appeared on the surface, but well into the twentieth century there was still no system for ensuring that builders working on a site did not just destroy anything they found, in the interests of getting on with the job in hand. In recent decades protection has become much greater and archaeology ever more skilled and scrupulous – but, paradoxically, this has generated its own nostalgic myths about what we have lost.

We know that our Victorian ancestors, while uncovering a great many ancient foundations of brick and stone during their works for underground railways, sewers, water mains and the other nineteenth-century public utilities which transformed urban living, also obliterated a great deal. As a result, subsequent accounts of what once lay under our feet and is now, alas, irrecoverable for modern scrutiny are not always as valid as one might like to believe. A normally reliable and insightful mid-twentieth-century historian, Michael Harrison, has written:

In August 1875, a gang of navvies, opening up the surface of Oxford Street just where it passes Stratford Place, came across the remains of an extensive stone structure . . . thick walls, pointed arches, decorative carvings, all in a fair state of preservation. In digging a sewer they had come across the surviving parts of the great reservoir constructed by the Mayor and Corporation of London, to supply the Conduit in Cheapside with pure drinking water.

This is convincing, and indeed is corroborated by a news item in *The Times* for 10 August that year headed 'Discovery in Oxford Street'. It was followed up by two letters from an out-of-town correspondent, the second more detailed than the first, pointing out correctly that the Stratford Place corner is exactly where the buried Tyburn stream crosses Oxford Street. The point was further made that in medieval times the Mayor was constrained to make an annual visit to inspect the reservoir (built in the mid-thirteenth century) and that this was made the occasion for a regular hunting party in Marylebone woods for foxes or hares, followed by a ceremonial meal in a banqueting house built nearby. *The Builder*, also in August, commented on the same discovery, though both it and *The Times* knew that the workmen were laying a gas main and not a sewer, and neither mentions the 'decorative carvings' that have crept into Harrison's description. The account in *The Builder*, evidently written by someone who had visited the place, even gave the dimensions of the several chambers within the structure, and remarked that it contained 'about 2 ft. of water and much foul air'.

So far, so well documented. But Harrison, writing a century later, goes on to mention an apparently quite separate Oxford Street discovery of what sounds like a very similar underground vaulted structure, with water in the bottom (this time 'a bubbling spring') and 'chamfered gothic arches'. This one was said to be a little further west, at the corner of North Audley Street. Harrison quotes what he describes as 'a contemporary source' but with no reference, giving the impression that the discovery was about the same time as that of the medieval reservoir but offering no firm date. His anonymous Victorian source appears to have decided that this second underground water construction was of Roman origin and 'from all appearances the place was originally a baptistry'. A remarkable and wonderful example of the complete preservation of an extremely ancient construction – if true.

Of course, none of this is impossible, and since the whole thing was allegedly destroyed by the construction of a sewer (or alternatively a new building) its non-existence is as unprovable now as its existence. However, unlike the medieval reservoir, I have not been able to find any reference to its discovery in the usual nineteenth-century sources. The comprehensive 1928 record of the Royal Commission on Historical Monuments, Roman (London) does not mention it, and the Museum of London team currently working on the archaeology along Crossrail's route have not heard of it either, though in digging at Stratford Place for the Crossrail station at Bond Street they did turn up the remains of the medieval water cistern just as their predecessors had. It seemed to have been reused much later, when Oxford Street became built up, as a cellar or ice-house.

The story of the Roman baptistry has been picked up by at least one modern commentator[8] and no doubt subsequently will be by others: it has thus begun to lead a life of its own. I suspect that here we are in the presence of an urban myth, one just as tenacious as the tales of secret passages or indeed of mysterious presences dwelling beneath the earth. The premise that two such similar and complete constructions were found so near one another at the same period, and that the less important one was noted and explained while the far older and more extraordinary one was not, seems to me unlikely, especially given the classically educated Victorians' respect for all things Roman. I think that the undoubted medieval reservoir has bred another, invented, version of itself, more fascinating, valuable and complete – and, of course, tragically lost.

CHAPTER IV

The High Road and the Low Road

And so to St Giles-in-the-Fields and its High Street, long-term marker of the end of the road from Oxford and, for several centuries once the fields had begun to retreat, the western entry point into London proper. The site is better known today as Tottenham Court Road, from the name of the Underground station that opened there in the summer of 1900, and which is, as I write, being transformed into a major Crossrail interchange point with other lines.

It is the crossroads at which the Charing Cross Road, running north, becomes the Tottenham Court Road, and Oxford Street becomes New Oxford Street to the east. Here too, since the late 1960s, has stood the 385-foot glass-and-concrete skyscraper Centre Point tower, designed by Richard Seifert. Its construction, and that of the lower-rise Centre Point building behind it, linked by a sombre gantry, involved the destruction of a substantial part of St Giles High Street, the remainder of which is now hidden immediately behind the tower. This led to considerable public indignation at the time,[1] and although the building complex acquired Listed status, Grade 2, in 1995, it seems fair to say that the Listing owes less to any intrinsic quality than to the iconic status the tower has achieved due to its position, and also for the way it is emblematic of the sometimes-visionary but insensitive and ill-regulated property market of the post-war era.

In fairness, too, one has to say that the intrusion of Centre Point was not the first space-changing assault on St Giles High Street's key position in relation to the surrounding townscape. Today's important crossroads is, in terms of St Giles's long history, relatively new.

St Giles church, late nineteenth century

Tottenham Court Road is old: it has nothing to do with the district of Tottenham in the far north of today's Greater London area, but gets its name from Tottenhall, an early Tudor house that stood for about three hundred years on a site just north of where Tottenham Court Road and the Euston Road now meet. The road to this modest-sized manor house was also the Way to Hampstead, and it was for centuries the only significant highway branching off where the Oxford road met the first houses of St Giles village.

The other roads that, today, form the crossroads by the tube station, New Oxford Street and Charing Cross Road itself, are the result of nineteenth-century road improvements. New Oxford Street was cut through an agglomeration of small streets in the late 1840s, to enable traffic from Oxford Street to reach Holborn without negotiating St Giles High Street's ancient curve. Charing Cross Road, surprisingly, did not get laid out till the 1880s; before that, there was only a narrow way ('Hog Lane' on old maps) running south about as far as present-day Cambridge Circus and then a network of streets to navigate as far as Leicester Square. The older route was via St Martin's Lane which, going north from St Martin-in-the-Fields, finally emerged, under various names, a little to the east of St Giles church.

Before these modern roads came, the long-standing village of St Giles was perceived as the heart of the district and as a close neighbour to both the Soho and the Seven Dials area. The fields and one-time hunting grounds of Soho began to acquire a few substantial houses in the mid-seventeenth century under Cromwell's Commonwealth, and more followed after the Restoration of 1660, including Soho Square. The star-shaped development of streets that became Seven Dials, and now finds itself to the east of Charing Cross Road, was planned in the late seventeenth century too as a natural extension to Soho, neatly fitted in with the line of St Martin's Lane.

Tottenham Court Road tube station is a key one for the West End shopping streets, for Soho with its restaurants and night spots and for much of theatre land. It is also the interchange station between the Central line and the Northern line: it has therefore long been one of the busiest stations on the Underground system, with almost one hundred and fifty thousand passengers passing through it each day. Regulars have been murmuring for decades about the inadequacy of its cramped ticket hall and its rabbit-warren passages. But while a number of people, as the 2000s progressed, had vaguely heard of a project called Crossrail in the planning stage that might or might not happen, very few realised that the Tottenham Court Road station was scheduled to become a key Crossrail site and that willy-nilly the existing old-fashioned station would get swept up in this change. That was why nothing had been done about it before.

Some general concept of Crossrail had been part of the 1940s planning for post-war London and over the 1950s, '60s and '70s the project waxed and waned again.[2] But this was the heyday of motorway construction outside London and attempts at it within the metropolis, for there was a persistent belief that the future lay with the car. In 1974 something akin to the Crossrail trajectory as it has finally emerged did begin to take shape, but it was dismissed, not for the first time, as too expensive.

However, ideas did eventually move on, and in 1990 steps were taken to safeguard what then came to be substantially Crossrail's route, to prevent any more skyscrapers with their inevitably deep foundations from impeding possible future tunnelling. In the summer of 2000 the Labour government, inspired perhaps by the irrational but persistent sense of stardust and new beginnings that the millennium year had brought, declared that the project should go ahead. Two years later the grand plan was beginning to roll. After much shuttling to and fro between Select Committees and both Houses of Parliament, the bill to enable Crossrail finally received royal assent in July 2008, in spite of a distinct downturn that year in Britain's economic situation.

Work finally started in May 2009, though much of it was preparatory: sewers, water mains, gas and electric lines and various other underground mysteries had to be carefully rerouted before tunnelling proper could begin. There was also preliminary deep-piling work for the stations and the drilling of 'compensation grouting' shafts for injecting cement deep in the ground to protect the streets and buildings above from the potential ground-settling effects of tunnelling and train vibration. Explanatory websites were put out and exhibitions planned. Property owners whose possessions happened to be immediately above the projected line were reassured that an insulated tunnel thirty metres underground was unlikely to cause their own walls to subside: the same assurances had had to be given out a hundred years

before when the first deep tubes were built. But what was actually
going on behind the new blue hoardings remained a mystery to many
Londoners, some of whom in any case confused the new underground
line with a more recently launched and controversial plan concerning a high-speed train line from London to Birmingham. Many were
disconcerted, and even disbelieving, when high barriers went up east–
west right across the point where Charing Cross Road meets Oxford
Street, creating a de facto pedestrian space out of what had till then
been one of the busiest road junctions in London. All traffic heading
further north up the Tottenham Court Road had, for over two years,
to take a diversion down a side street and round the back of Centre
Point – where a piece of redundant roadway that had been a planning
folly in the 1960s at last found a temporary use as something other than
a bus-stand.

Centre Point tower itself was much in the way. As a Listed object it
had to remain; but the cramped 'water feature', complete with fountains, that had occupied the space between the tower and the roadway,
confining pedestrian movements there to a dangerously narrow and
splash-sprinkled kerb, was swept away. More disconcertingly, the run
of buildings on the west side of Charing Cross Road, which backed
onto those of Soho Square behind, also had to be removed. Of these,
Michael Hebbert, sometime professor of planning at Manchester University, has written:

> There was general dismay at the loss of the Astoria Theatre across
> the road. The closure and disappearance of this music venue in
> 2009 was the first public indication that Crossrail was for real.[3]

Since that stretch of road was by now entirely shut off and hidden,
'across the road' implies that the viewer is standing on a conveniently
elevated vantage point in front of Centre Point, gazing at a new view
of the backs of buildings in Soho Square, including the imposing apse
of the Roman Catholic church there. And this is exactly what the
viewer was able to do for a long time, due to the fortunate chance of
an external flight of steps leading from the pavement of New Oxford

Street up to the mezzanine level of Centre Point tower. Those in charge of Crossrail wanted to remove this, fearful perhaps of what unnameable problem might occur if members of the public could actually get a bird's-eye view down into the workings. However, the steps turned out to be Listed along with the rest of the building. They had to remain, and the view from the top of them was an ever-changing source of interest.

I first came upon it after dark, when the huge hole that had been gouged out of the earth behind the bland screens was at its deepest and rawest, a great muddy pit a hundred yards wide and a good hundred or more feet deep. In the bottom of it men were manoeuvring around, cautiously, crab-wise, with earth-shifting equipment: well-drilled demons in suits the colour of fire, in the glow of great arc lamps. *Facilis descensus Averno . . .* The next time I saw it, it was deserted and snow lay on it as if this were the cold hell of the Nordic races, not the red-hot inferno of the Mediterranean peoples that the Christian

Crossrail works at Tottenham Court Road, June 2013

tradition has inherited. Then, one spring day, a hugely tall crane was there in the pit, very slowly and delicately lowering an iron girder into place on the edge of a yet deeper gulf, on whose brink other obedient demons lay stretched out to judge its position exactly. On a later visit again, a forest of slim iron rods had grown like saplings and the view changed once more. Very gradually, the cavern that had seemed so terrible began to fill up. Concrete tunnels appeared and a very large, oblong box. Finally, I really could believe I was looking down into the unfinished but recognisable geography of the handsome new station into which light would filter. It had, after all, been promised all the while on the sheltering hoardings, in pictures, along with some pretty mock greenery.

What the hoardings did not say is why this site, and its related ones in Soho Square and Dean Street, is a peculiarly complex one. There is Centre Point; there are other buildings that have to be preserved, including an important seventeenth-century house on the edge of Soho Square full of fragile plasterwork.[4] There is also all the infrastructure of two working Underground lines already occupying the space. A particularly tight corner had to be navigated in the spring of 2014 when it was necessary to ease one of the great boring machines just above the existing Northern line tunnel and just below a set of working escalators, with a margin for error of only a few centimetres. It was successfully achieved, while a posse of engineers and workmen held their collective breath. And there has been yet another consideration to be taken into account. In the future, a Crossrail Two is planned to arrive here also.

The Crossrail being constructed is an east–west route, with its central underground section running at an angle that is actually south-east to north-west. It is logical to suppose that, one day in the not-too-distant future, London will equally require a north–south route – again, one running at an angle, in counterpoint to Crossrail One, north-east to south-west. So far, this exists only as coloured lines on planners' drawings but already the route has a name. It is, provisionally, the Hackney to Richmond line (or alternatively the Epping to Clapham one), and we shall hear of it again. Tottenham Court Road station is where travellers would be able to change from the one Crossrail to the other – a brand-new nexus on a site that has been a significant spot for nine hundred years already.

St Giles-in-the-Fields is not mentioned in William the Conqueror's survey, the Domesday Book. It first appears in the records in the very early years of the twelfth century, when Maud, also known as Matilda, the young wife of Henry I, founded a small hospice there for lepers. Henry, a son of William the Conqueror, became King in 1100, after his elder brother, William Rufus, was killed out hunting (probably on purpose) and another brother retreated temporarily to Normandy which was the home base of this quarrelsome dynasty. Henry set himself up to be a firmer and more just ruler than Rufus, and in the same year he married Maud-Matilda in the old, pre-Gothic Westminster Abbey. As she was a great-great-niece of Edward the Confessor and the daughter of Malcolm, King of Scotland, the marriage was designed to unite the Saxon line with the Norman invaders, which, for a while, it did.

Maud, who had spent much of her teens being sheltered in an abbey from the turmoil that was Britain, seems to have been a suitably serious and pious bride for Henry. She was twenty in 1100, and therefore only thirty-eight when she died in 1118, but such a brief lifespan was then commonplace. The omnipresence of death was a compelling reason, among other more ageless ones such as simple humanity and charity, for the wealthy to found hospices, chantries, priories and the like. The donors were acquiring a form of insurance that, after death, their good works would weigh in their favour on the Day of Judgement. Pictures of naked souls with good deeds in their hands being welcomed at St Peter's gate, while other identical souls without such provision were being hustled to a fiery pit, were standard doctrine. By the time, four hundred-odd years later, that the Dissolution of the Monasteries got under way, London was thick with religious institutions, both within and without the walls. Most were dedicated, at least in theory, to charitable causes: concrete evidence of faith and the power of Christian rule.

It has been suggested that there may have been a small church on or near the St Giles site already before Maud's shelter for lepers was built, but this seems improbable: why would there be a church with no settlement near it? Also, St Giles was the name bestowed on the chantry chapel alongside the leper shelter, and St Giles was the patron saint of lepers.[5] Churches dedicated to him were usually outside towns – St Giles Cripplegate, immediately outside London's northern wall, was another one. Lepers were the archetypal outcasts, often disfigured, chased out of built-up areas as they were supposedly unclean and in the misguided belief that leprosy is extremely catching. At the same time, it was recognised that the lepers' affliction was probably not their fault, and so they were quite a popular target for good works.

Today, when leprosy is almost extinct in Europe, it is hard to know how many of the long-ago recipients of a charity such as Queen Maud's actually suffered from this disease. Some may have been simply victims of scurvy (scrofula), which is associated with a very inadequate diet, or of one of the horrible skin conditions that are still with us, such as erysipelas. Leprosy seems to have been generally associated with dirt in the minds of our ancestors (who had more general concepts of hygiene and pure water than we tend to give them credit for) but it remained something of a mystery even as its incidence in the developed world gradually declined. In the Elizabethan era, when most of the early-medieval leper houses had gone, Richard Carew,[6] man of letters and one of the very first antiquaries, was of the opinion that

> much eating of fish, especially newly taken, and therein principally of the livers, is reckoned a great breeder of those contagious humours which turn into leprosy.

The inhabitants of the small colony at St Giles were not immediately beside any stream for fish. The nearest would have been the Tyburn, a mile along the rough track to the west. It was, at first, a poor little house: to call it a 'hospital' brings in much later connotations of medical treatment. It was, like other such colonies, simply a place of decent refuge for outcasts and of prayers for something better

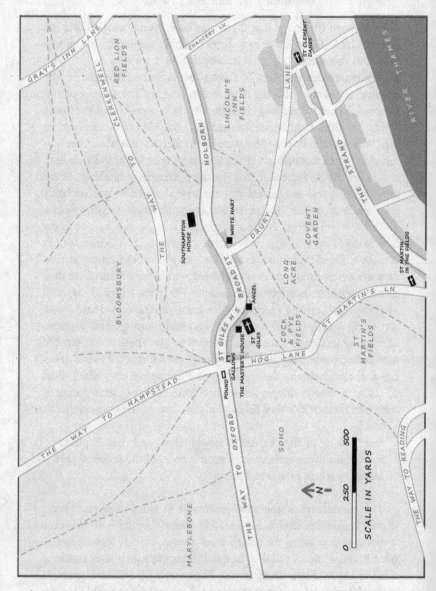

St Giles-in-the-Fields village, *c.* 1550, the built-up area shown in darker grey

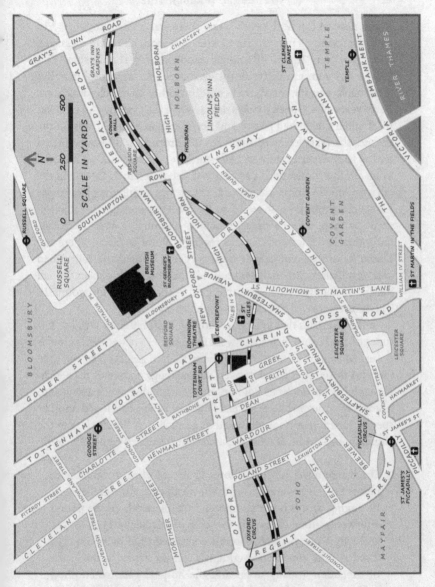

St Giles/Tottenham Court Road district today, with Crossrail

in the next world. In the early years there was a chaplain, a clerk to keep the records, a manservant to fetch provisions and carry messages, and about forty lepers. Its original endowment was only some £3 a year, a tiny sum in relative terms even then, but as a royal initiative it probably became a favoured cause for other charitable donations. Forty years after Queen Maud's death, when the anarchy and civil war of Stephen's reign had passed and her grandson Henry II was on the throne, the place received more royal patronage and became linked with a large leper hospice in Leicestershire. In 1212, about a hundred years after its foundation, a Master was appointed to St Giles, and the current Pope in Rome announced that he was taking the place under his special protection. It seems to have been a prestigious establishment by then, with its chapel rebuilt as a church, a Master's house, and other buildings and gardens reaching about as far as where the Dominion cinema now stands at the corner of Tottenham Court Road and New Oxford Street. By that time also, as you would expect, a small village of cottages with vegetable gardens had grown up around it. The future parish of St Giles was taking shape.

In the centuries that followed, until the Dissolution in 1537, the fortunes of the hospice came and went from one era to another, as it was governed well or ill. One must suppose that, in any case, by the time Henry VIII seized it and bestowed the buildings on one of his henchmen, the need for leper colonies around London was passing into history. But meanwhile St Giles-in-the-Fields had developed another specific function. A book compiled by a much later Vestry clerk to the church, John Parton, describes it, under the heading 'Peculiar Custom':

On the removal of the gallows from the elms in Smithfield, before 1413, they were erected at the north end of the garden wall belonging to this hospital, opposite the place where the pound afterwards stood; between the end of St Giles's High Street and Hog Lane, on which spot it continued until its removal to Tyburn. The condemned criminals, on their way to this place of execution, usually stopped at the hospital gate, where they, as their last refreshment in this life, were presented with a large bowl of ale – the 'St Giles's bowl'. (*Some Account of the Hospital and Parish of St Giles in the Fields, Middlesex*, 1822)

'Opposite . . . the pound . . . between the end of St Giles's High Street and Hog Lane' indicates more or less the site of Centre Point tower. A pound, usually walled, was where stray animals were sequestered until they were claimed. The short paragraph signals once again that what we are dealing with here at St Giles-in-the-Fields is a staging point on a journey. But this journey was not eastwards and down into London town but outwards in the opposite direction. The traitors, supposed heretics and common felons who travelled that one-way route, in increasing numbers between the fifteenth and the eighteenth centuries, quite literally 'went west'. It is their journey out of the City to their death that is referred to.

The phrase stuck, so that much later, in a changed world, it still persisted in use, often trivially, in relation to a monetary loss or just a broken plate. However, rather oddly, it also came to be used to indicate the death of men in the trenches of the First World War, where arguably death came from the eastern or German side. Perhaps the understated, euphemistic nature of the phrase suited the stoic, don't-distress-the-people-at-home mentality that characterised the unprecedented slaughter of that war:

> Once I came home on leave: and then went west . . .
> What greater glory could a man desire?[7]

* * *

Let us follow Crossrail in the opposite, eastward direction, and visit Smithfield.

Smithfield (today included in the jurisdiction of the City) was for centuries part of the external ward of Farringdon, bordered by Clerkenwell to the north and Holborn to the west, as far as the Temple and taking in part of Fleet Street. The name Smithfield derives not from any smithy but from 'smooth field'. The old wall of London avoided it with an L-shaped turn just past Cripplegate southwards to Aldersgate, and another turn there westwards to Newgate. Presumably this extensive green space of smooth field was recognised both by the Romans and by later Londoners to be more useful outside the walls than within. A generation after the Norman Conquest, in the same tradition of good works as the St Giles leper house, an Augustinian priory and hospital (St Bartholomew's) was established on the City side of Smithfield, and two centuries later the Charterhouse, for Carthusian monks, was built to the north of it. Unlike the large number of religious houses within the City, of which very little is now left but inconspicuous ceramic plaques on nineteenth- or twentieth-century walls, both St Bartholomew's and the Charterhouse survived the Dissolution, though in altered form, and flourish to this day.

Smithfield was a place of assembly and contests, friendly or otherwise, of archery, jousts, football, wrestling – and riots. It was where the Peasants' Revolt of 1381 ended in Wat Tyler's being stabbed by the Mayor of London, among others – though there was a popular story put about that the fatal blow was dealt by the boy-King Richard II. Smithfield was also the obvious open space for fairs and sales. Already, about a century after the Norman Conquest, a three-day annual cloth fair for English wool and linen was established there and attracted buyers from as far afield as Italy.

At this period, too, Smithfield began to be used for the City's chief weekly market for cattle, sheep and swine on the hoof, and also for horses. Cheapside, the City's only wide thoroughfare, had served this purpose in earlier days, but already, by the latter part of the twelfth century, this was becoming impossibly inconvenient, especially as the animals for the table, and fowls as well, were customarily slaughtered on the spot. So, by degrees, the whole noisy, chaotic enterprise was shifted outside the walls to Smithfield. Its presence there was ratified by a market charter of 1327, and within fifty years all butchery within the City was banned. Meanwhile, the muddy lanes leading into Smithfield from the countryside beyond acquired the names some of them still bear today: Chicks Lane, Cock Lane, Cow Lane – and Cowcross where Farringdon station stands today. The shambles, the stalls for already-killed meat, were shifted to Newgate Street, the westward extension of Cheapside, which ended at the Fleet ditch – a convenient place into which to throw skins, guts and other unwanted oddments.

It was inevitable that Smithfield, a place of knives and blood and the cries of frightened animals, as well as entertainments, should become a place of human slaughter too. A twelfth-century victim was the Scottish patriot William Wallace, whom Edward I had hanged, drawn and quartered there as a traitor. The quarters were sent for show to different places in the north as if, indeed, they had been joints of meat. If Edward hoped to make an example of him the effort misfired, for Wallace was adopted as a Scottish hero with a legend that is current to this day. A memorial to him adorns a wall in Smithfield near the hospital of Barts.

The chief London prison was the Tower, but the fortified gatehouses on top of London's great iron-bound gates were also used as holding places. The New Gate, not far from Smithfield, was in use as one by 1200. It was rebuilt on a larger scale when the City walls were being allowed to crumble, rebuilt again after the Great Fire and yet again in the late eighteenth century (twice, owing to the damage caused to it during the Gordon riots of 1780), and all this time the Newgate name persisted till the last substantial, grim building was demolished in 1902. The Old Bailey, the Central Criminal Court, now stands on the site. From Newgate, or all the way from the Tower, people were dragged by their heels to be hanged at Smithfield. John Stow, the thoughtful Elizabethan writer whose *Survey* is a mine of detailed information on the London of his own time and much earlier, writes of a large pool at Smithfield used for watering horses, which by his day had been diminished to a brick-lined pond. He adds:

In the 6th [year of the reign] of Henry V a new building was made in this west part of Smithfield, in a place then called the Elmes, for that there grew many elm-trees; and this had been the place of execution for offenders.

Henry V came to the throne in 1413. I don't know why Parton, the vestry clerk quoted earlier, thinks that the gallows were taken to St Giles before that date, but clearly it was around that time that executions were moved out to St Giles, starting with the especially gruesome one of Sir John Oldcastle.

The fact that this offender had given particular offence by holding a seditious meeting on the out-of-the-way St Giles Field (the place later known as Cock and Pye Field) may have had something to do with the choice of the St Giles crossroads for his ending; but perhaps also it was felt expedient to carry out the procedure away from the press of London crowds. St Giles and its surrounding buildings were then entirely 'in the fields' with just a few houses so far built along the lower reaches of Holborn. Essentially, what the Oldcastle execution marks is the time when the first stirrings of religious unrest, that were eventually to culminate in the Reformation, began to rattle those in power – though the protracted struggles between the rival Houses of York and Lancaster meant that power frequently shifted. John Wycliffe, who was arguably the first English Protestant, had died in 1384, but his followers, the Lollards, continued to proclaim his ideas.

Sir John Oldcastle was prominent among them. He was a member of the minor nobility, sometimes called Lord Cobham because he had married Joan, Lady Cobham, a Kentish heiress. He was a soldier by vocation, and seems to have been a genial, swashbuckling but bombastic personality. He was one of the many hangers-on who made up the royal household and was a friend of the young Prince Hal or Harry, who would go on to become Henry V. But when formally summoned to justify his religious views, Oldcastle refused to attend either a civil court or a religious one, and was given to such inflammatory statements as: 'The Pope, the Bishops and the Friars constitute the Head, the Members and the Tail of the Anti-Christ.' He was imprisoned in the Tower but somehow escaped, presumably with clandestine Lollard help, and set about raising a rebellion, which is when the assembly on the St Giles Field occurred. The authorities moved in on him, he escaped, but many of his associates were taken and hanged. Over the next four years he busily fomented revolt after revolt in various parts of the country, till he was finally captured on the Welsh border in 1417 and brought to London for trial, once more to the Tower.

An extra dimension is given to this long-ago story, of intemperate belief and equally intemperate retribution, by the fact that Shakespeare is thought to have based the character of Sir John Falstaff on stories of Oldcastle. Falstaff, who has been the jolly, turbulent, older drinking companion of the young Prince Hal, is set aside when the Prince becomes King (see *Henry IV,* parts 1 and 2). He reappears, fatter and more boastful than ever, in the comedy *The Merry Wives of Windsor.* There is assorted textual evidence that Falstaff's name in the plays was originally to be Oldcastle, and that Shakespeare altered it, and also uttered a hasty disclaimer, when an influential descendant of Sir John complained. In *Henry V* Falstaff does not appear, but his death is recounted to us just before the scene shifts to France and the build-up to the Battle of Agincourt. Several of the semi-comic minor characters meet before a tavern in Eastcheap, and the barmaid gives them the news that Falstaff is dead:

Nay, sure, he's not in hell: he's in Arthur's bosom, if ever man went to Arthur's bosom. A' made a finer end and went away an it had been any christom child; a' parted even just between twelve and one, even at the turning o' the tide: for after I saw him fumble with the sheets and play with flowers and smile upon his fingers' ends, I knew there was but one way; for his nose was as sharp as a pen, and a' babbled of green fields.

Alas for the real Sir John, more than a century and a half before this was written, he suffered a far less gentle death. Bishop John Bale, who was originally a Carmelite monk but, like many others, went over to the Protestant cause at the Reformation, wrote then:

Upon the day appoynted was he (Sir John Oldcastle, the Lord Cobham) broughte out of the Tower with his armes bounde behynde him havyinge a verye cheereful countenance. Then was he layd upon a hurdle as though he had bene a most heynouse traytour to the crowne and so drawne forth into saynet Giles's Felde where they had set up a new payre of gallowes. Then was

he hanged up there by the myddle in cheanes of yron and so consumed alyve in the fyre.[8]

Executing Catholic priests in 1591

It both horrifies and baffles us
today that such extreme cruelty was
ordered by men who, in many cases,
were astute, articulate, literate and,
what's more, were quite likely to
suffer a similar horrible fate themselves when the political tide turned
again. Having what was currently
deemed to be the wrong opinion
about God's Will was punished far
more severely than robbery or murder. The contest of brutal tit-for-tat
martyrdom reached its height in the
sixteenth century, as successive mon-
archs held different religious views
and sedition was therefore treacher-
ous to earthly as well as to heavenly power. But the more fundamental
explanation for it is that the perpetrators of cruel executions, on both
sides, believed that, by suffering earthly torments, the prisoner's soul
would have already begun to make reparation to God for his sins. The
sufferers themselves believed, almost to a man, that Heaven was now
very near and that through their extreme pain they would be gaining
an instant place there. Oldcastle, we note, looked positively cheerful at
the prospect. He could echo to himself, and probably did, the words of
Paul before his own execution:

> I have fought the good fight, I have finished my course, I have
> kept the faith. Henceforth there is laid up for me a crown of
> righteousness.[9]

Confusingly, Oldcastle has a pub named after him in the Farringdon
Road just by Smithfield. Although it seems clear that the gallows for
ordinary felons were moved to St Giles, probably because Smithfield

was now becoming so crowded with multiple other uses, burnings of successive waves of heretics continued in the traditional Smithfield location. But this was apparently not the hanging place where the elms had once stood but a spot further over by the west door of St Batholomew's church, near where today an ancient alley leads under a gatehouse to the churchyard that is the site of the pre-Reformation nave. In 1849, when new concepts of public health were burgeoning and sewers were being dug all over London's old streets, workmen uncovered there 'about 3 foot below the surface . . . unhewn stones, blackened as if by fire, and covered with ashes and human bone, charred and partly consumed' (*The Times*, 16 March 1849). It was said further that passers-by, and those who heard of this discovery, hastened to take bits of bone away as relics or mementoes, but, once again, no professionally recorded evidence of this discovery remains today.

The Smithfield–Farringdon district had some tradition of Protestantism. John Knox (*c.* 1514–1572) held discreet services there in a room in the Saracen's Head, a well-known inn at the corner of Snow Hill and Cock Lane. His friend John Rogers, vicar of St Sepulchre church just outside the wall at Newgate, was a follower of Tyndale, the Bible translator. At an open-air pulpit near St Paul's Rogers preached what, under Queen Mary, was sedition, an act of suicidal bravery not to say folly. Although anti-Catholic, he was opposed to very radical Protestantism also, and refused to condemn the burning of one fanatic on the grounds that this was a punishment 'sufficiently mild for heresy' – a remark that came home to roost with a vengeance when his own turn for trial came. He went to the stake attended on the way by his wife and ten children. Several of his associates were burnt with him; all in all some two hundred Protestants suffered the same fate during Mary's five-year reign (1553–1558). Known as the Protestant Martyrs, they are commemorated in various places around Smithfield and Clerkenwell, and in the subsequent centuries of Anglican England it was always these, along with the Oxford Martyrs, Cranmer, Latimer and Ridley, who were emphasised in history lessons.

However, a significant number of those who held to their Catholic faith suffered cruelly under Henry VIII, including the confessor of his first wife, Catherine of Aragon. Some of the earliest Catholic martyrs were the monks of the Charterhouse; those of Barts proved to be more adaptable. In the spring of 1534 the Carthusians reluctantly agreed to the Act of Succession, which ratified King Henry's divorce from Catherine and allowed him to marry Anne Boleyn. But the following spring the idea of recognising Henry rather than the Pope as head of the Church was a step too far for them. The favoured method of retribution for such defiant heresy (i.e. not doing what the King wanted) was hanging, then drawing and quartering while the victim was still alive. This was the fate eventually suffered by many of the monks, though nine out of the ten who had been chained upright to posts at Newgate for many days did not survive to suffer further pains. Others were eventually dragged westwards, not just to St Giles-in-the-Fields but all the way to Tyburn along the Oxford road, which for some time seems to have been regarded as a suitably out-of-the-way place to dispose of traitors. This was public punishment, but not so immediately accessible to the City that it might attract too large and possibly too sympathetic a crowd. Thirty-five years before, Perkin Warbeck, the mysterious fraudster who tried to pass himself off as 'Richard IV', the younger of the two princes who had disappeared in the Tower, had gone that way. Now it was the turn of Prior Houghton of the Charterhouse, and a number of others who found themselves at odds with the King and with his henchman Thomas Cromwell.

A further procession of Catholics was intermittently dispatched at Tyburn later in the century, after Mary's counterwave attacking Protestants had come and gone, and Elizabeth was crowned. All these, along with more commonplace criminals, passed by St Giles. No wonder the route out of Newgate, down the steep Snow Hill slope from the City wall, across the Fleet at Holborn Bridge, up the other side and along the gentle curve of Holborn, has come to be looked on by Catholic writers as a Via Sacra, the path to another place that was both actual and symbolic. 'I am the Way, the Truth and the Life, saith the Lord.' And no wonder those in charge of St Giles, whether the Masters of the leper hospital before the Dissolution or the successive vicars there once the chapel had become a parish church, continued to offer a last drink to the condemned. Stow, writing towards the end of Elizabeth's reign, mentions this offer of a 'bowl of ale' as if it were a past thing, but there is plenty of evidence of it in later days. It was indisputably an act of non-partisan Christian charity in the midst of so much sectarian judgement.

But the public houses that later became associated with the ritual Bowl were also the pubs used by cattle drovers going in the opposite direction. Odd to think that, on their last journey, the condemned must sometimes have come face to face with unruly mooing or baaing herds bound for Smithfield market, whose keepers tried hastily to drive them to one side of the rutted roadway. These creatures, too, were going to their deaths but, more fortunate than men, they did not yet know it.

Some of the men found that their journey ended at St Giles. In 1586 several Catholic conspirators from what became known as the Babington Plot met their fate at the gallows of St Giles. As with the Lollards a century and a half before, St Giles Field had been one of their meeting places. Their hope had been to assassinate Queen Elizabeth and raise countrywide enthusiasm for putting her cousin, Mary, Queen of Scots, on the throne. As we know, it was Mary who ended up headless. The first conspirators to be arrested and tried in a batch, including Anthony Babington himself, were sentenced to be hanged, drawn and quartered and this was carried out, but public feeling was now beginning to recoil from the disembowelling of still-living men. The second lot to be convicted were allowed to hang till they were dead before being eviscerated and quartered. These were mainly young, handsome, well-born men – one, Tichborne, wrote a poignant poem in the Tower the night before his ordeal – and perhaps those in authority felt uncomfortably aware that these were people of their own kind.

My glass is full, and now my glass is run,
And now I live, and now my life is done.

* * *

During the sixteenth century the Way from Holborn to St Giles was getting steadily more built up. There had long been settlement immediately to the west of the Fleet. On the rising ground there was the palace and grounds of the Bishop of Ely and, on the south side, the church of St Andrew and the various lawyers' inns beyond, running down to Fleet Street. There would have been a gradually increasing number of houses along the roadside as far as Holborn bars, and perhaps a few up Gray's Inn Lane. But once Elizabeth was established on the throne, relative peace and prosperity after so much earlier turmoil brought a building boom. Two of the earliest extant maps of London, the Agas map of 1562 and the Braun and Hogenberg one of ten years later, show the way to St Giles ribbon-developed at least halfway along, the houses fronting the road with gardens behind them. (The one imposingly large survivor of all these timbered Tudor habitations for comfortably off people stands today in Holborn, opposite Gray's Inn Road, just on the Westminster side of Holborn bars.) Then there was a short stretch of open field lined with hedges before a cluster of houses where the ancient country track, recently called Drury Lane after a big house built there by one of Elizabeth's courtiers, joined it slantwise from the south. Then another run of houses began on the opposite side of the road, continuing to St Giles. Behind all these, fields, mainly meadow and pastureland to supply London's ever-increasing need for hay to feed horses and cattle, still stretched open to the sky. But not for much longer. Stow, writing at the end of the century and of Elizabeth's reign, noted:

> Now the Highe Holborne street, from the north end of New street, stretcheth on the left hand [i.e. south side] in building lately framed, up to St Giles in the field.

A generation later, both sides, and the whole Drury Lane district, were filled with houses.

It was to be a long time, however, before the Way to Oxford, west from St Giles and hence to Tyburn, would have much building along it, although Marylebone to the north was an established hamlet. Tyburn continued to be regularly used as the last place seen by felons through the seventeenth and much of the eighteenth centuries, a countrified spot too far from London proper to be much visited. By the later days of Tyburn most of those who died there were not traitors or martyrs to their faith, but run-of-the-mill highwaymen and other still more ordinary wrongdoers who were unlucky enough to be caught rather too often.

On their last ride in the cart, most would have believed that they were going to a real Somewhere, to Heaven or Hell, rather than into nothingness. The apparently gentle song 'Loch Lomond' refers to this. A homesick Scot, who has come to London to seek his fortune, has got into trouble and then worse trouble and is now on his way to Tyburn, thinks of a girl he is leaving behind and sings optimistically:

> Oh, you'll take the high road and I'll take the low road,
> And I'll be in Scotland afore ye.[10]

It is the high road that is the ordinary, arduous path all the way to and from the north, which he himself took on foot when he made his fatal decision to come south. The low road, in Scottish folklore, is the magic route by which the fairies were believed to transport a dead Scot back to his homeland. It was called low because it was said to run underground. Another example of an underground in the mind predating reality by many centuries.

CHAPTER V

'No Man may by the Eye discern it'

It is time to continue the Crossrail journey further eastwards from Farringdon and Smithfield. It runs a little to the north of old London Wall, beneath the tracks of the Metropolitan and Hammersmith & City lines that now have a part of the 1970s Barbican complex sitting on top of them, and so under Finsbury Circus to Liverpool Street station. Thus the new line takes the route followed by the earliest Underground and also, hundreds of years before, by travellers wanting to bypass the crowded City lanes and get quickly to the other side.

A very long time ago the space next door to Liverpool Street station, where the Broadgate Centre now stands, was where the Walbrook ran. This stream bisected the City north to south, running down past where the central crossroads of the Bank now lies, to Dowgate just west of present-day Cannon Street, and so out into the Thames. To do this, it had to cross under London's northern wall – or rather, the wall when it was built by the Romans around AD 200 had to accommodate the stream. It may indeed have got its name 'Wall Brook'[1] because a culvert had to be made in the wall for it.

The Walbrook has long been the most deeply hidden of all London's buried rivers, but a street not far from the Thames still bears its name. It was here, nearly two thousand years ago, that a temple was erected to Mithras, a Persian god who was apparently popular with Roman legionaries. The temple was found during work for a new office block in 1954: it was very nearly destroyed before mounting public opinion, and the efforts of individual archaeologists, achieved a rescue – though at the cost of its removal to another site.[2]

One thousand years ago, the Walbrook was still navigable, several yards wide in some places, with bridges passing over it that were to be maintained by the adjacent householders. It was an administrative marker, dividing the wards of the City into east and west. But it seems that already at this time it was beginning to suffer the usual fate of streams near dense human habitation and was becoming a repository of human waste and general rubbish. From the early Middle Ages there are references to its being 'scoured' or otherwise dredged, and in about 1300 its meandering course was straightened and confined to a newly dug ditch slightly to the east of the original waterway. In 1374 a brewer, known by the street-sign of his address as Thomas atte Ram, undertook to keep the ditch cleansed, and in return was granted a seven-year lease enabling him to charge a rent for each privy (latrine) constructed over it – which one might think a somewhat contradictory bargain. By 1415, the stream was being referred to as 'the Fosse of Walbrook', so evidently it was undergoing the classic transformation from clear waterway into sewer. Fifty-odd years later the City prohibited the discharge of latrines into the Walbrook, and by the end of the century the inhabitants of London were being positively encouraged to bring their old debris and rubbish to fill the ditch up. Another hundred years passed and Stow, writing at the end of Elizabeth's reign, was able to pronounce the epitaph of the stream:

which was of old time bridged over in divers places, for passage of horses and men, as need required; but since, by means of encroachment on the banks thereof, the channel being greatly straightened, and other noyances done thereunto, at length the same by common consent was arched over with brick, and paved with stone, equal with the ground, where through it passed, and is now in most places built upon, that no man may by the eye discern it, and therefore the trace thereof is hardly known to the common people.

Early-twentieth-century speculative maps show the Walbrook rising very near the City and due north of it, on Moorfields, but more

recent research[3] suggests that its main tributary in fact rose to the
north-west as far away as Islington. Still more recent excavations on
the Crossrail Liverpool Street station site seem to indicate another
western arm much closer to London Wall, which may be the main
stream. A section of Roman road, complete with signs of cart ruts
and what seems to be a bridge-embankment, has been discovered at
the west end of Liverpool Street (junction with Blomfield Street).
There too have been found the Roman equivalent of horseshoes,
which were strapped on rather than nailed to the hooves, two horse
skulls, and also thirty-nine human skulls which were probably washed
down the stream during a flood from a Roman cemetery which is
known to have lain to the north of Finsbury Circus. Just skulls – no
accompanying bones. What hidden tale do they tell of gladiatorial
fights or ritual decapitations?

The Romans kept the culvert for the stream through London Wall
clear, but the very construction of the wall must have tended to create a
build-up of water on the northern side of it. After the Romans retreated
from Britain in the fifth century, and Saxon occupation of the City was
sparse and intermittent, culverts were neglected and became blocked,
and the swampy conditions on the north side would have increased.
Not for nothing did that area of open land immediately adjacent to the
wall and west of the Bishop's Gate become known as 'the Moor' and
'Moorfields'. In other words, the Moorfields were not the source of the
Walbrook, as was once thought, but were formed by it.
    The fields dried out in summer, but each winter they flooded. When
a Lord Mayor at the beginning of the fourteenth century was inspect-
ing the fields he had to make his tour by boat. Later that century a
house of monks was established near the Moorfields, a place which,
through time and chance, later became the most significant establishment of the area. The monks complained of 'great rains and water',
and said that because the Walbrook ditch became choked 'in winter
time, every year, a foot or more in depth overflowed', invading the
bridge into their priory. Earlier in the Middle Ages, when one William
Fitzstephen wrote an adulatory description of London in Latin as part

of his biography of the murdered Thomas à Becket, he gave a detailed description of the seasonal floods. Translated later by the indefatigable Stow, for inclusion in his own work, Fitzstephen's word-picture of wintertime fun on the Moor is as fresh as if it were written about goings-on a generation or so ago, whereas in reality some eight hundred years separate us from these vigorous, inventive people:

> When that great marsh which washes the walls of the City on the north side is frozen over, the young men go out in crowds to divert themselves upon the ice. Some, having increased their velocity by a run placing their feet apart, and turning their bodies sideways, slide a great way: others make a seat of large pieces of ice like mill-stones, and a great number of them running before, and holding each other by the hand, draw one of their companions who is seated on the ice: if at any time they slip in moving so swiftly, all fall down headlong together. Others are more expert in their sports upon the ice; for fitting to, and binding under their feet the shinbones of some animal, and taking in their hands poles shod with iron, which at times they strike against the ice, they are carried along with as great rapidity as a bird flying or a bolt discharged from a crossbow.

Mock battles took place with these poles, and accidents, he added, such as the breaking of arms and legs, were not uncommon, 'but youth is an age eager for glory and desirous of victory'. In recent Crossrail excavations at Finsbury Circus, whose central garden is a last remnant of the Moorfields, one of these bone-skates came to light.

It is clear that, what with repeated medieval efforts at dredging and channel-cutting, for much of the year the Moorfields were made dry enough for all kinds of other sports. We hear that, on Shrove Tuesday:

> after dinner, all the young men of the city go out into the fields to play at the well-known game of football . . . The more aged men, the fathers of the players, and the wealthy citizens, come on horseback to see the contests.

The division into teams belonging to the various schools in the City also seems of all time, though the ritual cock-fighting in schoolrooms in front of the masters, which preceded the football, is more alien to us. Other mock battles with blunted lances included spirited horses, if the participants were the sons of gentlemen, and Easter was marked by a strike-the-quintain competition with a target on a moving boat on the Walbrook – currently confined in its banks.

The Moorfields had become Londoners' principal playground. What Fitzstephen does not mention, presumably because it would have seemed quite ordinary to him but would fill a time traveller from the present with delight and wonder, would have been the number and variety of birds that were then present, even so close to a built-up area. We see them disporting themselves on the borders of medieval manuscripts: lapwings, peewits, woodpeckers, jays, kites, merlins, ravens, buzzards and others now driven into remote corners of the British Isles or into extinction, were then part of the common scene. So, on the Moorfields would be waterbirds and herons. Cuckoos would have been calling loudly every May only a short flight from the bells of London's numerous church towers. Geoffrey Chaucer – who was living for a while in the late fourteenth century in the gatehouse over the Ald Gate – did not have to rely only on literary sources for the population of his Parliament of Fowles. They were there, accessible and visible to him on any spring walk just beyond the City.

By the end of the fifteenth century, with the digging of drainage channels and the gradual covering and paving over of the Walbrook, the erstwhile marsh had became pastureland. In the mid-century the Moor Gate itself had been built, as a new entry-and-exit point for Londoners between the older Bishop's Gate to the east and Cripple Gate to the west, and this could hardly have happened if the space beyond it had still been full of rushes and reed beds. There were now small 'summer houses' there, little wooden pavilions; 'dog-houses' too, where the Mayor of London kept his pack of hounds for hunting in the hills and woodlands further north. Garden plots began to appear, nibbling away at the public space, and there were instances of parties of young men with picks and shovels breaking down newly planted hedges to free the land again for sports. A little later brick clay was dug out on the Moor, and after that the City took the opportunity to level the land for archery practice, the social obligation that those in power had laid on the ordinary populace over many generations. A ribbon of houses began to creep up the edge of Bishopsgate-Without-the-Walls, as that part of the high road was by then called.

By a lucky chance, we have a detailed bird's-eye view of exactly this area dating from the mid-sixteenth century, just before the building boom of Elizabeth's reign transformed it into a suburb. The 'Copper-plate map', of which only three sheets have survived, is thought to have been the original from which Agas, and then Braun and Hogenberg, took their less detailed but more comprehensive plans of London. One of the sheets shows the district immediately to the north of London Wall beyond the Bishop's Gate and the Moor Gate with extraordinary, indeed exaggerated, precision, as if the viewer were seated in an open, low-flying plane.[4] Water is confined to a ditch running immediately below the wall (the Town Ditch) and to other cut channels further north that then go into underground sluices. At one point on the Town Ditch are two tiny sheds that are presumably public latrines. Over the open, grassy spaces washerwomen are laying out clothes to dry. Others are spreading out larger lengths of cloth, one of them pegged to the ground to keep it from blowing away, and to the west and to the north are 'tenter grounds', as used by dyers and fullers of cloth, to dry their products by hanging them on racks. One washerwoman seems to be remonstrating with a man equipped for martial practice in a cuirasse and helmet, as if telling him he is in the wrong part of the fields. Elsewhere, people stroll; two ladies play with a little, bouncing dog; some-one carries a heavy jar on his head; a horse and cart are being led up the track from the Moor Gate; an old man trudges with a stick; horses and cows browse, and pigs trot freely. Over towards Finsbury, where there are windmills, some gentry seem to be meeting. In several spots archers practise, though the presence of 'Artillery grounds' on the east-ern side of Bishopsgate suggests that by this date archery had become less of an essential skill for the defence of the realm and more of a congenial pastime – the sixteenth-century equivalent of golf, perhaps.

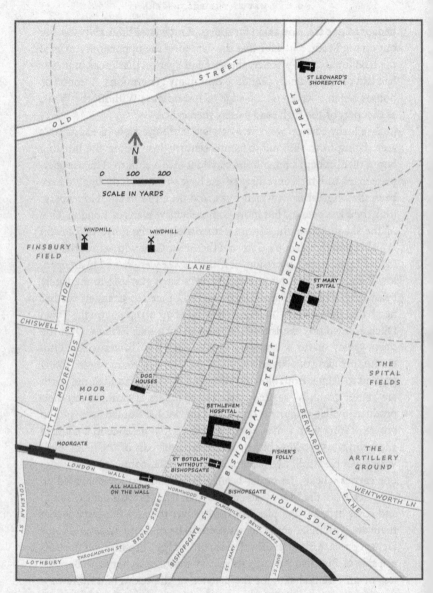

The way north from the Bishop's Gate, *c.* 1550, the built-up area shown in darker grey

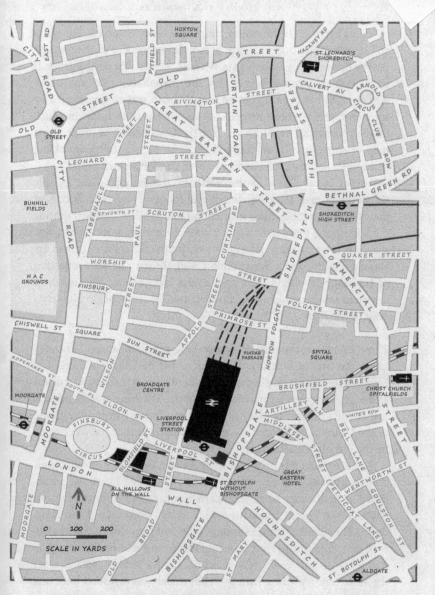

Bishopsgate/Liverpool Street/Shoreditch district today, with Crossrail

In this happy and informative scene scale is not observed. The shirts and towels spread out to dry are in fact almost the size of the roofs of nearby houses along Bishopsgate Without. Clearly the drying grounds were seen as more important by the map-maker than the buildings were. It has been suggested that the map was commissioned by someone with business interests in the thriving cloth trade, in which English merchants exported much to the Continent. The cruder Agas map of some years later then followed the same pattern, sprinkling giant shirts and also oversized cows over London's home fields.

Almost immediately to the north of the Bishop's Gate on the Copperplate map stands a church and its graveyard. This is one of the four St Botolph's churches then in London, all placed just outside the City gates, since St Botolph, a seventh-century Saxon abbot, was a patron saint of those setting out on journeys.[5] A little further up, about a hundred yards from London Wall, the map shows a collection of buildings set within their own courts and gardens. This is where the monks had complained of flooding two centuries before. It is now marked 'Bedlam'.

These buildings, the dust of whose long-ago foundations lies today under the Great Eastern hotel on the corner of Liverpool Street and Bishopsgate, did not begin their chequered life as a madhouse, still less as the generic name for madness anywhere. The place was founded in 1247 as the Priory of St Mary of Bethlehem. It was a dependent house of the Order of Bethlehem, which was based in France but was owned by the Bishop of Bethlehem.

To understand this fully is to enter the mindset of our distant ancestors. Essentially, a diocese of the Roman Catholic Church was established in Bethlehem when Jerusalem was captured from the Fatimid Arabs in the First Crusade, in 1099, and was declared a 'Latin Kingdom'. The Greek Orthodox monks who had been living there unobtrusively were thrown out, as being the wrong sort of Christians; in Bethlehem a new monastery was built, and a bishop's palace. Over the next century and a half the Holy Land was wrestled back and forth between European Christians and Muslim 'Saracens'; at intervals bishops, driven out by strife, would find refuge in the French house of

Bethlehem, in Burgundy. In 1244 the Saracens took Jerusalem again, and there were tales that the current bishop had sold off some of the Church possessions there to his own profit. It was three years after this that an Englishman, a City alderman and one-time sheriff, decided to make a present to the Order of Bethlehem of some three and a quarter acres of land that he owned off Bishopsgate Without.

He seems to have been a charismatic figure, but controversial and sometimes ruthless, even by the standards of those brutal times. He had enemies, but also influential friends. His name was Simon FitzMary, which sounds like a matronymic and has led some commentators to speculate whether he, like the Christ Child, was born of an irregular union. This appears not to have been the case; his mother's family were themselves prosperous and respectable, but on account of his name he may always have felt particularly under the patronage of the Virgin Mary. This was an era when the celestial population of saints was as real and present to believers as were the secular powers, and FitzMary may have been a genuinely religious man. There is a legend, which may or may not have any truth in it, that he went crusading to the Holy Land himself and nearly fell into Saracen hands there, but that a bright star over Bethlehem guided him back to his own camp.

What is more convincing evidence is that he met the exiled Bishop of Bethlehem at a formal reception in Westminster, and bonded with him. His aim in founding a Priory of the Order of Bethlehem was threefold. On a worldly level, the place was to serve as an alms-raising centre and an English refuge for bishops and other clergy from the Latin Kingdom – a shrewd move at a time when Henry III's attempts to seize back lands lost to the French were failing. But the members of the Priory were also to offer shelter to the poor and needy. Thirdly, and crucially, they were to pray for the soul of Simon FitzMary after his death. He was eventually buried near the altar of the Priory chapel, but his tomb, like the chapel, did not survive the vicissitudes of time and chance in the centuries that followed.

At much the same time that the Priory, complete with its own orchard, herb and vegetable gardens, was established, the conduit was built to bring fresh, clean water from the Tyburn near Marylebone all the way into Cheapside. London was expanding. By the end of the thirteenth century its population may have been sixty or seventy thousand. (The population of England then is thought to have been about six million, considerably more than at the Norman Conquest two centuries before, though it was to reduce again with the Black Death fifty years later.) In strictly relative terms most of the thirteenth century, during which Henry III reigned from childhood into old age, was, in spite of uprisings, a little more peaceful than either the preceding one or the one that followed. Magna Carta was ratified. Comprehensive records of land ownership were made. The concept of Parliament was born. The City of London developed a proper system of government. Earls did not have their heads cut off.

But even in prosperous London, the 'mart of many peoples', the mass of the population was poor by the standards of later centuries, often ill-nourished in winter, defenceless against all kinds of sickness. Life could be merry and sweet but it was also fragile: its end could come at any time. Huge numbers of people scraped by only on the charity of the better off. In the early days of St Mary Bethlehem, whose name had not yet been contracted by unlettered speech into 'Bedlam', the monks themselves were mendicant friars, going out into the streets and lanes to solicit alms for their Order. Bishopsgate Without, as the start of a major route north, was a good location for begging – from travellers just setting out on an inevitably hazardous journey and therefore likely to buy, as insurance, celestial credit and protection. The same was true of St Giles-in-the-Fields, on the north-western route out of London, and there too in its early days before its endowment improved, the monks of the leper hospital probably begged for alms.

There was another Order of monks just a little further up Bishopsgate Without, but on the eastern side. This was another St Mary's, St Mary Spital, which had been founded by a London citizen and his wife a little earlier than St Mary Bethlehem. Part of its ruined chapel was unearthed (literally) in recent years when large blocks were going up in Spital Square, and has been preserved under glass many feet below the modern pavement. Both places were soon to be described as 'hospitals', hence the appellation 'Spital', but 'hostel' would be a more appropriate term. St Mary Spital was 'a house of relief for the needy' and apparently could find floor space for nearly two hundred of these. St Mary Bethlehem was much smaller, and it was more a general religious house that was prepared to shelter deserving guests in its infirmary.

It is not quite clear when St Mary Bethlehem began to receive the insane; evidence that it was doing so early in the fourteenth century, as some have claimed, is scant. The Black Death in the mid-century dislocated the social order; the poor became less submissive about their lot, wages rose – but the most significant events of the time for the Order of Bethlehem were probably a series of bloody encounters between England and France. In these circumstances 'foreign' priories, such as St Mary Bethlehem, whose mother house was in France, risked having their assets seized by the King. It seems probable that in emphasising their hospital role and specialising in the care of the insane, the friars established a new justification for their existence. In the late 1370s they acquired 'the Stone House', a religious property in St Martin's Fields near Charing Cross, that was already in use as a shelter for the mad. Richard II wished to have these neighbours removed from the vicinity of his Westminster palace, so they were taken over to Bishopsgate Without. By 1403, Bethlehem Hospital is recorded as having care of 'six men who had lost their reason'. The place continued in this mode throughout the fifteenth and into the sixteenth century, though it also seems to have gone on functioning as a hostel for travellers newly arrived at London's northern gate. In addition, it began to capitalise on some of its ground by building tenements which were let to people who had nothing to do with the hospital. This is 'Bethlem' as depicted at the moment of the Copperplate map, still with plenty of garden space around it.

Popular history-porn, which runs on a condescending pity for the past, has looked to descriptions of what Bedlam may have become by the seventeenth century, and to the lurid fantasies of Jacobean drama, to portray late-medieval Bethlem/Bedlam as a place where half-starved maniacs sat on the ground loaded with chains, sticking straws in their

hair while being jeered at by well-heeled visitors. There is no evidence
for this in the pre-Reformation period, or indeed for long after. It is
true that the mad were chained if they made a nuisance of themselves, and that medieval 'treatments' for insanity, such as purging,
cold showers or confining in a dark place, cannot have been pleasant,
but treatments for physical ailments then were often grotesque and
counterproductive also. Bedlam was called 'a hospital for distracted
people', with the implication that 'distraction' could be a passing affliction, like vomiting, or the 'ague' which was the then-commonplace
malaria fever. Some of the inmates, in any case, would probably not
have been insane at all in present-day terms, but were subject to epilep-
tic fits or were brain-damaged, suffered from senile dementia or were
just of very limited intelligence. Tolerance of oddity was much greater
in the distant past, and still in the early modern period, than in our own
times, and descriptions of the hospital accommodation make it clear
that patients judged to be harmless could wander about the Bedlam
buildings and yards at will and even roam outside the gatehouse. The
fourteenth-century poet William Langland – who was a little odd
himself – regarded some of the mad as 'god's minstrels and merry-
mouthed jesters', and there was the long tradition of those judged to
be fools being treated as mascots and allowed special tolerance to say
whatever came into their heads.

It seems most likely that, like many other institutions, Bethlem/
Bedlam jogged along, a refuge of a sort, with few amenities and few
comforts because most of the ordinary population of England did not
have these anyway. Sometimes it would be in the charge of a decent
Master, who might bestir himself to procure new palliasses for the
lodgers, sometimes prey to a more incompetent and venal one who
stole hospital property, let the mad get drunk, and allowed in rowdy
layabouts.

Then came the Reformation, with the royal seizure and closure of
religious houses up and down the country, and thus a terrible dislo-
cation of the ad hoc welfare system they represented. St Mary Spital
was closed then, being apparently in a somewhat ruinous condition –
but, even so, some remaining inmates must have been left to roam the

streets, fields and commons as 'poor naked wretches' with garments of 'loop'd and window'd raggedness'. It is not hard to see, in Lear's madness and Edgar's sympathetic feigned madness – and in their abandonment on a storm-blasted heath – a comment, some sixty years after the event, on Henry VIII's brutal Dissolution. Edgar, calling himself 'Tom o'Bedlam', cries: 'No one cares for poor Tom.' Many religious foundations may indeed, by then, have become decadent, but the King's own quest for riches and power led to the wholesale dismantling of charitable structures that had taken hundreds of years to evolve.

However, Bedlam survived. Not as a religious house any more, but as a simple madhouse. Evidently it was, like Bartholomew's hospital for the sick in body, too useful to be shut down. Indeed, the specific reference in *King Lear* probably owes something to the circumstance that the Curtain Theatre, halfway up the road to Shoreditch, was Shakespeare's main base between 1597 and 1599. The wandering deranged would have been a common sight on that stretch of highway:

> *Bedlam beggars, who, with roaring voices*
> *Strike in their numb'd and mortified bare arms*
> *Pins, wooden pricks, nails, sprigs of rosemary.*

In 1547, just three hundred years after Simon FitzMary had founded it, Bedlam had been given by the King to the City of London, and they maintained it as an established institution. At the end of the century, Stow wrote:

> The church and chapel thereof were taken down in the reign of Queen Elizabeth, and houses built there by the governors of Christ's hospital in London. In this place people that be distraught in their wits are, by the suit of their friends, received and kept as afore, but not without charges to their bringers-in.

So, no longer a charitable asylum for the most wretched, but a madhouse charging fees presumably on a scale relating to the accommodation offered. The relations of the poorer inmates were expected to visit with supplies of food, as in some parts of the world today.

Hospitals, asylums, prisons and poorhouses have always tended to be established just outside urban centres, where there is for the time being spare land, and where the ailments and/or behaviour of the inmates will not trouble respectable townspeople. But it is also in the natural order of things that the town spreads and that the one-time green-field site becomes coveted building land. By the late sixteenth century the way up from Bishopsgate to Shoreditch was becoming a sought-after location. Trades and manufactures, as well as houses, were beginning to crowd round – and within – the precincts of the old hospital. There had long been a prosperous inn immediately to the south, the White Hart, which survived through the centuries, having been rebuilt several times, till this book was being written.[6] There was at least one alehouse, the Black Bull, actually within the site of Bedlam, and a distillery and a dye-works nearby. There were other demands on its space also. In 1568 a Sir Thomas Roe, who was a member of the Merchant Taylors' Company and was that year Mayor of London, paid for a brick wall to be put around almost an acre of Bedlam's garden land. This was henceforth going to be used 'for burials and ease of such parishes in London as wanted [i.e. were lacking] ground convenient within their own parishes'. This was not an exploitative act but, rather, a protective measure for land that would otherwise have disappeared under more tenements.

So, the burials on Bedlam site began. We shall meet the bodies again – literally. Since it has been widely assumed in recent times that this was a despised pauper graveyard filled mainly with dead lunatics (more history-porn), it seems worth mentioning that Sir Thomas Roe's lady wife, who had encouraged him in his generous enclosure of a new burial ground, was herself interred there when her time came. He, however, was buried in the parish church of Hackney, a little way outside London to the north. For much of the expansionist sixteenth century, gentlemen like Roe had been colonising, with fine houses,

London's ancillary villages. It was in Hackney too that Thomas Crom-well's ward, Ralph Sadler, had built himself a brick mansion house – today almost the only one of that period that has survived in the London area. We shall meet the Cromwell family again in Stepney, another one-time village on the Crossrail route.

Other Elizabethans, however, remained true to the City, building in areas which would once have been regarded as right outside but which more and more were being subsumed into an extended town-scape as the walls ceased to be needed for defence. The garden-suburb idyll, which was eventually to become so characteristic of England, was already being established. On the east side of the high road, more or less opposite Bedlam but set well back, was 'a large and beautiful house', according to Stow, 'with gardens of Pleasure, Bowling-Alleys and such-like, built by Jasper Fisher'. As this gentleman, though a goldsmith, was apparently 'of no great calling or possessions' but had many debts, the house became mockingly known as Fisher's Folly. Another substantial house was built nearby by the Vaughan family and yet another by Christopher Campion: this may have been the one in which Sir Anthony Babington, he of the 'Papist Plot', was hidden fruit-lessly for a few hot days in the summer of 1586.

Right at the end of Elizabeth's reign, another mansion of a trad-itionally timbered kind was built on the western side of Bishopsgate Without by one Paul Pindar. He was a Merchant Taylor, and was profitably involved in the growing trade with Turkey and Persia. This was a town house, three and a half storeys high, gabled and jettied, with big, expensive, carved and glazed windows, yet it had a garden almost the size of a park behind. There was a grove of mulberry trees, and deer from the country were fattened there for the table. The Venetian ambassador, who stayed in this house for some time, described the locality as 'an airy and fashionable area . . . a little too much in the country'. But then his standard was the close-packed palazzos of Venice, separated only by waterways and by hidden gar-dens of the medieval kind.

Between 1611 and 1620 Pindar was sent by James I as ambassa-dor to the Ottoman Empire, where he was well liked and trusted. A

Paul Pindar's house, when a tavern

man of exceptional ability and decency, he would have done well in any era, but his friendship with Charles I and his generosity to that fatal monarch left him finally with large debts. He died during the Commonwealth, aged eighty-five, a very long life for those times. Some of his extensive garden had already been sold off to the City Corporation, and at the end of the century they built a poorhouse upon it – a sign of the area's then-accelerating change. Because of its situation well north of old London Wall, the Pindar house survived the Great Fire of 1666 which destroyed so many other fine houses of that kind in the City. A hundred-plus years later, in the eighteenth century, it became a tavern, the 'Paul Pindar'. Another hundred years and it was demolished to extend Liverpool Street station's goods sidings. Today, the site where the deer browsed is straddled by platforms 14 to 18. The carved wooden structure of its façade alone was saved, and is to be found in the Victoria and Albert Museum. The place where it stood is now occupied by a weighty stone and granite block at 137 Bishopsgate, part of the general Broadgate development of the 1980s. A pedestrian way leading through an undercover car park and then up some steps bears the name 'Pindar Passage'.

Stow disapproved of the growth of London that he had seen in the course of his life. Another long-lived citizen, he was almost eighty when he died in 1605, and came of a well-established City family. The persevering erudition of his great work does not disguise his nostalgia for a lost past which (though he does not say it in so many words) seems for him to be located before the Reformation, the world in which he grew up, or perhaps in the more distant medieval days described by Fitzstephen. He had a fondness for time-honoured rituals, folk festivals and old-style charity, and a mistrust of more lavish and urban entertainments. There was also his expressed regret at the destruction of ancient monuments, which at one point in Elizabeth's reign led to him being fingered as a closet Catholic. He managed to escape from that particular awkward corner, and the truth is probably that, like most people in the sixteenth century, he watched the way the wind blew, prudently veering this way and that as sovereigns succeeded one another, and kept his head down to avoid the storms.

The feeling that some period in the past, often the fairly recent past, represents a golden zero-summer since which there has been a decline, is of all time. When a playwright called Munday, who had known Stow personally, produced a revised and augmented edition of his *Survey* in the early seventeenth century, it was Stow's own world that appeared to Munday as a time of lost stability before the Fall – the 'days of Good Queen Bess' syndrome. For a later editor, Nathaniel Crouch, after the Restoration, the pre-Civil War time of the early seventeenth century was the lost country, whereas by the eighteenth century, when John Strype revised Stow's work yet again and added much to it, the Restoration era itself was coming to figure as the static Good Old Days. This forward displacement of nostalgia has continued unabated ever since.

Disapproval of urban growth and consequent physical change in the landscape of people's lives is also something that tends to resurface in every era, though that is not to say the feeling is unjustified. Stow had witnessed at first hand much of the in-filling and building on back gardens that characterises any town under pressure of space, but in later life he also noted London's relentless expansion outwards. During his lifetime the population of the capital probably more than doubled, from under one hundred thousand to almost two hundred thousand. Writing of the area north of the wall a few years before his death, he remarked that the ward of Cripplegate 'consisteth of divers streets and lanes, lying as well without the gate and wall of the city as within it'. It seems clear that the wall had ceased to be an efficient barrier and, though it continued to appear solidly on maps for the next hundred-odd years, it may already have been crumbling in parts or had unofficial door and window spaces knocked through it to accommodate houses that were built up against it.[7]

As for the adjoining Smithfield area, occupying the section of land beyond the wall's southward turn after Cripplegate and its westward turn at Aldersgate, this was obviously going to get built up. The cattle market spaces remained open, though full of pens, but the district had already had St Bartholomew's at its centre for hundreds of years, with the Charterhouse to the north and the separate settlement of Clerkenwell up the hill. Now Stow wrote of Long Lane, 'which reacheth from Smithfield to Aldersgate Street' as it still does today:

> This lane is now lately built on both sides with tenements for brokers, tipplers and such like; the rest of Smithfield from Long lane end to the bars is enclosed with inns, brewhouses and large tenements.

Aldersgate Street itself, leading north from the gate, was lined with houses: a generation later Milton lived in that street and wrote *Paradise Lost* there, and on his death he was buried in the yard of St Giles Cripplegate. He lies there to this day, somewhere far down beneath the Barbican Centre paving.

Stow also had things to say about the developments on the other side of the City, east of Aldgate and the Tower, where other fields that he had played on as a child, and where he had fetched milk from cowkeepers in his boyhood, were now becoming urban sprawl related to London's river traffic:

> this common field, I say, being sometime the beauty of this City on that part, is . . . encroached upon by the building of filthy cottages, and with other purprestures, inclosures and Lay-Stalles.

This expansion was the downside of the relative peace and consequent prosperity of Elizabeth's reign, which attracted many foreigners, as well as people from all parts of Britain, to London's booming trade. Elizabeth herself and her counsellors were not happy about this uncontrolled urban growth, which was widely if vaguely perceived to lead to outbreaks of plague. In 1580 a proclamation had been issued prohibiting any new house from being built within three miles of any London gate where no house was earlier known to have existed 'since the memory of man runneth not to the contrary'.

The edict was reissued in 1593, this time including in more general terms a situation that anyone from any era, including our own, will recognise: countryside becoming willy-nilly a suburb of a sprawling town. Socially, the district becomes less select:

> great mischiefs daily grow and increase by reason of pestering the houses with diverse families, harbouring of inmates and converting great houses into several tenements, and the erecting of new buildings in London and Westminster.

The same diktat was expressed again in 1602, the year before the Queen's death, but to little effect. Versions of it reappeared over the next sixty-odd years, as rulers rose and fell, but no prohibition seemed to make much difference. Then the Great Fire burnt out large parts of the City and precipitated a change in the whole concept of what a town should be and how it should be laid out. With the development of the St James's and Soho districts the idea of curbing London's development seems to have been, for the time being, shelved.

There is a lack of a good overall map of London through the reigns of James I, Charles I, through the Civil War (when London's civic and physical structures received a considerable battering), the Commonwealth and almost to the Restoration. Then, at last, several new maps appear within a few years of each other. Wenceslaus Hollar, the last and most skilled executor of the traditional bird's-eye map, planned a splendid one the very summer that Charles II returned in triumph to reclaim his throne. Had Hollar received funding to research and engrave all the six sheets he proposed, we would have had not only an incomparable survey of London's pre-Fire layout but a record of the actual appearance of thousands of streets and buildings. But Hollar could only afford to engrave one sheet on spec, and this one covers the area that was fast being developed around Holborn, the Strand, Lincoln's Inn, Drury Lane and St Giles-in-the-Fields – interesting and significant in itself, but telling one nothing of the heart of old London.

That heart, the City, was within half a dozen years to be almost obliterated: the ashes of the Fire were still warm, and smouldering in places, when Hollar – ever a tireless worker – drew his famous plan-cum-view of the area that had been destroyed, and that is in itself a precious record. But it is understandable that in the immediate post-Fire period, when grandiose schemes for rebuilding the City to a new design were being overtaken by a mass determination to rebuild the landholdings as they had been before, and when huge numbers of its citizens were settling in a rapidly changing townscape further west, a new map was not really feasible.

Ten years later Ogilby and Morgan produced a detailed plan of London conforming to our modern concept of the word 'plan', with every plot of ground meticulously surveyed. And after Ogilby's death Morgan produced a further refined edition in 1682, complete with illustrations and an extra (optional) panorama. Apart from some deer in St James's Park, a few token figures training on the 'new Artillery ground' north-west of Moorfields, and copious boats on the river (which were probably contributed by Hollar the year before his death), the Morgan map is a radical departure from the old way of seeing things.

The surroundings of the City had changed radically too. On these maps of the 1670s and '80s, the entire area to the east of Bishopsgate Street, running over the Spitalfields to Aldgate and Whitechapel, is semi-urbanised with houses mixed with gardens and tenter-grounds. To the west, where old Bedlam stood for nearly four hundred and fifty years, there is a similar mix, with Moorfields still there but reduced to a public garden laid out with tree-shaded walks. Beyond Moorfields to the west, the Smithfield district, Farringdon and a great swathe of Clerkenwell beyond it are now dense with houses. The Charterhouse and its gardens are surrounded, and London has now jumped the Fleet and fully colonised much of Holborn.

On the south edge of Moorfields, immediately facing London Wall, is a large institutional building which was completed within a few months of the new map's appearance in 1676. It is marked 'New Bethlehem': a new, purpose-built madhouse far bigger than before. Mad behaviour was less well tolerated by society than it had been in earlier times. The land of Old Bethlem/Bedlam was still the property of the hospital and would be for the next two centuries, but the place itself was now nothing but dilapidated dwellings and manufactures, a fading memory, and a burial ground encroached upon by builders but still in use. When the use ceased, the name 'Old Bedlam' remained attached to a narrow cobbled way alongside it that would eventually be widened and rechristened 'Liverpool Street', and so suppress still further the memory of what had once occupied that space of London earth and, in one important sense, still did.

It slept. But eventually the railways came. They did their best to obliterate it, but did not quite succeed. Another hundred years went by, and the place was remembered again but, once again, tucked away. A further generation has passed, and now at last Crossrail has arrived and the forgotten dead have, in a fragmented sense, lived again. It has been their last appearance.

CHAPTER VI

Going East

After Liverpool Street, the next Crossrail station is at Whitechapel, partway along the Mile End Road, bypassing Aldgate which lies a little further to the south where London's wall once ran down towards the Tower. Whitechapel might also seem, therefore, the logical next place to explore physically and historically. But in fact we are going to travel fairly rapidly through it.

Passing under Bishopsgate, Crossrail curves to the north, skirting the old market of Petticoat Lane (Middlesex Street), tunnelling underneath an eighteenth-century chapel-turned-synagogue in Sandys Row, and thence just south of the one-time artillery ground that, in the late sixteenth and seventeenth centuries, occupied the land that had been St Mary Spital's. It skirts, too, Christ Church Spitalfields, the beautiful, rescued shell of the Hawksmoor church where once London's Huguenots gathered. It crosses beneath the busy curry houses of Brick Lane, and then runs straight along the line of Hanbury and Princelet Streets.[1] From there, it continues under post-war housing estates, through what was once known as Mile End New Town, to meet the section of the Mile End Road that is called Whitechapel High Street.

Here it slots in behind the existing line through Whitechapel station, which was an early extension of the Metropolitan. At that point it is crossed by the Overground that, further south, dives under the river Thames and was originally built to get dockers to and from work. For much of the later twentieth century, as the docks died, this orphaned line only ran in a dispirited and partial way between Shoreditch station to the north and then via Wapping and Rotherhithe to New Cross. Now it has undergone a triumphant revival, with an extension northwards over previously disused Victorian viaducts to form a link with the old North London line via Hackney, through Canonbury, to Highbury and Islington. Southwards, the line now continues from Rotherhithe to Canada Water and Surrey Quays. It then goes westwards, via Peckham and Denmark Hill, to Clapham Junction, and hence to an unexpected link with the North London line coming down from Willesden Junction and Shepherd's Bush. You can thus travel right round the perimeter of inner London, if you so wish, much of the journey at rooftop level, offering fleeting and unfamiliar views of known townscapes and fugitive embankments. Though many of these have become wooded, bracken-choked, and radiant with buddleia in early summer, I like to think that our great-great-grandparents, who built so much of this infrastructure that the twentieth century almost lost, would feel that their investment has been vindicated in the twenty-first.

So the Whitechapel complex of stations is destined to be an interchange point almost as important as Farringdon, its geographical twin on the western side of the City. And the layers of history associated with Whitechapel surely make it as important a site in its way as St Giles-in-the-Fields? The actual white chapel that gave its name to this stretch of the main road east out of London was built only a century or so after St Giles, as an extra place of worship for the spread-out parish of Stepney. Like St Giles, it later became a parish church in its own right, and it survived through seven centuries and several rebuildings till German bombs ended its life in 1940. A public garden, Altab Ali Park, named after the victim of a racist assault in the 1970s, now occupies its space; it is a daily haven for heavily draped women with pushchairs, and their menfolk who stand apart and smoke. A little way along the High Road to the east is the large and well-endowed mosque, complete with dome and minarets, attended by Whitechapel's present-day predominantly Bangladeshi population.

Whitechapel is a rich field for study, dense with history. Famously, it has long been the 'back door to London'. As early as the end of the fifteenth century a group of young courtiers on a night out got into an argument outside Aldgate, and this became a mass brawl. Gentlemen usually carried daggers at that time, and three men – commoners – ended up dead. No courtier got punished. A hundred years later, at the end of the Elizabethan era, there were taverns along what had become Whitechapel High Street, and a playhouse, and Stow was complaining that the street was 'pestered with cottages and alleys'. By and by the district's nearness to the Pool of London, below London Bridge, where the seagoing ships docked, made it a natural first place of settlement for successive waves of immigrants.

The French Protestant Huguenots, who were mainly weavers, silversmiths and other skilled artisans such as cabinetmakers, began arriving after 1685, when Louis XIV revoked the Edict of Nantes, which had given them a century of protection from persecution. Once settled in London and prospering, they were the principal builders of the late-seventeenth- and early-eighteenth-century terraced houses of Spitalfields, which were constructed over the gardens and tenter yards immediately east of the City. Here had been dumped the great mass of charred, broken timbers, ash and charcoal to which the medieval and Tudor buildings of the City had been reduced by the Great Fire of 1666: thus, the fine new houses of the silk manufacturers in Elder Street, Fournier Street, Folgate Street and the rest are sitting upon the cemetery of earlier homes.[2]

Two hundred years later, the new houses, now dilapidated and soot-darkened in their turn, their looms silenced, had become the crowded lodgings of a different wave of foreigners: Eastern European Jews. The Huguenots' chapel, that had been built in the corner between Princelet and Fournier Streets, belonged briefly to the Wesleyans and then became the Great Synagogue.

Another eighty or ninety years passed. The children and grandchildren of the Jewish clothing-trade workers prospered and moved to London's northern suburbs, and the Bangladeshi influx of still greater numbers took over Whitechapel. Leviski's tailoring shop became Al-Akbar Sarees, Bloom's kosher restaurant a halal curry house. The Great Synagogue is now a mosque. It still bears on its wall-mounted sundial the Latin inscription put there there by its first occupants, *Umbra sumus* – 'We are but shadows'. The building's history would seem to validate this view of human beings and their varying convictions.

The progression chapel-to-synagogue-to-mosque will already be familiar to many readers. I have seen it often cited in a faintly self-congratulatory way, since it is supposed to exemplify (and perhaps does) Britain's record in welcoming downtrodden strangers. But the changing saga of the house of God also desirably offsets the image of the whole of the East End of London as 'Jack the Ripper-land', which is now promoted as a feature of downmarket tourism. The reality is that the six squalid Ripper murders of street prostitutes between August and November 1888, which all took place within five hundred yards of Whitechapel High Street, were no more typical of the East End in general than were the psychopathic activities of the Kray gang over much of the same territory a century later.

What the 'sinister East End' preoccupation does tell us, however, along with Stow's four-hundred-year-old remarks about Whitechapel being 'pestered with cottages and alleys', is that the contrast between the wealth and power of the City itself, and the quite other way of life that is in evidence soon after you pass the frontier of Aldgate, has at various times been marked. It is so again today. The enormous glass towers of modern City offices would like to take over and destroy Spitalfields: this is known as 'corporate creep'. They have fortunately been prevented – just. But they loom ever nearer over the market stalls which have lined Whitechapel High Street for generations, and which these days are full of plastic and steel kitchenware, mint, sweet potatoes, okra, fish, cheap ornamental shoes, and shawls and headscarves for Bengali daughters and wives.

I am not, however, going to give the Whitechapel district its own full account in this book, or go into the above brief history in any greater detail. This is not because this stop of Crossrail's route lacks interest: far from it. On the contrary, it is such a complex site that only a whole book could begin to do justice to it – and a number have been written already. From Arthur Morrison's *A Child of the Jago* (1896) to Rachel Lichtenstein's *Rodinsky's Room* (1999), Monica Ali's novel *Brick Lane* (2003), and Jeremy Gavron's brilliant historic evocation *An Acre of Barren*

Ground (2005), the rich vein continues and is being mined and extended now by the anonymous 'Gentle Author' of the blog SpitalfieldsLife. Add to this the living novel/ghost-story/stage-set/museum that is the house of the late Dennis Severs in Folgate Street, now maintained by other devotees of the persistence of the past in the present – and it will be clear why I think that Whitechapel does not need me.

Instead, my most eastern stop of this Crossrail journey is half a mile down the road and a little to the south, at Stepney Green, by St Dunstan's church, the true heart of the old East End. There is not actually going to be a Crossrail station at Stepney Green. But it is there that the line divides, with the northerly branch going mostly overground, via Bow, Stratford, Seven Kings and Romford, to Shenfield, and the southerly branch to Canary Wharf in the Docklands development and thence to Woolwich and Abbey Wood. As originally planned, it was to go further, to Erith, Dartford and the as-yet-unbuilt Ebbsfleet. Who knows what the long future may bring?

So Stepney Green is a significant junction, and a large ventilation and access shaft is situated there. There too, conveniently in the middle of an open space which is a legacy of bombs and post-war planners, is an important archaeological site, that of a Great House. For Stepney, in contradiction to the myths and prejudices about the East End having always been the poor relation of the metropolis, and despite the century and a half of genuine poverty that came to the area with the streets built from the 1820s onwards – Stepney was not always thus. Once, it was like St Giles, a pretty place well beyond London's smoking chimneys and sickness-breeding alleys. It was somewhere where gentlemen built big houses with courtyards and even moats, fine gardens and orchards. It is actually part of London's grander history.

The journey we have been making, from west to east round London, is also made by London's traditional church bells, passing on their chimes from one to another:

> *Oranges and lemons, say the bells of St Clement's;*
> *You owe me five farthings, say the bells of St Martins . . .*

Now a nursery song, and once a traditional round-dance and game, the old chant is also a testament to the extent to which parish churches and the faith they represented were interwoven with everyday and worldly affairs. The tune itself echoes the changes of ringing, with one bell picking up on the next.

St Clement's seems to be St Clement Danes in the Strand, outside old London because beyond Temple Bar: the bells of the rebuilt church today ring out the tune of the rhyme. Several candidates have been suggested for St Martin's, but I think it is St Martin-in-the-Fields, out of London once too, in the direction of Westminster. Thus the churches on the western extremities of the expanding town call to their fellow churches nearer the walled City:

When will you pay me? say the bells of old Bailey;
When I grow rich, say the bells of Shoreditch . . .

The Old Bailey church (the enduring name comes from a narrow lane running up near Newgate) is St Sepulchre, just outside the wall in the ward of Farringdon Without, while the Shoreditch church is similarly beyond the wall on the opposite, north-eastern side of the City.

When will that be? say the bells of Step-ney . . .

Now we have gone further east again, to the last outpost of London settlement when the song was first recorded in the sixteenth century:

I do not know, says the great bell of Bow.

Bow, a good mile and a half from Aldgate, was then a village out in the fields, like St Martin's at the other end of the carillon.[3] Bow church would indeed pick up the chime from Stepney. Off the Mile End Road a side-track curved southwards, long ago, and still does today, down to Stepney church.

* * *

St Dunstan's church in the late nineteenth century

The church of Stepney was, and is, St Dunstan-and-All-Saints. It was established as the counterpart to another St Dunstan, in what became Fleet Street, the two big parishes framing the City at a little distance from it. St Dunstan was Bishop of London and Archbishop of Canterbury a hundred years before the Norman Conquest; both churches are of ancient origin although both have been rebuilt a number of times. The parish of St Dunstan, Stepney, originally covered all the land to the east of the City, including Spitalfields, Whitechapel, Mile End, Wapping, Ratcliffe, Limehouse and Poplar – everything that was eventually to be included under the resonant term 'East End'. Only gradually, as these hamlets grew in size, were other parishes created out of them with churches of their own.

Stow speaks of 'Stebunheth' (Stepney) as a huge old manorial holding stretching from the City walls to the Essex marshes, and mentions a Bishop of London who held the manor under St Paul's. He had a manor house out there called Bishop's Hall where he 'fell sick and died', but there is no indication that this was a particularly substantial residence. I believe, from later references, that it may have stood just north of Stepney church, at the south end of what is now White Horse Lane.

The peasants of the manor of Stepney were freed quite early from serfdom, which meant that their traditional strips for cultivation in the common field were gradually consolidated and could be amalgamated into substantial properties. The earliest clear trace of a wealthy London citizen owning such land and having a house on it out at Stepney is that of one Henry Waleys or le Wallais, who had Edward I to stay there for a fortnight in 1299. It was not a purely social visit: the King's meeting house at Westminster had burnt down, and the King wished to call the Parliament of barons to get some more money out of them to pursue his ongoing wars in Scotland and France. Waleys was of Gascon origin, a Vintner and a very prominent merchant in the wine trade with the Continent; he was concerned in the running of the Cinque Ports on the south coast of England through which so much merchandise passed. He had been Sheriff of London (a new appointment) in 1273 and again eight years later, when he had built a roundhouse on Cornhill to serve as a lock-up. In 1283 he was Mayor of London, and again in 1298. (The year before, his roundhouse was broken into, to rescue prisoners, by 'certain citizens . . . for the which they were grievously punished'.) In between his London appointments he was, for a while, Mayor of Bordeaux in south-west France, which then came under the English Crown. He helped fund Edward's wars and became his man of 'special affairs'. He owned a great deal of property besides a house in Stepney grand enough to receive the King, his retinue, a number of barons and presumably their attendants as well. There must have been servants bedded down in their cloaks at night on any convenient floor space and possibly in the gardens as well. I hope that the weather was fine that May. No doubt Waleys's financial shoulders were broad enough to support the ostentatious display of food and entertainment his King required. Two years later he was dead, and his son Augustine of Uxbridge inherited the Stepney property. But where exactly was this great house?

Some historians, hoping I think for a neat pattern, have identified it either with the 'Great Place' that was owned later by Henry Colet, or with the house that stood north-west of the church, on what is today the central open space where Crossrail has been at work. There is, however, no reason to suppose it was either of these properties, and good reason to think that it was not, in that both these fairly well-documented houses date from the second half of the fifteenth century, some hundred and fifty years after Henry Waleys's death. It has been suggested, rather, that an old inn called the Red Bull that stood opposite the west end of St Dunstan's church, and was cleared for rebuilding in the nineteenth century, may have been a surviving part of Waleys's domain. When it was demolished, fragments of fine medieval pottery were found there, originating from the south-west of France, where, we know, the Waleys family had connections.

The house in the centre of the area, where Crossrail have been conducting a detailed archaelogical dig, was long known to local inhabitants as 'King John's Palace' or 'King John's Court': it appears as such on nineteenth-century maps, though Stow said nothing about any such Palace or Court in his *Survey* of two hundred-odd years before. It has been said that whenever the origins of an ancient building have passed from the memory of men, it tends to be ascribed to King John. Presumably this is because he was the only John and somewhat infamous, and therefore easily identifiable among the bevy of Henrys, Edwards and Richards. It may also be because a time so distant as the turn of the twelfth and thirteenth centuries can be readily perceived as a kind of mythological golden age of which anything may be safely believed.

Since recent excavations have shown that the house dates from some time after 1450, and King John reigned from 1199 to 1216, it seems improbable that he had any connection with it. It has been revealed as a late-medieval or early-Tudor brick courtyard mansion with a moat

round it, possibly built on the site of still-older constructions. It seems
to be the same property that was at one time known as 'Fenne's Great
Place', having been conveyed to a John Fenne in 1466. ('Great Place'
was then a standard term for any impressive, free-standing house.)
This mansion was let to Lord Darcy in 1519 for 35 shillings a quarter,
when Stepney was becoming increasingly popular as a dormitory
suburb with 'courtiers and citizens' – in modern terms, high-ranking
civil servants and City men. Darcy and another occasional Stepney
resident, Sir John Neville (later Lord Latimer), were made 'commissioners for suspects' in the area, a kind of local magistrate possessed
of arbitrary powers. Some fifteen years later Lord Darcy, who had
opposed Henry VIII's wholesale Dissolution of the Monasteries and
joined in Robert Aske's Pilgrimage of Grace in the north, lost his
head on Tower Hill.[4]

Seventy-odd years and several tenants later, an extensive revamp
of the house was undertaken by Henry Somerset, later Marquis of
Worcester, who bought the place in 1597. A 'moated grange' is characterised by Shakespeare in Measure for Measure as something a little
dilapidated, belonging to the old, pre-Reformation world: moats and
gatehouses were now more for ornament than for defence. It was probably Worcester who filled in the moat and altered the general composition of the buildings, but he kept the gatehouse of diapered brick with
rooms above it and a hexagonal tower to one side. Worcester backed
the Royalist cause in the Civil War with large sums of money, and so
the house was summarily taken away from him under the Commonwealth. By the time the family got it back after the Restoration it had
begun its long and gradual transformation into a quite other collection
of buildings, to which I will return later in Stepney's chequered history.

Henry Colet's Great Place is better documented, though all physical
trace of it has now gone. In the mid-fifteenth century, about the same
time that 'King John's Palace' was taking shape, a house was built
by a London citizen called John Crosse just south-west of Stepney
church. It was a timbered house, so more traditional and slightly less
grand than the brick mansion. It was later acquired and enlarged by
Henry Colet, who was a leading member of the Mercers' Company.

He was, like Waleys a century and a half before, Sheriff of London and then twice Lord Mayor, and was knighted. His wife, too, came from an influential and highly placed family, the Knyvets. She bore Henry twenty-two children, according to the record, of whom only the eldest one, her son John Colet who was to go on to be more famous than his father, survived. This figure is sometimes quoted as indicating the huge scale of infant mortality in those days, even for the rich who could afford clean houses, fine linen, good food and the best of care available. However, the fatally persistent pattern would suggest rather that some rhesus-incompatibility problem affected Dame Colet's pregnancies after the birth of her first one. The transfer of a stillborn or rapidly dead infant from the big house to the nearby churchyard must have become an annual pilgrimage of sorrow, with hope endlessly deferred.

Henry died in the house in 1505: the bare altar of what was once his more elaborate tomb can be seen in the church to this day. His wife outlived him for some eighteen years, in fact outliving her distinguished son too, and kept the Great Place as her home. She has been described as 'an old lady of wonderful charm, who bore all these losses with exemplary sweetness, and whose beautiful house . . . was always open'. When she finally died, she left the house to the Mercers' Company. It is documented that they then passed it on to a Sir John Alleyn, for his lifetime, in return for his doing repairs on the house and also paying for the completion of the chapel at Mercers' Hall in the City. But this arrangement seems to have broken down: ten years later in 1533 we find Thomas Cromwell, who was by then Henry VIII's right-hand man, taking a fifty-year lease on the house.

Cromwell apparently leased the nearby Vicarage and the 'Church House' (Prebend House?) as well. His main place of business had been at the Austin Friars in the City (he had once imperiously caused a garden house there belonging to Stow's father to be shifted on runners, in order to give himself more space). Cromwell was a cloth merchant, a lawyer and a moneylender, among many other activities. As he rose in power he seems to have decided to make Stepney into his principal seat. His wife and two daughters had by then died, probably of the 'sweating sickness', but he had in his household his mother-in-law, his sister- and brother-in-law and various children including a nephew, Richard Williams. Many of his surviving letters are dated from this 'Great Place' and, as the Dissolution was getting under way, the house has been called 'a hub of monastic suppression'.

But Cromwell's personality and energy were evidently such that, in addition to his works for the King, he became a de facto Stepney squire; he was asked to resolve disputes when local manorial tenants had grievances against either the Bishop of London or each other. Would Sir Thomas use his great influence to intervene with the Bishop? Would he rent a small garden that was on the edge of his domain to Robert Studley? And, alternatively, would he do something about Robert Morley, who lived in a cottage by the church and had been stealing herbs out of Studley's garden?[5] It is a little hard to reconcile the confidence that Stepney people evidently had in Cromwell's judgement with the historic image of a powerful and sinister figure, who used his Stepney retreat as a place to interrogate several of the courtiers he afterwards sent to their deaths in connection with Anne Boleyn's trial, and who dispatched his neighbour Lord Darcy to the block.

Seven years after he had established himself in the Great Place, Cromwell had fallen from favour and was himself beheaded – as Darcy, in a heartfelt speech at his own trial, had prophesied that he might be. The Great Place was forfeited to the Crown. Two years later, by which time Henry was apparently regretful that he had destroyed his most useful advisor, the house was returned to Cromwell's heir, his nephew Richard Williams.[6] Richard took Thomas Cromwell's name, and was destined to become the great-grandfather of Oliver Cromwell, who had Charles I beheaded rather more than a hundred years after England's King had beheaded Thomas.

So we know what happened to Sir Henry and Dame Colet's house after their deaths. But what of their son John? Known to posterity as Dean Colet, he was perhaps the most distinguished of all Stepney's early gentlefolk. A number of commentators seem to have assumed that John simply went on living with his mother after his father's

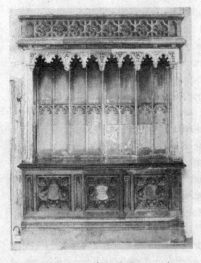

Henry Colet's tomb in St Dunstan's

death, but the arrangement he made for his house after his own death in 1519, four years before his mother's, shows that there were in fact two separate houses not far from one another. A manuscript history of Stepney written by someone[7] with access to Mercers' Company records in 1844, and therefore at a time when the unbuilt Stepney of fields and the remnants of ancient houses was still well within memory, makes this clear. Henry Colet's mansion, it says, was 'a little to the west of the church . . . [it] has been considerably altered and divided into several small tenements'; whereas John Colet's house was well south of the church, beyond where the Mercers' almshouses were later built and stand today.[8]

A fine, large-scale tinted map that was made in 1612, a century after the Colets' presence, hangs in Mercers' Hall in the City. It shows the extensive landholdings of the Company in Stepney, especially to the west, south and south-east of the church. To the west are the remains of a moat surrounding a collection of grouped buildings and enclosing also gardens and an orchard. I think this is what was left of Henry and Dame Colet's house. A little way down the trackway running south from the churchyard that was then called White Horse Street, just before the corner with 'the road to Blackwell' that is now Salmon Lane, is an enclosure with a building on it marked 'Copt Hall'. This is presumably a garbled local version of 'Colet' since, a century later again, on Gascoyne's map of 1703, the same parcel of land is marked 'belonging to Pauls' school', and we know it was to the school, which he had founded, that John bequeathed his house and this land on his death.

Born as he was into extraordinarily fortunate circumstances, John Colet became one of a group of gilded intellectual figures of what, in the early sixteenth century, was called the New Learning. He went to Oxford at the age of seventeen, was ordained a deacon and later a priest and travelled on the Continent. He became friends with Erasmus, the brilliant Dutchman and man of letters who had been an Augustinian friar but had left the Order to pursue his studies further. In Florence, John Colet met other radical thinkers and scholars and may have encountered Savonarola – who was not then the fanatical book-burner he was later to become. Back in London, John's associates included Lord Mountjoy, who was tutor to the young Prince who would become Henry VIII; Linacre, who was a pioneering medical doctor; and also Thomas More, who was the youngest of the group. John gave a series of lectures at Oxford, in Latin, on the need to 'love God rather than knowing Him', and made clear his views on the worldliness and corruption that had crept into the Church.

This was rather dangerous stuff, at a time when Protestantism was stirring all over Europe and the new printing presses were able to disseminate mass copies of material that in previous centuries had been confined to laborious handwriting. Indeed at one point John was suspected of being a Lollard and was accused of this by a Church court, but the great storm that would blow up into the English Reformation, forcing citizens to take sides for or against the Catholic faith, still lay a generation ahead. The charge was dismissed: no doubt Henry Colet's son had protection in high places. He was already Vicar of Stepney and held various other ecclesiastical posts; in the year his father died he was made Dean of St Paul's. Most famously, he used some of his considerable inherited wealth to found, under the auspices of the Mercers' Company, a school in St Paul's churchyard for one hundred and fifty-three bright boys who had already learnt to read and write. The school, grown into one of the most academically prestigious in England, flourishes in west London to this day.

A man in his forties once Henry VIII came to the throne, Dean Colet was chaplain to the young King for a while, and was sent by him on diplomatic missions. One may wonder whether, if a third bout of the sweating sickness had not brought his life to a close in 1519, he might have ended up being executed for holding firm to his own views, as his friend Thomas More eventually was. But all this lay in the unguessed future, and in the promising early years of the century both Erasmus and Thomas More stayed with John Colet in Stepney. Indeed, it was Thomas More who had encouraged him to acquire a house of his own there – further proof that John did not simply make use of his parents' Great Place. More wrote:

> The beautiful landscape refreshes, the fresh air exhilarates and the sight of heaven delights you . . . If you dislike the town, yet your country parish of Stepney . . . will offer you as many attractions as the place where you are now; and from thence you can now and then pass into the City, where you will find a great field of merit.

A later letter from John Colet himself to Erasmus, inviting him to stay, promises:

> Wheresoever you look, the earth yieldeth you a very pleasant prospect . . . [My house] is set among orchards, and the summer seems to linger in the garrets where the fruit is stored.

On the Mercers' Company map of a hundred years later, the section containing this house and running south down White Horse Street is marked 'Tenements, gardens and orchards'. This was the property that, on his death, John Colet had bestowed on St Paul's. A print of the late eighteenth century shows an old-style timbered house with a more modern extension fronting part of it. In another print, twenty-odd years later, a further classical-style façade has been added. The back land was, by then, a Nonconformist burial ground. It has been persistently said that this was the house Colet intended for the Master of St Paul's as a country retreat, and so he may have, but in fact at some point in the seventeenth century, a hundred years or so after Colet's death, a quite other brick house, with an imposing pillared central doorway and a carved head on the top gable, was built for the Master on the opposite corner of Salmon Lane.

Dean Colet's house in 1797

The same house, slightly later, having been extended with a more fashionable frontage

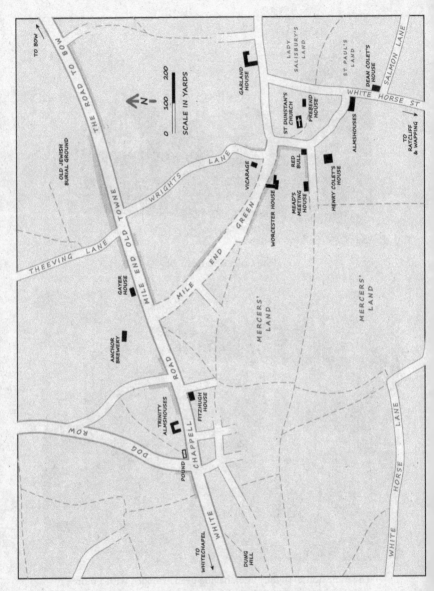

Stepney, *c.* 1710, the built-up area shown in darker grey

Daniel Lysons, writing about the area at the end of the eighteenth century, remarked:

Stepney having in great measure lost its rural <u>delights</u>, the Masters have not visited these many years. On the site are now two mes-suages called Colet Place, of which the Master receives the rents; on the front is a bust of the Dean. (*The Environs of London, 1796*)

Within a few years a workhouse had been built adjacent to it. Today, the workhouse, the brick house that became Colet Place, and the ancient, rambling, part-timbered one are all long gone.

One may well regard the area round Stepney church, an easy walk or a quick horse-ride from the City, as having been, in the sixteenth century, something like what Hampstead or Chelsea were to become in the nineteenth century, or the Sussex Downs and the Cotswolds in the early twentieth. For there were yet other grand houses dating from before the Reformation of which little has been written. There was one, for instance, north-east of the church where Ben Jonson Road now runs. It is just off the Mercers' map (as is the Marquis of Worcester's house), presumably because the Mercers did not hold land on that side of the parish, but it appears on Gascoyne's detailed 1703 map as an apparently still-complete, substantial, late-medieval courtyard house. By this time it was called Garland House, after the family who then owned it. They were not old gentry, for when John Garland, said to be of Stratford (i.e. further east again from Bow), figured on a deed of sale as buying some land in 1589, he was described simply as a 'yeoman', a minor owner of some farming land. A century later, in 1651, his descendent Ralph Garland was a 'mariner', an example of the social evolution of Stepney at that time. Ralph Garland was buying 'a mansion-house, garden and orchard in Stepney, late in the occupation of Dame Hellen Sleaford and Sir Edward Waterhouse': this was the old courtyard house.

On this fragile parchment deed, darkened by the London soot of three hundred and fifty years but with its ribbons and seals still intact, the actual owners of the property are mentioned as Sir Henry Herbert

and Sir Henry and Dame Vere Every. Both were established aristocratic names, the Herbert family being related to the Earls of Pembroke. Earlier in the century, before the Garland buy-out, a daughter
of Sir Philip Sidney, of the Pembroke clan, is said to have been living
'somewhere on Mile End Green',[9] where she entertained the poet John
Donne among other figures of the age. So one may reasonably conclude that the mysterious old house, which disappeared at some point
in the eighteenth century, was earlier a nexus of culture and influence
even as the Colet houses were.

Much clearer to posterity, and obviously part of the sixteenth-century
Stepney intelligentsia, are the Harrington family, although accounts
of them are sometimes confused because there were two poets of
the same name in successive generations. Alexander Harrington
'of Stepney' died there in 1539, in what is referred to as the Prebend or
Parsonage House, an imposing building near the church on the eastern
side. (It was demolished when a new rectory was built in the eighteenth century.) Harrington was allegedly, and perhaps in reality, the
illegitimate son of the Dean of York which may explain how he came
to live for many years in a house owned by the Church. His son John
was born in this house in 1525 and as he grew up he made the most of
claims, possibly imaginary, to be related also to a grander Harrington
family. Alexander had entertained a number of significant people at
the Prebend House, including Thomas Tallis, the composer of church
music; his son John became a courtier and a poet and a close friend
and protector of the young Princess Elizabeth. John married an illegitimate daughter of Henry VIII (that is, a half-sister to Elizabeth) and for
this he was rewarded with money and property. When Henry finally
died and the boy-King Edward took over the throne, the Harrington
star was in eclipse, and John suffered a spell of imprisonment in the
Tower of London. Here he probably first met Isabella Markham, who
was the daughter of the then Lord Lieutenant of the Tower. (Evidently
Harrington's was a fairly polite form of imprisonment, but imprisonment none the less.) He was released in 1550 and retreated to a family property in the West Country, where he remained for some years,

through the reign of Catholic Mary during which Elizabeth herself
was for a while in the Tower.

Elizabeth's coming to the throne in 1558 brought back good times
for the Harringtons. Isabella Markham was now one of the Queen's
waiting women. She was apparently beautiful, and it is clear that John
Harrington was in love with her, judging by letters that he wrote to
her from Somerset while his first wife was still living. That wife died
the following year, and John and Isabella promptly married. Their
son, the second John, was born in 1561, and they went on to have several more children. Following the family tradition, they made Stepney
their London home.

Beautiful she may have been, and prepared to receive love letters
from a married man, but Isabella seems to have been a strong-minded
lady with the right ideas about the conduct of a household. It was
surely she who drew up the list of house rules and fines[10] that have
come down to us:

Item, Maids to be kept shut . . . None to toy with the maids on
pain of 4d.

Item, That none swear any oath, upon pain for every oath 1d.

Item, that none of the men be in bed, from our Ladyday to
Michaelmas, after six of the clock in the morning; nor out of his
bed after ten of the clock at night; nor, from Michaelmas to our
Ladyday, in bed after seven in the morning; nor out after nine at
night, without reasonable cause, on pain of 2d.

Item, that no man make water in either of the courts, upon
pain of, every time it shall be proved, 1s[hilling].

Item, that no man teach any of the children any unhonest
speech, or baudy word, or oath, on pain of 4d.

Item, that meat be ready at eleven or before at dinner, and six
or before at supper, on pain of 6d.

Item, that the court gate be shut at each meal, and not opened
during dinner and supper without just cause, on pain the porter
to forfeit for every time 1d.

The fines were to go to the relief of the poor. The fact that 'making water in the courtyard' was the most severely punished offence indicates that Isabella Harrington had high standards of hygiene, though since horses would have clattered in and out of the yard it must have made it rather difficult, one feels, to prove the origin of any pungent puddle. The importance of set mealtimes in what must have been a large and disparate household where apparently all ate together is typical of the times: the separate 'servants' hall' was a much later development. Nor was it only servants who had to obey the house rules. It is recorded that when Lord Hastings came to dine 'he walked out in the garden while the prayer were saying' (that is, the grace before the meal) and so the hostess refused to eat with him that day.

Where exactly was this house, clearly a large courtyard one? It has been claimed, once again, that it is identifiable with Sir Henry Colet's Great Place, and this may in fact be true, since we are now twenty years further on from the downfall and partial rehabilitation of the Cromwell family. When his own son John was seven, John Harrington-the-first received a grant of heraldic arms, the first step on the way to aristocracy, and a typical move in the rapidly evolving society of the time. Young John was always said to be a godson of the Queen, who referred to him as 'boy Jack'. Schooled at Eton, then Cambridge, then an Inn of Court, the perfect gentleman's education of the time, this second John is reported to have been handsome, charming and clever. He was, like his father, a poet; he was witty and was much admired by his contemporaries. A complex translation from Italian that he made is still used today. His mannered style has little appeal to modern generations, though one of his poems strikes a chord with us in that it refers to a child saying grace at a great family table.

Apparently he was rather *too* witty, and given to indecent compositions, for in 1583, the year after his father's death, he fell out of favour with the Queen who more or less banished him to the property in Somerset. It may or may not be coincidental that 1583 was also the year he married a very young wife. Eight years and quite a few children later the Queen relented, so the story goes, and paid him a visit during which he showed her an invention with which he had been occupying himself. This was the very first water closet, and workmanlike drawings of his model survive. He christened it 'Ajax' after the Greek warrior-god – a pun on 'a jakes', the standard word for a chamber pot. It would seem that his mother's insistence on clean habits in the courtyard at Stepney had taken root in his mind. I wish I knew whether he had an Ajax installed there. The Queen was apparently delighted and ordered one to be made for herself. Surprisingly few other people seem to have taken up the idea, and it was to be another century and a half before the reinvented flush lavatory began to appear even in the wealthiest London houses.

The Queen was rather less delighted at a satirical treatise he wrote called *The Metamorphosis of Ajax*, which was a scatalogical covert attack on the corruption, spying, backbiting and use of torture to extract confessions which went on in court circles. He was, however, partially forgiven towards the end of her reign, and was allowed to join the Earl of Essex during the Irish campaign in 1599, for which Essex, without consulting the Queen, bestowed on him a knighthood. It did not improve his situation that the Queen had Essex beheaded for treason in 1601, thereby confirming all that he, Harrington, had insinuated about the brutality of court life. After the death of the Queen and the accession of James I things continued difficult for him; there were family disputes and debt problems, but he hung on at court. Eventually he became tutor to Prince Henry, he who died before he could come to the throne, leaving the way open to his younger brother, the luckless Charles I.

When John Harrington died in 1612 there was no shortage of other prominent families within easy reach of Stepney church. The Great Place to the north-west of it was now Worcester House, modernised and made grander by its present occupant, the Marquess. Next to Worcester House lived the Morley family, who were connected by marriage to the Monteagles through whom the Gunpowder Plot of 1605 fatally came to light. Lord Morley's son, Lord Monteagle, was sent an anonymous letter warning him to stay away from Parliament on 5 November. Stories about both the letter's origin and its subsequent trajectory vary, but one version is that Monteagle showed the letter to his father, who passed it on to his Stepney neighbour Sir Thomas Lake, who was the confidential agent of Robert Cecil, who was principal Secretary of State to the King . . . We know the final outcome: seven high-born Catholic or Catholic-sympathising men were horribly executed, as was their soldier of fortune Guy Fawkes. Lord Morley and Lady Lake both lie in or beside Stepney church, along with many other wealthy contemporaries and neighbours who, as the seventeenth century progressed, continued to colonise Mile End Green.

Mile End Green was the original name for Stepney Green, which is a relatively modern term, and its original nature and aspect have been confused by the physical upheavals and changes that Stepney has suffered. Today, you might be forgiven for thinking that the small, rather bare park that is called 'Stepney Green', well to the west of St Dunstan's church, along Stepney Way, is the last relic of a space of open land, and that it once included most of the area where Worcester House has been excavated by Crossrail and where there is a city farm with cows, pigs, chickens and geese. This is not, however, the case; in the nineteenth and early twentieth centuries much of this central area was covered with buildings.

Long ago the Green – Mile End Green, as it was – was a swathe of common land, communal grazing space for manorial tenants, that ran along part of the south side of Mile End Road and then down at a slant to Stepney church. The road that is today called Stepney Green marks its course, and this road itself is simply there because of the common land: naturally a footpath will develop across land where anyone has the right to walk. The narrow park with big trees that runs down Stepney Green between the houses and the roadway is the surviving remnant of the true green. It had traditionally been used for fairs and pageants and other gatherings. Wat Tyler assembled his peasant forces there in 1381 before marching on Smithfield. It was used for more orthodox trooping from the late-Elizabethan period, when the City artillery grounds became too crowded, and it was also a place for hangings, but it was getting nibbled away. Humble and unauthorised dwellings were erected by local farm labourers; then people rich and powerful enough to get what they wanted began building substantial homes there for themselves. By the late seventeenth century there was a sprinkling of rather fine houses down it from Mile End Road. A couple of them, defying the time and chance that have been unusually hard on London's East End, survive today. Records of their occupants, and sometimes of the wealth of silver, glassware, bound books and fine carpets that embellished these houses, have also come down to us.

Meanwhile, the Marquess of Worcester had fallen foul of the Commonwealth, and a change came over the occupation and use of Worcester House which was to have a far-reaching effect on the whole character of Stepney.

CHAPTER VII

'Man goeth to his long home'

The dust of one-time houses – stone dust, brick dust, charred wood, small shards of tile and glass, fragments of lead from old cisterns – is everywhere, metres beneath our feet. But almost as ubiquitous is the dust of humans: shards of bone, red-brown stains in earth, coins once used to cover dead eyes with the intention of paying the way into another world.

Frequently, when a new railway line, a bypass or a roundabout has been announced, there have been justified protests that the invasion passes through old burial ground. Very many known graveyards did disappear under new constructions in the mid- to late nineteenth century, when the concepts of progress and modernisation were particularly dominant and conservation almost non-existent. But, paradoxically, it is only in our own times, when recognised graveyards are heavily protected by law from casual redevelopment, and when belief in bodily resurrection on the Day of Judgement is all but extinct, that indignation about disturbing old bones has become a popular cause. And, just to add to the complexity of the issue, many old stones that still bear traces of memorial inscriptions have been reused for paving; they no longer cover any named individual.

I do not, of course, advocate the brisk obliteration of sites where our ancestors, however humble, were 'laid to rest'. But if the possible presence of human bones on a site were an overriding reason for calling the diggers off, we would never build anywhere in central London again, for the truth is that vestigial human matter is everywhere. It is to be found not just in what were once unconsecrated plots adjoining

Dissenting chapels, nor yet in the one-time precincts of churches that were never rebuilt after the Great Fire. It lies on the sites of the more than forty-five religious communities that disappeared at the Reformation; it pads the earth of any crossroads where executions took place. It is particularly thick just outside what, for over a thousand years, were the walls of old London. Roman remains have been dug up in Moorfields, Spitalfields, south of London Bridge and at the foot of Fleet Street by what is now Ludgate Circus. This last site in particular was conveniently situated just beyond the long-time boundary of the Fleet river. It seems to have been used and reused over many centuries; pagan holy places were readopted as Christian ones and a Celtic saint, born in AD 453, was put in charge. The old burial grounds of St Brigid, today's St Bride's, were far more extensive than the present small churchyard; they stretched over Shoe Lane and part of what is now the bottom of Farringdon Road, running down to Blackfriars Bridge. Just to the north were more grounds, those of St Andrew Holborn, which were extensively disturbed when Holborn Viaduct was built in the 1860s. Archaeologists who excavated the whole area in the late 1940s, when rebuilding was taking place after the London Blitz, formed the impression that most of those stacked one upon another in these grounds were people regarded at their deaths as being of little social consequence: many of them probably came from the nearby Fleet or Bridewell prisons. Indeed, extra grave space near the Fleet prison for debtors was donated to St Bride's in 1610 because the upper churchyard was so crowded.

And then there were all those more privileged bodies, in lead-lined coffins, that ended up piled twelve feet deep – 'jostled together', in the words of one seventeenth-century sexton – in the capacious crypts of St Bride's and of many other London churches. Nearly all of these crypts have, in the twentieth century, been emptied for public-health reasons, and sometimes (I have been told) the lead has been recycled for more profitable purposes. A great many of the bones from these and from other sites all over the London area have been reburied in mass graves, but a substantial number have found a last resting place, of a kind, in the Museum of London. Currently, the museum holds around seventeen thousand skeletal remains, some semi-complete but most fragmented and depleted, and so ancient that the idea of reburial seems unrealistic. It is also pointed out that in the future, with the evolution of analytical skills, especially the science of DNA, much might be learnt from them. All are neatly packaged in strong cardboard boxes, with their geographical provenance, and with an individual name if known.

Some, for space reasons, have been boarded out again back to their parishes of origin. Currently St Bride's, one of whose erstwhile crypts is now a peaceful subterranean office for the vicar, holds in safekeeping what is left of some of the earliest printers, with whose trade the church is particularly associated. I have touched with my living fingers the poignant, eggshell fragments of the skull of Wynkyn de Worde, the aptly named pioneer of printed type. He died in 1535, just as the coming Reformation was turning books into increasingly dangerous objects. It was the same year that John Colet's friend, Thomas More, was executed for his faith.

In the stories periodically generated by the construction of Crossrail, none have been seized on so eagerly by newspapers as those that relate to old bones. Typical was a headline in the *Evening Standard* in May 2009, when preliminary, explorative boreholes were being made before the works themselves started: 'Crossrail works stopped after human bones found on site', with the strapline, 'Remains linked to workhouse are tested for anthrax and plague'. Accompanying it was a late-nineteenth-century photograph of capped and aproned female workhouse inmates, mainly old ladies, at dinner.

Animal remains from Smithfield, a pauper burial ground resited, and a present-day obsession about the horrors of workhouses – all seem conflated here. The bones in question were not so much found as revealed again in an already-known location. When Farringdon station had been constructed for Pearson's brand-new Metropolitan line at the beginning of the 1860s, it will be remembered that it ran down the Fleet valley, close to the river but just to the east of it. Then, after passing under Cowcross Street, it curved further eastwards in the direction

of the new Smithfield market buildings, which were then still being
built. The line was designed to carry goods as well as people, goods
in this instance being meat for the market. A dozen years earlier the
slaughter of animals on the hoof had been moved to the new Metropolitan Meat Market well north of King's Cross, up the Caledonian
Road. The centuries of live beasts milling around on the edge of the
City were at last over. It was first planned that the basement beneath
the glass-and-iron market buildings was where the whole railway
line would terminate – only, as we know, it proved so popular as a
form of human transport that within a year or two of the opening
of Farringdon station extra rails were laid, bypassing the market, to
carry passengers on to Moorgate in the City and also to link with the
London, Chatham and Dover railway coming from across the Thames.

In order to reach its special terminus beneath the market, the line
had swept aside a number of lanes and buildings, including Sharps
Alley (famous for the stinking industry of catgut manufacture), Red
Lion Alley, Green Hill Rents and Field Lane Ragged School. Green Hill
speaks for itself, and a field lane was just that in Stow's childhood. But
in 1862 the journalist John Hollingshead wrote of the disappearance
of 'the old traditional by-gone dens of Field Lane . . . Jonathan Wilde,
Jack Shepherd and other similar criminals are said to have haunted
this spot.' For several hundred years, in spite of periodic attempts to
clean the Fleet up, both physically and socially, there had been tales
of trapdoors and secret passages leading down to the water, ways of
escape and ways of disposing of unwanted evidence of crime. Now
these were gone, obliterated by the railway, and St Sepulchre's Workhouse had vanished as well. It was known that the workhouse had
been built on land that had earlier been an overflow parish graveyard
for St Sepulchre church by Newgate. It was this square of parish land,
or what was left of it after the workhouse was built, that became a pauper burial ground and was excavated in 1862 by the railway company
(see Chapter II). The remains they took out were then walled up in a
newly constructed vault – the vault whose wall collapsed, embar-
rassingly, along with one side of the railway cutting when the Fleet
sewer flooded. The whole mess was expensively repaired and walled

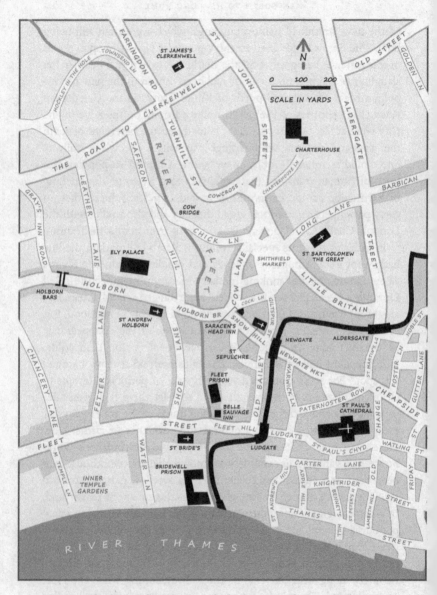

Farringdon and Holborn, *c.* 1550, the built-up area shown in darker grey

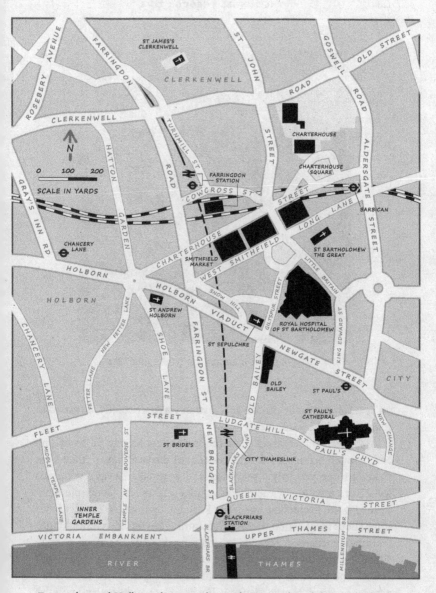

Farringdon and Holborn district today, with Crossrail, and the north–south overground route over the original Metropolitan line

Collapse of the Metropolitan works, June 1862

up again, so naturally no one at Crossrail was particularly surprised in 2009 to find bones still there.

A spokesman remarked that the bones (apparently all from one body) 'might belong to a former resident of the workhouse'; they were thought to be '200 to 300 years old' and were taken away for various tests. But a mention of their being routinely tested for 'contamination' by the Health Protection Agency at Porton Down set off a wilder news story about meat contaminated with anthrax having been brought into Smithfield markets in 1520 and having caused the deaths of 682 people. While it is true that anthrax spores can lie dormant for centuries, 1520 was a good hundred years before the establishment of St Sepulchre's parish graveyard. In 1520 Henry VIII was still a handsome and popular young King, and the area concerned was then an open field. The anthrax scare seems to have been started by a member of the House of Lords who had opposed the building of Crossrail from the start.

As for plague, the various forms that bubonic plague (*Yersinia pestis*) can take have only been identified relatively recently, and the idea put forward in every school book that it is always rat- and flea-borne is now questioned. What seems to have been established, however, is that there is no risk of infection from the remains of long-dead victims. Nevertheless, horror stories about plague pits, and especially about ones dating from the Black Death of the mid-fourteenth century, are understandably popular, as if the untamed and noxious spirits of the long past might come back to wreak vengeance on the careless, living, privileged people of today. Plague, 'the Pestilence', was, among all the various ills and fates that our ancestors suffered, *the* one of which people seem to have been most afraid. Not till tuberculosis became a widespread and stealthy killer in the nineteenth and early twentieth centuries has the same atmosphere of dread surrounded an illness, although in practice deaths from all sorts of other epidemics occurred repetitively throughout the medieval and early modern period.

The site for the Crossrail eastern ticket hall at Farringdon, just north-east of Smithfield on the edge of Charterhouse Square, has been a coveted field both for archaeologists and for news hounds, since a substantial Black Death burial ground has long been known to lie there. Indeed, the Carthusian monastery that became the Charterhouse, and survives to this day through time and chance as a residential community for distinguished old men, owes its very foundation to the Black Death.

Bubonic plague first arrived in Europe, apparently from India, in 1347. It spread rapidly across the Continent, reaching England in the summer of 1348 and continuing for the rest of that year and until Whitsun 1349. In the City of London the graveyards became overwhelmed:

Very many were compelled to bury their dead in places unseemly and not hallowed or blessed; for some, it is said, cast their corpses into the river.

At this point, one of King Edward III's right-hand men, who had been a chief commander at the recent successful Siege of Calais, decided on effective and charitable action. This was Sir Walter de Mauny or Manny; he leased from St Bartholomew's a plot of thirteen acres in the west part of Smithfield and donated it as a graveyard, building a chapel in the middle. Some adjacent land was also bought and donated by the Bishop of London.

The same plague reappeared in 1362 and again in 1369. By this time de Mauny's plans for founding a Carthusian monastery on part of the site – no doubt an excellent insurance for his soul – were well advanced. He was said to be 'in all things laudable, both in matter relating to religion and those of human knowledge'. The required papal licence for the monastery finally came through in 1371, the year before he himself died. He was buried within the precincts of the Charterhouse, and his coffin came to light during bomb-damage repairs after the Second World War, some five hundred and seventy years later. Its contents were examined; it was resealed and reburied in the same place, and a memorial service was held. Occasionally, continuity is stronger than change.

The Black Death shocked and frightened by the very speed at which it killed: the iconic late-medieval image of the grinning skeleton mingling with a crowd of the living is born of that experience. But the few chroniclers of the time, mostly writing some years after the worst epidemic was over and sometimes a whole generation after, probably tended to overestimate the mortality – 'Not one in ten left alive' etc. There is little evidence, from most parts of England, of whole villages laid waste and deserted as happened in France, and the often-quoted speculative figure of one third to one half of the English population dead of the plague seems to have little to back it up. In the peak winter of 1348–49 mortality would have been high anyway, because the climate of Britain was deteriorating and, it is reported, 'rain fell from midsummer to Christmas'. That would have wiped out most of the harvest, creating conditions of famine among the poor and malnutrition in all classes. It is thus hard to tease out a realistic figure for plague deaths from the general death rate in a bad time.

In the crowded lanes of London itself, the death rate that winter seems to have been extremely high, especially towards the end of the winter when you might expect plague itself to decline with the cold, but deprivation would have been increasing. Some commentators have suggested that over fifty per cent of the population died. But given that the figure for burials in the new Smithfield ground appears to have been much exaggerated, one may question other assumptions also. Two years after this first and most lethal bout of the Black Death, a papal bull recorded that sixty thousand victims were buried at Smithfield – a figure revised twenty years later, when the negotiations for the Charterhouse were still going on, down to fifty thousand. Since the entire population of London before the plague came was probably well under eighty thousand, and many of the dead in plague times continued to be buried in churchyards, both totals are improbable. The recent Crossrail excavations on the site seem to confirm this.

The term 'plague pit', which has long been used for what was thought to lie beneath Charterhouse Square, conveys an image of bodies tumbled pell-mell, unshrouded, without prayers, into one mass grave. This indeed appears to have happened on other sites at the height of the Plague of London, some three hundred years later. Yet what the Crossrail archaeologists found early in 2013, when an exploratory shaft was sunk in the appropriate place, was not that kind of burial. On the contrary, the dead were laid down individually, in neat rows, aligned south-west to north-east.

Of the twenty-five bodies obtained from the 4.5-metre-diameter shaft, three were identifiable as women and thirteen as men, ranging in ages from eighteen to forty-five. Significantly, on analysis of the bones, more than half showed signs of malnutrition, vitamin C deficiency or anaemia. One person had had a dental abscess eating into his jaw, which must have been excruciating and possibly lethal anyway. There was no trace of plague in the bones, for it is an illness that acts swiftly, but later analysis of teeth confirmed that eleven of the bodies *had* contracted bubonic plague, though of a variant, pneumonic kind rather than the classic kind of the seventeenth-century Plague of London. Two of the burials appeared to have taken place a little later than the first layers, and a dozen rather later again. Were these from the 'second plagues' of the 1360s, or were they just a sign that by then the burial ground was in general use?

In addition, when an electronic geophysical survey was undertaken on the rest of Charterhouse Square, still no signs of communal pits were discovered but, rather, quite a light density of burials. In many places there are not even layers of bodies, but single interments. And much of the designated land does not seem to have been used at all. Any of the City's old parish graveyards, some of them now little gardens ringed by skyscrapers where office workers eat their lunch sandwiches, would produce a far greater density of packed-down remains.

After the fourteenth century, the plague never really went away, although it is only the major outbreaks that history remembers. It had rivals, such as the mysterious 'sweating sickness' that was rife in the late Tudor period, eventually killing Dean Colet, Thomas Cromwell's wife and daughters, and many others. But swift, deadly bubonic plague, which, untreated, will kill three-quarters of sufferers within four days, was the one that preyed on people's minds. It is incidentally present in Shakespeare's *Romeo and Juliet*,[1] when the sealing-up of a house because of supposed pestilence prevents Friar John from conveying a necessary message to Romeo; and indeed Juliet's faked death was presumably meant to suggest the all-too-familiar situation of a sudden plague attack. There were bad epidemics of it in Elizabethan London, in 1564 and in 1593, and particularly severe ones under the Stuarts in 1606, 1625 and 1636, but in a great many other years also the weekly Bills of Mortality showed a significant number of deaths considered to be due to plague along with those ascribed to other causes. In contrast with the situation at the Black Death three hundred years earlier, plague in the seventeenth century was often said to be under-reported because people were so afraid of it, but it was an established, endemic anxiety.

What upset and shocked the population of London when the Great Plague began to make its presence felt at the end of 1664 was the combination of haunting familiarity along with quite exceptional numbers, which after a while began to be fairly carefully counted. It may also have been hoped that in these modern, Restoration times, with the Stuarts back on the throne in the popular form of Charles II and a new prosperity in the land, the plague belonged to the Bad Old Days that were over and done with. In fact, it did – but this, its last appearance, was to be a devastating one.

One of the first places it appeared was the parish of St Giles-in-the-Fields, a still-countrified district well to the west of London proper. It was thought (probably wrongly) to have 'come in' with bales of cloth or boxes of ribbons that had arrived from Amsterdam, where plague was rumoured to be present, and were delivered to a Drury Lane shopkeeper. There was soon an increase of burials in St Giles's churchyard: we will come across its effect on one distinguished parishioner and his family in another chapter.

But soon the plague travelled, just as people and animals travelled, on the time-honoured route into London, and began to show itself much nearer to the City. Burials increased in St Andrew's churchyard at the foot of Holborn, near where the bridge went over the Fleet, and at St Bride's further south by the other bridge. Soon it had hopped over the dirty stream, but instead of making for the heart of the City it chose, with the travellers, to go round just to the north of it though still moving steadily east. Burials increased in St James Clerkenwell, then at Cripplegate and Bishopsgate, then round the walls to Aldgate. The weekly figures in these parishes were as yet quite low while at St Giles-in-the-Fields by May 1665 they were up in the hundreds. Houses began to be forcibly shut up there, and also in the nearby parish of St Martin-in-the-Fields and in that of St Clement Danes in the Strand. The Inns of Court were closed round Holborn and the young lawyers, along with all Whitehall, went away to the country. On the other side of town less privileged people began streaming out of Aldgate, through Whitechapel bars, always eastwards, escaping, as they hoped, on the road towards Essex. In this way the plague reached Stepney, then still a retired, semi-rural spot with a sprinkling of gentlemen's houses and a newly established Dissenting presence.

By the height of the summer, the travelling sickness was beginning to vacate the western suburbs where it had already killed so many and was steadily worsening in the east. In the last two weeks of July the plague totals for Stepney were 33, and then 58, followed by 76 in the first week of August. Then, by mid-September, the Stepney figure had jumped to 716, higher even than crowded Whitechapel (532), and in the last week it was still 674. After that, with the unusually hot summer finally over – there was a particularly good fruit harvest in the orchards of Stepney that year, if anyone cared to pick it – the rates quickly declined. But the human damage had been done. The plague, which for eight months had seemed inclined to bypass the City, finally settled in there too. Between August and early October, 59,870 people died in and around London proper, 49,705 of whom were considered to be plague victims. In one week, according to a physician who lived to tell the tale, twelve thousand died, four thousand of them in one single night.

In Stepney, as in the City, most of the wealthier citizens had fled, but those mainly ordinary men responsible for running the parish stayed and many did not survive. The Vestry minutes are scantily kept for that year, not surprisingly, and there seem to have been few meetings held. Daniel Defoe, in his *Journal of the Plague Year* (which is not a true journal, since it was concocted from research a generation later, but is an outstanding exercise in investigative journalism), wrote:

> when I say that the parish officers did not give in a full account [of the numbers of the dead] or were not to be depended upon for their account, let anyone but consider how men could be exact in such a time of terrible distress, and when many of them were taken sick themselves, and perhaps died in the very time when their accounts were to be given in . . . The parish of Stepney had, within the year, 116 sextons, gravediggers, and their assistants; that is to say, bearers, bellmen, and drivers of carts for carrying off the dead bodies.

The parish of Stepney, of course, then included the Thames-side areas of Ratcliffe–Wapping, Limehouse and Poplar. Great numbers died there, and ship-owners shut themselves up in their berthed ships, all sails furled under the relentless sun, to see the disaster out. Water-borne trade was almost at a standstill and many boats were forbidden by the Lord Mayor to come up to the Pool of London.

Although anyone of any class might die of the plague, it hit the poorest citizens the hardest, probably because their houses, bedding and clothes were less likely to be kept clean and free of infestations, which the better-educated knew was in general a good idea though they did not know exactly why. To accommodate those without the means to have something better organised for them, huge plague pits were dug, one at Aldgate and another in Finsbury Fields just beyond the Moorfields. Defoe says there was one off Bishopsgate Street: this appears to have been on the east side, more or less opposite Bedlam. It was open ground then, but with the pressure on land for building a mere few years later this particular space came into private hands. Houses were

> built on the very same ground where the poor people were bur-
> ied, and the bodies, on opening the ground for the foundations,
> were dug up, some of them remaining so plain to be seen that
> the women's skulls were distinguished by their long hair, and of
> others the flesh was not quite perished; so that the people began
> to exclaim loudly against it, and some suggested that it might
> endanger a return of the contagion.

Human reactions have not changed that much with the passing centuries ('Remains . . . are tested for anthrax and plague', 2009). On this occasion the barely rotted bodies were all bundled up and carted off to be packed into a new, narrow but deep pit not far off which, it was understood, was not to be built upon. It soon became an alleyway.

Stepney parish, stretching as it did right to the edge of London, acquired extra land for plague burials in Shoreditch and on the as-yet-unbuilt Spitalfields. There was also a large piece of land added to the south-west of the existing St Dunstan's churchyard, which never got built over and is there to this day. It is the part of the present churchyard that has been entirely cleared of monuments and where people are allowed to exercise their dogs under the spreading plane trees.

Defoe – who was eventually to be buried in Bunhill Fields, to the north of the City, in 1731 at the decent age of seventy – also mentions in his account plague burials in 'a piece of ground in Moorfields, by the going into the street which is now called Old Bethlem'. We have been here before.

This was the acre of garden belonging to Bethlehem Hospital – Bedlam – that was walled around by the Mayor of London in Queen Elizabeth's reign to provide extra burial space for London parishes that were running out of ground of their own. It was a respectable and even prestigious ground, and, apart from plague times, when bodies were buried hastily wherever they could be, it seems to have remained so for much of its visible existence.

The earliest burials were in shrouds, as was normal in the sixteenth century for everyone but the wealthy. Later burials were coffined, when that became the general usage. In the seventeenth century two passionate and endlessly contentious Levellers were buried there. One, Robert Lockyer, was executed for mutiny while an officer in Cromwell's Model Army, and the other, the famously outspoken Lilburne, died when on parole from his third or fourth prison sentence. Lockyer was a St Botolph's parishioner in any case, but the Bethlehem ground, being extra-parochial, may have been considered particularly suitable for Dissenters. There were also a number of occupants who were commemorated by more than the wooden crosses that were all most families then aspired to. Twentieth-century excavations in what was left of the place revealed a grave slab (which had been reused in a wall) for a Sarah Long who died in 1672, and whose bereaved husband could afford Portland limestone to commemorate her. Another fragmented slab, seeming to commemorate three men, was of Derbyshire slate.

There were also two conjoined vaults containing members of the distinguished if slightly eccentric Jenkes family. The chronology of the vaults' contents was thought by those who unearthed them to be a little complex, with the remains from a number of wooden coffins having been gathered together at some point into one lead coffin. But, judging from surviving coffin plates, an early occupant appears to have been one Francis Jenkes, who died in 1686 at the age of forty-six. Other sources reveal that he was probably a Quaker, and that he may have been a member of the 'Wallingford House party' which conspired to overthrow Oliver Cromwell's son Richard near the end of the Commonwealth. But Jenkes seems to have been one of nature's contrarians, since a speech he made in the Guildhall in 1676, long after the Restoration, was regarded by the King and his Council as seditious. He was committed to prison, from where he petitioned to be either bailed or brought to trial, but because it was vacation time for the courts the unsympathetic Lord Chancellor said that a writ could not be issued. This created something of a public scandal, and the lasting result was the Habeas Corpus Act of the following year.

A decade later, in the year of his death, we find Jenkes again in dispute, this time over monies due to Sir Christopher Wren for work on Wallingford House, near Charing Cross, for which Jenkes was apparently responsible. Later the same year his widow was petitioning 'for the removal of the stop which is put upon her' – i.e. the family money had been distrained because of the debt. If Sarah ever came to rest in the vault too her coffin plate has gone missing, but two daughters in their twenties joined their father there in 1694 and 1698 and a third, married one, in 1714. A brother of Francis Jenkes also arrived there in middle age, and what may have been a son-in-law or a young grandson. In contrast to this toll of early mortality, the vaults also sheltered an Ann Halford, born nine years before Francis, who died in 1712 at the age of eighty-one. A beloved spinster cousin or aunt? In 1714 or soon after, the vault was probably sealed. Other members of the extended Jenkes family must have enjoyed good health, for a number of them went across the ocean to the New World where they prospered and became eminent.

In 1676, the same year that Francis Jenkes had been at odds with the ruling powers, Bethlem Hospital, we know, moved to much larger and more important-looking new premises especially built in Moorfields facing onto London Wall. The architect was the scientist and poly-math Robert Hooke, and the monumental gates of the building were adorned with two alarming recumbent figures labelled 'Melancholia' and 'Raving Madness'. The new hospital was built to contain far more inmates than the old, informal buildings had harboured; and, notori-ously, visitors unrelated to the mad were allowed in to stare at them and laugh at them as if at an entertainment.

In a map drawn the year the hospital opened, the burial ground is marked 'Bethlehem Church Yard' and has no houses encroaching on it. But on the Rocque map of 1746 small houses have been built round two sides of it. Recent excavations have revealed that most of the old stones had been removed and were reused in nearby walls or for pav-ing. Their removal would also have made it possible to dig new graves into the ground that was already heavily sown with bodies – as hap-pened routinely in churchyards up and down the country – digging old bones in deeper and piling extra earth on top. The plot was now both reduced in size and becoming quite crowded. It was called by Rocque 'Bethlem Burying Ground', probably just because of its con-tinuing vicinity to the hospital. However, this has led to a burgeoning modern myth that it was actually or predominantly the burial place of despised lunatics, and therefore (by our modern ethical standards that have largely replaced formal religious beliefs) particularly deserv-ing of our attention and pity. In fact recent research has revealed few, if any, records of Bedlam inmates being laid there. They were all just Londoners from many different parishes, crowded together in death as they were in life.

And yet there continued to be a symbiotic relationship, presumably based on land ownership, between the long-ago garden of the Priory of St Mary Bethlehem and the institution that continued to bear the same name. By 1799, Hooke's hospital, so prestigious when it had been built one hundred and twenty years before, was considered to be in such bad repair that it was being demolished. A new hospital was situ-ated on the far side of London, in Lambeth. A map of that year that shows the old hospital half gone marks the old burial ground simply as 'gardens'. It was still a garden in the 1820s and as late as 1862, though by this time buildings had encroached on all four sides of it. What the garden had originally been had now faded from living memory.

The narrow cobbled street that ran across the southern edge of the ground and went by the name 'Old Bedlam' had been widened in 1829 and renamed 'Liverpool Street' after Lord Liverpool, a recent prime minister. Even the nineteenth-century antiquarian Charles Roach Smith, who in his later years lived at 5 Liverpool Street, does not seem to have known the place's history, though he was an authority on Roman London and responsible for identifying and saving several tracts of London's rapidly diminishing walls. He wrote near the end of his life:

Opposite my house on the other side of the street was a long, dead wall, which separated the street from a long piece of garden ground. When my man buried in it a deceased favourite cat, he said he came upon the remains of human skeletons. A few years later the cat's coffin and epitaph were brought before the directors of the North London and Great Eastern Railways as a very puzzling discovery!

*　*　*

And so we are back with the 1860s and the tendency of the new railways to sweep away not only the living but also the dead.

The successful North London line, which had up to then taken its passengers in a wide arc round to the eastern side of London before depositing them at Fenchurch Street,[2] constructed a new junction near its Kingsland station in Hackney to run a spur line almost to London Wall. The cul-de-sac street that had encroached on the north side of the old burial ground early in the eighteenth century, parallel with Liverpool Street on the south side, was inappropriately called Broad Street. On Stanford's detailed map of 1863 (the useful A-to-Z of the time) a patch of green with symbolic bushes on it appears between these two modest streets, but within a year this was obliterated. Broad Street station was now rising on the site, together with a swathe of railway lines for goods as well as passengers cutting through the old lanes to the north. The ground landlords of much of this land to the west of Bishopsgate Street were still the same family that had acquired it from Henry VIII at the Reformation, when a minor religious house up there had been seized at the same time as St Mary Spital to the east. The family received a substantial sum in compensation from the North London Railway while the actual inhabitants of the crowded lanes, being only tenants, received nothing.

Six hundred and forty-three houses were demolished between Hackney and Broad Street, displacing something between five and seven thousand people. The way such railways cut through the poorer and more crowded districts was still widely regarded as 'solving the slum problem'. While the new station was in the planning stage, *The Times*[3] wrote that north towards Shoreditch was:

> one of the most poverty-stricken, dirty and unhealthy clusters of thickly populated houses in this part of eastern London . . . broken windows mended with paper or rags, ever-open doors with begrimed walls and blacker floors, ill-scrawled notices of lodgings at 2d. and 3d. a night.

By the time the demolitions had taken place the public conscience was roused: there were protests, and even a petition to Parliament for the evicted people. But it was not till the mid-1870s that the expanding Metropolitan Board of Works, together with various philanthropic associations, began to assume responsibility for housing displaced people, building the great blocks of Workers' Dwellings that characterised the end of the century.

As for the dead, they were evicted too. The bones of some three to four hundred people were recorded as having been removed (along with Charles Roach Smith's cat) when part of the 'garden' was dug up. The human remains were all supposed to have been reburied wholesale in a pit in the huge new City of London Cemetery that had been established in open country, seven miles to the north-east. However, some hundred and twenty years later, in the 1980s, when Broad

Street station itself was being demolished to create the Broadgate Shopping Centre, Museum of London archaeologists found the bone fragments of at least four hundred more bodies, and also the deeply buried vaults of the Jenkes family. It became evident that all these bits and pieces from the cemetery's earlier period of use had simply been shoved back into the ground under the newly constructed station as backfill beneath the booking office. Somewhat naturally, this example of brisk entrepreneurial progress and modernity had not been documented in the 1860s. I imagine that a foreman of the works, faced with another, deeper layer of bone fragments that he had not expected, took a robust decision early one morning and that was that.

So was this the very last vestige of the walled acre of land that Mayor Thomas Roe secured for the parishes of London in 1568? Well, not quite, as we shall see.

Even as the North London Railway was building its new line, the directors of the Eastern Counties were planning their own incursion and arguing with the Corporation of London about it. Following the ruling made in the 1840s that mainline railways should not invade central London, the line from East Anglia had had to settle in that decade for a terminus at Shoreditch. Quite a grand Italianate station was built there, of which not a rack remains today except that the Overground station is on its site, and the one-time Bishopsgate goods station survives and is the object of competing plans as I write. (The name 'Shoreditch' for the terminus was later changed to 'Bishopsgate' in an attempt to disguise the fact that it was situated many hundreds of yards from the City proper. This fudge may partly explain the fact that the names 'Shoreditch' and 'Bishopsgate' began to be used interchangeably by the late nineteenth century, though earlier Bishopsgate had become entirely built up at a time when Shoreditch was still on the edge of fields.)

However, by the 1860s various lines that had, till then, been kept penned south of the river Thames were making their way further into London; and once the North London line was coming all the way to Broad Street the traditional objection to having a main line nearer to the City collapsed. The Eastern Counties Railway, now renaming itself the Great Eastern after various amalgamations, would have liked to put its station on Finsbury Circus, to the west of the new Broad Street station. Since Finsbury Circus was the small park that had been laid out on what was left of the Moorfields about 1816, the idea of turning it into a railway terminus was not popular. The company had to settle instead for the land on the other side of Broad Street station, adjoining Bishopsgate. So it came about that what was pragmatically but confusingly christened 'Liverpool Street Station'[4] ended up occupying the very plot on which the Priory of St Mary of Bethlehem had been built over six hundred years before. To be exact, the edge of Charles Barry's monumental station hotel, the Great Eastern, at the corner of Bishopsgate and Liverpool Street, is where the Priory gatehouse once was.

As with Broad Street station, much of the land the railway company needed was still owned by a body who had held it for hundreds of years – in this case, the Bethlehem Hospital governors. They had retained the land, even though the hospital had moved to Moorfields two centuries earlier and had later moved again to Lambeth. The governors asked the railway company for £95,000, a huge sum in the 1860s,

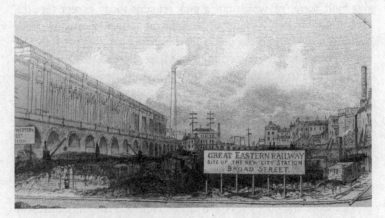

Demolition for Liverpool Street station, 1871

but £67,000 was the sum eventually settled on. Others who benefited from the land grab were the Corporation of London and various livery companies. The new station and its sidings eventually extended far up Bishopsgate, creating for a while a vast open space into which had disappeared Paul Pindar's house, the workhouse that had been built and then rebuilt alongside it, a theatre, a gasworks and numerous old dwelling houses, courts and lanes. The *Illustrated London News* noted in October 1871:

> The works in progress for the City terminus Extension of the Great Eastern railway have involved the demolition of many buildings to clear the ground . . . On the west side of Bishopsgate Street the line [coming down diagonally from Shoreditch] will turn in a southerly direction, crossing Worship-street, Primrose-street, Skinner-street and Sun-street, to reach the site of the proposed City terminus. This will occupy a large piece of ground about 700 ft. long by 400 ft. wide.

It was to be lined up with Broad Street station facing Liverpool Street.

Many of the small businesses and artisans that had flourished in the area lost their trading premises and, once again, three thousand were made homeless. With the two stations and their shunting yards side by side, the City's oldest suburb had effectively been wiped out.

This extraordinarily cavalier destruction of townscape, not just of thousands of Londoners' homes but of the very setting and context of their lives, had never been practised on such a scale before the late nineteenth century, and it was not equalled again till the vision of 'comprehensive redevelopment' obsessed planners and architects in the two decades after the Second World War. It is hardly surprising that in the 1850s, '60s and '70s the dead had no security of tenure either, and that the physical obliteration of burial grounds tended to be seen as another form of slum clearance.

In 1832 London had its first cholera outbreak, and more cases appeared in 1834. There was trouble about where and how cholera victims might safely be buried, and that year a count was done of London graveyards. It was noted that in the whole of the metropolis there were under five hundred acres of burial space, most of it already overfull. Churches whose cramped churchyards were now surrounded by buildings had at varying times acquired for themselves extra grave space a little further out of town, even as Thomas Roe had done for the City parishes in 1568. St Giles-in-the-Fields had done this, so had St Martin's and also St James Piccadilly, but these extra grounds were themselves filling up fast. In addition, there was a widespread perception that graveyards were a permanent source of disease – that a 'miasma' could at times be seen hanging over them, and that this in itself generated fatal illnesses.

Cholera actually derived from India and had worked its way gradually via Russia and then across Europe. The cholera vibrio is usually passed on by contaminated drinking water, but the miasmic theory of infection was so firmly entrenched that it was decided that Something Must be Done. It had been obvious in any case that putting so many bodies into churchyards, raising the level of the earth several feet around the church walls, was bad for the fabric of the building. St Giles had had to be rebuilt twice in two successive centuries partly on account of this, and St Dunstan's in Stepney had had problems as well. And that was before you even began to discuss the evil of putting dead bodies not into supposedly cleansing earth but into crypts immediately beneath the floor on which the congregation stood, sat, sang and listened for hours every Sunday . . .

Dickens, in *Bleak House*, which was serialised in 1852–53, describes, in the burial of 'Nemo', exactly the kind of inner London graveyard that was by then being seen as a source of death in itself. Indeed, it is sometimes said to be St Giles-in-the-Fields' ground that is being described, since Nemo dies in Cook's Court near Lincoln's Inn, which was then just within St Giles parish. 'Phiz's' illustration of the place where Jo, the poor crossing-sweeper boy whom Nemo befriended, plies his trade undoubtedly depicts the Resurrection Gate that was by then a feature of St Giles. However, the graveyard Dickens envisaged was probably in Russell Court off Drury Lane, one of numerous pauper yards which were destined to disappear under buildings once they were of no more use:

> the body of our dear brother here departed [is borne off] to a hemmed-in churchyard, pestiferous and obscene, where malignant diseases are communicated to the bodies of our dear brothers and sisters who have not departed . . .
>
> With houses looking on, on every side, save where a reeking little tunnel of a court gives access to the iron gate – with every villainy of life in action close on death, and every poisonous element of death in action close on life – here, they lower our dear brother down a foot or two: here, sow him in corruption, to be raised in corruption: an avenging ghost at many a sick bedside: a shameful testimony to future ages, how civilisation and barbarianism walked this boastful island together.

Bleak House is, like many of Dickens's novels, set back twenty years or so in time. In any case, when it was published, burials such as Nemo's had ceased. Big new cemeteries such as Highgate, Brookwood and Kensal Green had opened on the then-edge of London. By 1849 agitation about unhealthy old graveyards had reached such a pitch that a bill was introduced in Parliament, and from 1851 they were all closed.

It is not surprising that, in spite of further regulation in 1857 regarding burial places, railway companies thought they could sweep away old grounds with impunity, and even be congratulated for doing so.

In the 1860s, when the Midland Railway was building its new terminus at St Pancras, slotting in between King's Cross and Euston, they confidently expected to be allowed to buy up Old St Pancras church (whose foundations date from the fifth century) and use the site and its surrounding burial grounds for their shunting yards. 'Grounds' in the plural, since the old graveyard of St Pancras itself had had another parcel of land joined to it in 1803 to accommodate some of the dead parishioners of St Giles-in-the-Fields. The Midland did not entirely get their way: instead, they were told to dig a tunnel beneath the land at a depth of fifteen feet. Evidently no one had worked out that, with multiple burials, the land had risen so much that fifteen feet was not nearly deep enough to avoid tunnelling through a solid mass of coffin wood and human remains. The resulting scandal has become a well-known story, complete with the fact that the writer Thomas Hardy, then a young architectural student, was sent there to supervise the grisly scene.

Less well known is the fact that in 1874, with its Gothic extravaganza of a station up and in full use, the Midland had another try. This time, they accepted that they would not be allowed to remove the church or the graves (those that had not been removed willy-nilly during the failed tunnelling of the 1860s) but they still hoped to be allowed to run some further railway lines over the site. With veiled and optimistic hints about compulsory purchase and 'the enlargement and ever-increasing growth of their traffic', the company declared that it 'did not propose to create thoroughfares or to take the ground by high-handed powers'. They did not actually intend 'to break the soil', they said. They had promised the Secretary of State they wouldn't. All they wanted was:

> to use the ground for lines of rails and light sheds . . . It is also proposed to allow monuments and remains to stay . . . but the ground would be raised 10 ft. to bring it on a level with the other property of the company.

Grave owners, they implied, might still visit the place (*The Times*, 28 May 1874).

How can they have imagined for a moment that this surreal scheme would be accepted? Did they suppose that those visiting Dear Papa's grave (between the light sheds and rails) would climb up and down ten-foot-high railway embankments in their crinolines and top hats, hoping not to be hit by a train? It was immediately made clear to the company that they would not win this one: not only were the Vestries of St Pancras and St Giles totally opposed, but the European Roman Catholic interest was roused in anger against it, since that ground had been much used for refugees from the French Revolution. The Midland company backed down, and the graveyards remain as gardens to this day. Ever since, any attempt to remove a burial ground has met with formidable legal obstacles and a public outcry. The railway companies brought it on themselves.

Today, Crossrail Two for tomorrow is tentatively planned to pass beneath St Pancras Gardens, as Crossrail One does beneath the burial ground of St Dunstan-in-the-East. But at thirty metres or more below ground, it is very unlikely to disturb the remaining dead.

And what, finally, of the Liverpool Street ground? We last saw it in the 1980s, when the archaeologists investigating the site of Broad Street station before it was covered over once again discovered that, rather more than a hundred years before, ancient bone fragments had been shoved back into the earth under the station booking hall. These finds, and a few other deep survivals such as the old and broken tombstones and the Jenkes vaults, were carefully documented as far as they could be. Surely, you might think, the site could yield nothing further? Particularly as, when the excavation was done, concrete was apparently poured into the trenches with the well-meant but misguided intention of leaving the dead in situ and 'in peace'. 'That wouldn't happen today,' a retired civil engineer said to me. And indeed, in the summer of 2013, the concrete was being carefully picked out again by a new generation of archaeologists. But how, you may wonder, was there any of the old Bethlem graveyard site left for them to get at?

The answer lies in Liverpool Street itself, the street to the south of the station where Roach Smith once lived and which replaced the eighteenth-century lane called Old Bedlam. A roadway is a great preserver of what lies immediately beneath it. What was once an earth or gravel path gets paved over, first perhaps with small cobbles and then with granite sets, but unlike land used for building it is not fundamentally disturbed. The odd water main, gas pipe, cesspit or drain may make a cut across it, but otherwise the earth and its contents remain what they have always been. Just such a piece of land has lain all the while under Liverpool Street – the last dozen-metres-wide sliver of the very old burial ground.

As this book was being written it was disappearing. For that segment of street is the place for the just-beneath-the-ground hall and ticket office of the new Crossrail station. The rectangular box placed in the earth occupies all the space. In the spring of 2015 a great sheltering canopy was raised over the ground, complete with arc lights for night work. The tarmac was stripped back, then some old cobbles, and then the sooty earth began to be turned over once again for a final time. Two teams of archaeologists worked for a month in double shifts from seven in the morning to eleven at night, scraping, sifting. Skulls and ribcages, thigh bones and finger joints lay exposed in their vulnerable quietness only a few yards from the noise of continuous traffic and the brisk footfall of the living. The last of the dead, which had been expected to number some hundreds of bodies of various different periods but which turned out to be as many as two and a half thousand, were finally going to vacate their long home. But before they disappear for ever, probably into a cemetery on distant Canvey Island near the mouth of London's river, the sophisticated archaeology and analysis of today has been deploying all its new skills to document their living and their dying. These people are receiving more minute attention in death than most of them ever received in life, and some of them may be brought back again from the nameless oblivion that will cover nearly all of us. Crossrail, with its state-of-the-art technology, is their final destroyer. But it is also their saviour and preserver.

CHAPTER VIII

St Giles Before the Fall. And After

We last had a clear view of St Giles as a pleasant village set among fields on the western route out of London. By the final years of Elizabeth's reign a ribbon of houses was creeping fast along both sides of Holborn to join with the village, but unlike those on the opposite side of the City at Whitechapel these were good-class homes with gardens behind them. Under James I and after him Charles I, further development began to line Drury Lane and then fill the space between that and Lincoln's Inn to meet the new Covent Garden district to the south. The parish of St Giles-in-the-Fields which, in the Middle Ages, had numbered only about one hundred inhabitants now had about two thousand, but they were quite widely spread; the old village centre still remained a sought-after location and had a number of grand residents.

Yet something revolutionary was clearly going to happen to it. For we also paid it a fleeting visit in the previous chapter, some two hundred years later in the early nineteenth century. At that point its parish churchyard – where Jo the orphan boy sweeps a crossing – figures in *Bleak House* as a particularly dark spot in a whole Holborn circle of darkness, mud, fog and the metaphorical fog and obfuscation of the Chancery lawyers sitting in Lincoln's Inn, the novel's sinister nexus. It is on the route of the cattle being driven towards Smithfield:

> The blinded oxen, over-goaded, over-driven, never guided, run into wrong places and are beaten out; and plunge, red-eyed and foaming, at stone walls . . . [A dog appears –] a drover's dog, waiting for his master outside a butcher's shop . . . a thoroughly

vagabond dog, accustomed to low company, and public houses;
a terrific dog to sheep; ready at a whistle to scamper over their
backs, and tear out mouthfuls of their wool.

Jo lives a little walk away, but in the same district:

> in a ruinous place, known by the like of him by the name of Tom-
> all-Alone's.[1] It is a black, dilapidated street, avoided by all decent
> people; where the crazy houses were seized upon, when their
> decay was far advanced, by some bold vagrants, who, after estab-
> lishing their own possession, took to letting them out in lodgings.
> Twice, lately, there has been a crash and a cloud of dust, like
> the springing of a mine, in Tom-all-Alone's; and, each time, a
> house has fallen. These accidents have made a paragraph in the
> newspaper and have filled a bed or two in the nearest hospital . . .
> As several more houses are nearly ready to go, the next crash in
> Tom-all-Alone's may be expected to be a good one.
> This desirable property is in Chancery, of course.

Even allowing for Dickens's hyperbole, it is not hard to identify Tom-
all-Alone's with a particularly notorious area of courts and yards just
north of St Giles High Street whose ownership had indeed become a
cat's cradle of subleases. Part of it was pulled down in the 1840s as a piece
of early slum clearance and to create New Oxford Street, but it lingered
long in the public consciousness. Parton, the Vestry clerk whose book
on the history of the parish was published just after his own death in
1822, summed up in its preface the change the district had seen:

> The astonishing increase in [St Giles's] buildings and popularity
> since the reign of Queen Elizabeth, when nearly the whole of it
> was solitary fields: the high rank and celebrity of numbers of its
> parishioners, when it came afterwards to be inhabited; the pecu-
> liar character of its poor, and a variety of other circumstances,
> concur to produce that sort of contrast between its antient and
> present states, which it is pleasing to contemplate.

Why it should be pleasing to contemplate an area's marked social decline is not clear – except that Parton may have derived satisfaction from knowing about its past grandeur. Also, many people have a sort of pride in the reputed celebrity of their slums and 'the peculiar character' of their poor – not any old poor, it is implied, but a specially interesting kind. In the case of St Giles, these tended to be immigrants: Huguenots in the late seventeenth and early eighteenth centuries, who had not been as successful as their cousins in Spitalfields and elsewhere; and also Irish, those proverbial creators of 'County Kilkenny in London', supposedly all oyster shells, drunken men, 'slatternly women', and *not good Church of England parishioners*.

Let us return to the days when St Giles could still, like Stepney that other suburban village, be said to be known for 'the high rank and celebrity of numbers of its parishioners'. The film rewinds rapidly backwards: crowded, soot-imbued tenements shake themselves out into old, timbered buildings with vegetable plantations and orchards between, or diminish into thatch-roofed cottages. A gallows rears up at the western end of the wide-open roadway, and here and there are the middens of animal and human manure that were to be found anywhere outside of towns in the centuries before sewage systems; but the country air is mingled with nothing worse than woodsmoke, and there are some fine houses adjoining the church.

In the late 1530s, when Henry VIII and his henchmen were busy seizing Church property, it is probable that the leper hospital had already more or less abandoned its original function as leprosy seemed to be retreating into the past. However, the formal transition from hospital chapel to parish church only occurred after Henry's death, under his resolutely Protestant son Edward VI. The buildings east of the church, the 'Spital houses' where the sick had lodged, were variously let, and the one nearest to the church became the Angel Inn. This hostelry took over the monks' benign practice of offering 'the St Giles bowl' of liquor to condemned felons, passing the door on their way either to the adjacent gallows or further west along the Oxford road to Tyburn. A rebuilt Angel inn stands on the same site today.

The hospital Master's house, on the opposite side of the church, was acquired at the Dissolution on a Crown lease by John Dudley, otherwise known as Lord de Lisle, from a family which had already had a chequered though illustrious past as the Tudor dynasty came to power. He was an ambitious careerist who rose, under Henry and then under Edward, to become Lord High Admiral, Earl Marshal and then Duke of Northumberland, successfully seeing off the claims of the rival Seymour family to run the country. (His eventual downfall, in 1553, was his attempt to put his newly-wed daughter-in-law, Lady Jane Grey, on the throne during the chaos that surrounded the death of Edward, and he was executed for treason as his own father had been over forty years before.) In the 1540s, so Parton tells us, John Dudley 'fitted up the principle part' of the Master's house, now known as the Mansion House, 'as a residence for himself, and leased various subordinate parts of the structure out to different tenants, as well as portions of adjoining gardens etc.' A few years later he passed on the lease to Wymonde Carewe, another of Henry's associates, who became the patron of the newly established parish. Assorted other gentlemen occupied other parts of the extensive ex-hospital property, including a Geoffrey Sutton who was related to the Dudleys, and Dr Borde or Boorde. This eccentric and much-travelled ex-Carthusian monk was helped by Thomas Cromwell to become one of the many physicians appointed to attend King Henry in his long physical decline. However, he later got into trouble for proselytising, and also for selling quack remedies at fairs – hardly behaviour becoming to a gentleman. A street named after him survived as a turning off the High Street till it was demolished for Centre Point in the 1960s.

The Mansion House stood just west of St Giles church, on the opposite side of the lane that is, today, Flitcroft Street. There was then no pathway where Denmark Street, with its music shops, runs today; other ex-hospital buildings adjoined the Mansion, continuing in an irregular line. This is where, behind a late-Victorian block of flats in what is left of St Giles High Street, Denmark Place runs. Here, after the Dissolution, there was adapted from the hospital buildings another gentleman's residence, which may have been where Dr Borde lived.

This other substantial house later became known as the White House and was given in 1646 to the rector of St Giles for his own use, thus returning one-time Church property to the newly reconstituted (and by then reconstructed) church. As late as the nineteenth century, by which time the house itself had long gone and Denmark Place, then called Dudley Court, had become 'an obscure thoroughfare inhabited by low people', the rector of the parish was still receiving the rents from it as his personal perquisite (see map p. 221).

As the name of the alley suggests, the Dudley family had kept their interest in the one-time hospital property. The giver of the White House was a Lady Dudley, who was then living herself in the Mansion House. She was to be a significant figure in St Giles for much of the seventeenth century. Urbanisation was creeping up on the village enclave; the open fields of Bloomsbury to the north were just beginning to be laid out for housing, and one or two very grand detached houses in the latest style even began to appear there. Lady Dudley may be said to have represented the old village order, for certainly her own predilection was for the old ways of benign aristocratic patronage.

The Dudley family constitute an English saga stretching over generations. John, Duke of Northumberland, had several sons including a Robert, who came near to losing his head too during the Lady Jane Grey debacle, but managed to weather life under Catholic Mary through military exploits. His career blossomed when Elizabeth came to the throne. Famously he became, as the Earl of Leicester, one of her chief statesmen, favourites, and probably her lover. Many expected the Queen to marry him, but a persistent rumour that the death of his wife had been an arranged murder clouded that prospect. He did not remarry for eighteen years, and when he did his new wife was promptly banished from the court. His only legitimate son died in early childhood, but he had an illegitimate son (also, confusingly, called Robert, like both his father and his half-brother) to whom Leicester gave a first-class education and to whom he left the bulk of his substantial estate, including Kenilworth Castle.

This Robert Dudley – the illegitimate one – became part of that band of late-Elizabethan and Stuart explorers and cartographers which was pushing the boundaries of the known world. After a secret teenage marriage to an aristocratic girl as young as himself (who soon died), he led a roving sea-dog existence, gathering wealth by raids on Spanish possessions and claiming new lands for the Crown. In his twenties, he married again: his bride was Alice, daughter of a baronet, Sir Thomas Leigh of Stoneleigh in Warwickshire, and she it is who was to become the presiding spirit of St Giles parish.

The marriage produced five daughters within seven years, but can hardly be said to have been a success. In the early years of James I's reign, when Robert was about thirty, he was encouraged by a shady hanger-on to believe that his parents had in reality been secretly married and that he was therefore the legitimate heir both to his father's titles and to his uncle's estate of Warwick Castle. He failed in his attempt to get this ratified: the Star Chamber discredited several of the witnesses and rejected his suit – upon which he left for the Continent and never set foot in England again. Ostensibly, this was because of the great insult he had received, but the reality of the situation probably had more to do with the female cousin who accompanied him. The pair set up house together in Italy, where Robert became naval advisor and ship-designer to the Grand Duke of Tuscany, who was one of the super-wealthy Medici. He wrote an important treatise on navigation; he began illicitly using his father's titles, and produced fourteen more children with his cousin, some of whom eventually acquired Italian titles of their own.

When Robert Dudley refused to come home and provide for his deserted wife and daughters, James I declared him an outlaw and gave the family titles away to other people, but the King's eldest son, Henry, still had some dealings with Robert, who had been a close friend. Henry wanted to buy Kenilworth Castle from him, but the deal foundered, and after Henry's untimely death the future Charles I favoured the deserted Alice's cause and got Parliament to let him buy the castle from *her* for a substantial sum of money.

It seems clear that general sympathies in England were very much on Alice's side, and that she understood the value of this. Far from trying to take revenge, or yet to reconfigure her marital situation (Robert had somehow managed to wangle a papal dispensation to marry his cousin), she slid into a role of dignified reticence and universal charity. Meanwhile, her absent husband had persuaded the Holy Roman Emperor of the time to declare him 'Duke of Northumbria'. This may have infuriated James I, but eventually, in 1644, Charles I confirmed the title for Alice's sake – 'having a very deep sense of the great injuries done'. So she was now addressed as Duchess Dudley, even though she had no lands to go with the title and her husband had been gone for nearly forty years. This must have been one of Charles I's last acts as a sovereign before his own dark fate began to catch up with him.

Meanwhile, Duchess Dudley had carved out a place for herself in the house next to the church as the Good Woman of St Giles. When she finally died, aged ninety, in 1668, it was in a world that had changed profoundly since her Elizabethan childhood, not once but twice over, and the son of her champion, Charles I, was at last back on the throne. No wonder she came to be regarded as 'a living chronicle', as the rector of St Giles claimed: 'In divers accidents and things relating to our parish I oft appealed to her stupendous memory.' The year after she died, this rector (Robert Boreman) composed a memorial sermon that was one long eulogy on her life and character. It was delivered in front of a large congregation, including the only daughter who survived her. He must have been rather proud of his effusion, for he had it published in pamphlet form, of which there are copies still in existence today.[2] According to him, Lady Duddeley (his chosen spelling, which he maintained was hers too) exemplified:

The precious balme of Grace that was poured by God's blessed Spirit into the Soul of our Renowned Dutchess at her Baptism, or in her Infancy . . . broke forth in such a sweet perfume, even from her Childhood to her riper years, that she was looked upon as an Earthly Saint, and Angel clothed in Flesh, a lawful image of her Maker and Redeemer, a model of Heaven made up in Clay, the living Temple of the Holy Ghost.

Spurning other offers (according to the rector, though one does rather wonder how any suitor could have felt equal to such virtue), she became a 'spouse of God'. It is probably true, however, that her conversation was 'amiable, pleasant and Venerable to all her Equals and Inferiors' and that she possessed

a winning and obliging way or disposition, that sweetly scatters favours . . . By this . . . a desire of doing good to all, even to our very enemies, we attract friendships and make friends even of those that hate us . . .

When she bestowed any favour, or gave Alms, she gave it cheerfully without grudging . . . She had a great command over her Tongue and Passions . . . Her ears were ever open to the complaints of the poor, but shut against all calumny and Detraction.

The giving of handouts to the poor at the rich man's gate was a fundamental feature of life in the seventeenth century, and indeed for long after, and the numbers of poor frequenting St Giles were increasing with the spread of London. The Poor Accounts of the Vestry reveal that as early as the 1630s there was anxiety about this, and also a first passing mention of people living in cellars – something that was later to characterise the famous slums of the district. But references to sums given to beggars in the mid-century still suggest that they were well-known village figures rather than the faceless multitude of later accounts. There was 'the Ballad-singing Cobbler', 'old Friz-wig', 'mad Bess' (who needed a shift to make her decent), 'Tottenham Court Meg being very sicke' and 'old Osborne, a troublesome fellow'. One may assume that these and others were familiar figures to Lady Dudley. On her death she left many bequests, listed by Boreman, including a pension for the sexton and £400 to 'the Hospital near the church' to produce 'twenty pounds a year forever'. This, of course, cannot be the long-defunct leper hospital: I think it refers to a row of almshouses that had been built on the widest part of the High Street (also known as Broad Street) a dozen years before. She left £50 to be distributed among the poor of the parish on the day of her funeral, and 'to fourscore and ten Widows (according to the Number of the Years she lived) to each one a Gown and Fair White Kerchief to attend the Hearse wherein Her Body was carried, and one shilling a piece for their dinner'. She also, with a sudden mental leap out-side her own world, left money 'for Christian captives in slavery'.

But Boreman was particularly intent on listing in detail everything that she had given to his church. This was highly relevant at the period when she was settling into St Giles with her growing daughters and with the money from Kenilworth, for the medieval church building that had belonged to the leper hospital was showing signs of serious physical deterioration. According to the earliest Vestry minutes that have survived, attempts were being made to shore it up and to rebuild the collapsing bell-tower, but after a few years it was clear that the whole place must be substantially rebuilt, which it was between 1623 and 1631. Lady Dudley, who had subscribed to try to mend the old church, helped to have the wall erected round the churchyard (with a special door in it by the side of her house for her own use). She paid for paving the new church nave with marble and for six new bells, and also gave a remarkable number of objects to furnish and beautify the new building, all of which the rector scrupulously notes:

hangings of Watched Taffity to cover the upper end of the Chancel, and these bonded with Silk and Silver Fring . . . Rich Green Velvet Cloth with three Letters in Gold IHS embroider'd on it . . . 2 cushings for the Altar Richly Imbroider'd with Gold, large Turkey carpet, a beautiful skreen of Carved Work, gilded Organs [and a] very Costly altar rail.

Another source (Vestry accounts) mentions 'a fine long lawn cloth, with very rich bone lace'. As well as all this, she gave assorted communion plate of silver and gold 'which is as large and Rich as any in the City and Suburbs'.

There was a subtext to this remarkably material and (one might think) worldly inventory. For in her later years Lady Dudley had lived through the execution of Charles I and then through the Commonwealth that followed. Adherents to the Church of England later referred to this as the Interregnum, for, as if it were a second wave of the Reformation of the previous century, what was acceptable and seemly was once again changed. Altars were stripped, popular religious festivals and saints' days banned, stained-glass windows smashed and costly and decorative objects discarded. Discarded too, for the time being, were very many rectors and vicars as being insufficiently Puritan in their outlook – the previous, devoutly Royalist and high-church rector of St Giles, who had been responsible for the rebuilding, suffered this fate. He got into trouble for his views during the run-up to the Civil War, and was replaced by another who was also forced to resign. He was succeeded by a William Heywood, who was himself thrown out into penury during the Commonwealth in 1651, as Puritanism took a greater hold.

After that there was a 'minister . . . giving a lecture every Sunday afternoon' (according to the rather sparse and evasive Vestry minutes of the time) for which parishioners were forced to subscribe. From 1651 to 1660 the rector was a man described by a contemporary and friend of Lady Dudley's[3] as 'a common preacher of rebellion'. Heywood was brought back as rector at the Restoration in 1660, but he died in 1663; he was succeeded by Robert Boreman who was himself a fervent Royalist and sympathised greatly with his predecessors' misfortunes. No wonder that, at the end of his list of valuables bestowed by Lady Dudley, there is a further passionate paragraph:

> Onely [one large] Bell and the foresaid Plate excepted, all the fore-named Ornaments of the Church (being counted Superstitious and Popish) were demolished and sold (under a pretence of relieving the poor out of Money Received for them) by the deforming Reformers (as they were call'd) in the late bloody rebellious times.

Whether the poor genuinely benefited from the sale of taffeta curtains and embroidered cloths, I cannot say – there must have been rather a lot of such merchandise coming on the market just then – but the Vestry minutes for 1645 indeed show that a number of the pretty things were sold. The 'beautiful skreen', which apparently featured Saints Peter, Paul and Barnabas with the keys of Heaven, plus winged cherubim and lions, was regarded as particularly undesirable: it went for 40 shillings (£2). As for the wall paintings of the Twelve Apostles on the organ loft, these were simply 'washed off', so no one benefited. Some of the efforts under the Commonwealth to help the poor were, however, genuine. It was then that the almshouses were built in the High Street, and two years before that Oliver Cromwell himself gave £40 to the parish to buy coals for the poor. Wood had always been the traditional fuel, but the gradual depletion of Britain's forests meant that by the seventeenth century it was becoming something only the wealthier households could afford. Nor could the poor of St Giles parish any longer go seeking sticks in the woods of Marylebone which were themselves fast disappearing.

In March 1646, 'the Rails that stood about the Communion Table were by a mutual consent sold to Major Walter Bigg'. He gave £2 for them. This major (an officer in the Commonwealth army, of course, and previously a captain at the Basinghouse siege) was also a church-warden: several generations of the eponymous Bigg family were Vestrymen of St Giles. This was the same year that Lady Dudley made the White House over to the rector and his successors. The coincidence of date makes me think that she perceived where matters were heading and was hoping to protect the rector (then Heywood) from storms to come – though there is some indication that the lease of the house was already held in trust for the parsons. One can imagine all too well the tensions that split St Giles parish, and so many others in those times, with some prominent citizens triumphalist and many others anxious only to keep their heads down and avoid trouble. The rector's peroration also makes dark reference to

> plundering Persecutours . . . those who did persecute [Lady Dudley] with their hands robbing her of her goods (because she would not be as they were, bad, rebels against the King and Church) . . . not dreading to report she was a Papist . . . Or something like one.

As the Biggs were her near neighbours, and the bells of the church had been rung to celebrate the victorious return of Walter Bigg from the wars, one may well imagine it is the Bigg family that are here referred to.

However, as we know, in the end things turned out all right both for the Royalist rectors of the parish and for Lady Dudley. Her famous patience and humility were rewarded, and she was loved, I hope, by others beside the besotted Robert Boreman. I like to think that she was not a sanctimonious old lady 'offering up' her well-known misfortunes rather too complacently to her God (though she may have been), but a genuinely sunny-natured person who enjoyed giving, and whose sumptuous presents to her beloved church betrayed her own personal weakness: love for discreetly fine bone lace against a sober black dress, a hint of a suppressed girlish pleasure in the texture of silk and velvet, a private sensuousness that had been cut off over sixty years before. She was buried far away in Warwickshire, but a daughter, one of four out of five who predeceased her, lies recumbent in stone in the church to this day, even though it has been rebuilt once again since her time. I wonder if she ressembled her mother? I have measured her, guessing her to be much the same height as myself.

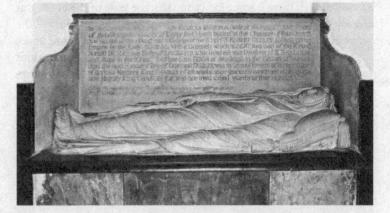

Lady Dudley's daughter Frances Kniveton

Indeed, she is about five foot six, tall for the times in which she lived; a slim figure with an oval face and heavily lidded eyes.

As a footnote, it is worth mentioning that the retribution exacted on the bodies of Oliver Cromwell and two other regicides, Henry Ireton and John Bradshaw, once Charles II was on the throne in 1660, seems to have had a close connection with St Giles parish.

Ten still-living signatories out of the fifty who had signed Charles I's death warrant were pursued and rapidly executed, while others escaped abroad. But the dead did not escape. Cromwell's body was exhumed from Westminster Abbey, where it had been interred with pomp only two years before. With the two others, Ireton and Bradshaw, it was given a symbolic trial in Westminster Hall before being (it is always said) 'dragged to Tyburn'; the bodies were left hanging there till sunset, then decapitated and the heads returned on poles to Westminster. However, there is also a persistent story that, after the trial, the corpses were kept for an intervening night at the Red Lion inn on the north corner of what was then Red Lion Fields – later to be Square. This open space is just off Holborn and near St Giles.

From Westminster, this would be the wrong direction for Tyburn, near the present-day Marble Arch – but is it really geographical Tyburn that is meant? The astute suggestion was made in Edward Walford's many-volumed 1878 book *Old and New London*[4] that 'Tyburn' had at that time become a generic term for any public execution site, and that perhaps it was actually St Giles, just down the road from the Red Lion, for which the corpses were destined? This idea is given further credence by the fact that, when the bodies were cut down and decapitated, Red Lion Fields was apparently where they were reburied, or so a persistent story goes. The King had passed up on his prerogative of having them quartered and exhibited round the country as traitors. The modern thinkers of the Restoration might still be capable of the atavistic ceremony of hanging dead men, but these bodies were already far from fresh meat. A few living regicides suffered the extreme, traditional fate, but it was beginning to be seen as a piece of outdated coarseness: twenty-five years later would take place the last ever English execution of this kind, and the last of a Catholic for his faith.[5]

So Cromwell and the two other corpses ended up in Red Lion Fields. And, once the centre of the Fields had become the Square, a discreet memorial obelisk was erected there by a local apothecary called Ebenezer Heathcote. He was living on High Holborn after the Restoration and he was married to the daughter of one of Ireton's associates.

No obelisk remains today. The symmetry of the once-quiet square has been semi-wrecked by a 1960s road scheme down one side of it. But no one has apparently gone looking for three headless skeletons somewhere under the central garden, so they may be there to this day. Directly beneath them, but much further down, runs the Crossrail line on its way to Farringdon and the City.

Another important London event occurred in the final years of Lady Dudley's long life. This was the plague.

As mentioned in the previous chapter, this last but greatest epidemic of the dreaded Pest actually began in the parish of St Giles, where it killed many before travelling further east. As was usual, many early cases tended to be put down to other causes. Daniel Defoe wrote that:

the weekly bills [of Mortality] showing an increase of burials in St Giles parish more than usual it began to be suspected that the plague was among people at that end of the town, and that many had died of it, though they had taken care to keep it as much from the knowledge of the public as possible.

This was in February 1665 – which still counted as 1664 until mid-March, by the old-style calender then in force. As the weather warmed into spring official figures fluctuated, and there were intermittent hopes that the danger was abating, but once the weather grew hot in early June:

the infection spread in a dreadful manner, and the bills rose high . . . all that could conceal their distempers did so, to prevent their neighbours shunning and refusing to converse with them,

and also to prevent authority shutting up their houses, w..
though it was not yet practised, yet was threatened, and people
were extremely terrified at the thoughts of it.

In the second week of June St Giles's churchyard received one
hundred and twenty bodies (a usual number would have been four
to six, including infants) and 'though the bills said but sixty-eight of
the plague, everybody said there had been a hundred at least'. The
bell-ringers, exhausted, said that they were giving up: no more tolls
would be rung. The graveyard had run out of fresh space, and further
land seems to have been added to it from Cock and Pye Fields, but
the Vestry entries are so sparse for that year that it is hard to tell what
was decided. By the week of 4–11 July, in the two adjacent parishes of
St Giles-in-the-Fields and St Martin's of the same designation, almost
four hundred died. By the week at the end of July three hundred and
twenty-five deaths in St Giles were attributed to the plague; 2 August
was declared a day of fasting to atone for 'God's displeasure against the
Land by Pestilence and War'.

I doubt if Lady Dudley was then still at home. In common with
almost all her class, and with the court at Whitehall, she had surely
made tracks for some of her country-based relatives, in Warwickshire
or elsewhere. As Defoe wrote:

> the richer sort of people, especially the nobility and gentry from
> the west part of the city, thronged out of town with their fam-
> ilies and servants in an unusual manner . . . indeed nothing was
> to be seen but waggons and carts, with goods, women, servants,
> children, &c; coaches filled with people of the better sort, and
> horsemen attending them, and all hurrying away; then empty
> waggons and carts appeared, and spare horses with servants,
> who, it was apparent, were returning or sent from the countries
> to fetch more people.

But the then-growing class of 'people of the middling sort',
tradesmen, skilled artisans employing apprentices, printers, saddlers,

surgeons and the like, had fewer options of a safe escape. They could hardly abandon their livelihoods, even though trade was said to be at a near standstill, and anyway most of their contacts would have been London-based. This class was very well represented in the Holborn–St Giles area, and among them was the man to whom we owe most of our pictures of seventeenth-century London and maps of the town both before and after the Great Fire. This was the gifted engraver of Bohemian origin, Wenceslaus Hollar. Hollar's first wife had died in 1654 and was buried in St Giles's churchyard, so clearly the family were already lodging in that neighbourhood then; though Hollar also kept a room further south, in the streets towards the Strand in the parish of St Clement Danes, as a workshop.[6] Some two years later, his second marriage was registered in St Giles church, with an Honoria Roberts, 'spinster of this parish'. The Roberts family lived a few minutes' walk away in a high, timbered house that had been built about fifty years before on the south side of what is now High Holborn; their next-door neighbour was a surgeon and there were several decent inns along the run. (The last traces of these houses or their foundations disappeared when Kingsway was sliced through the traditional geography of the district about 1900.)

The burial records for St Giles show that between late June and mid-July nine members of the extended Roberts family in the parish died. Honoria did not die, nor did her daughters by Hollar. It is possible that he had sent them for safety just as far as the fields of Islington, since that heavy summer he made a series of pictures of the Islington Water House – a reservoir and pumping station for the New River that supplied part of London. But his only son, the boy he had had with his first wife, variously described by contemporaries as 'very promising' and 'an ingeniose youth, drew delicately', did succumb to the plague: 'a great loss'. Like many victims as the epidemic reached its height, he has no recorded place of burial.

Robert Boreman the rector stayed at his post, ministered to the sick and did not die. So did William Boghurst, an apothecary who lived and traded at the sign of the White Hart (later a somewhat notorious pub) on the corner of Holborn and Drury Lane. This intelligent and cultured man, who has left us his own account of the Great Plague,[7] confessed that he had difficulty in believing God had created it to punish man. He understood that though plague might not actually be engendered by dirt (as some thought), the greatest and simplest remedy against infection was cleanliness – much hand-washing, much changing of linen, much care in the preparation of food, 'good fires, good dyett . . . good conveyances of filth' – and evidently practised this successfully himself. He dressed sores, took pulses, let blood and sat by the bedsides of the dying, yet he survived in good health. But William Green, the extremely good-hearted constable for the Holborn side of the parish, died with £44 owing to him for money he had spent from his own purse on food for the sick and destitute. I wonder if his model of Christian charity had been Lady Dudley, though he can hardly have enjoyed her means.

The Great Plague was followed the next year by the Great Fire of London, which is inseparably linked with it in history books since it was widely if inaccurately credited with destroying the sources of infection along with much of the old townscape. What is undeniable, however, is that the destruction of nearly all the City, along with the relentless expansion of London's population, created a profound shift in the very idea of what London might be. The Fire reached to the west only as far as the lower end of Fleet Street, burning down St Bride's church but just sparing St Andrew Holborn and the Hatton Garden district to the north of it. It did not get near to St Giles parish; nevertheless, soon after that, the Hollars, like many other Londoners, moved further west again, and went to live off Whitehall, a district of orchards not yet taken over by government offices. Many people also began to colonise Soho, nearer at hand. A few houses had been built on these one-time royal hunting fields in the 1640s, but after 1670 building progressed rapidly, Soho Square was properly laid out and the whole district began to assume something of the air it has to this day. St Giles-in-the-Fields and its High Street were no longer right on the edge of town: instead, town was absorbing and inexorably changing them. It is almost as if Lady Dudley's death there in her Mansion House in 1668 were a coded signal for the ending of an old village world and the first stages of something very different.

Some part of the Mansion House was taken on by a man variously described as 'Colonel', 'Lord' and 'the Duke of' Wharton. One later writer, Rowland Dobie, describes him as having been 'dissolute', which appears to mean that after the flight overseas of James II in 1688 he espoused the Stuart cause of the Old Pretender: not a good career move. He seems to have remained in his quarters till at least the end of the century, arguing with the Vestry about windows to be opened onto the graveyard but closed when the bells were ringing. Much of the Mansion House, however, was pulled down in the early 1680s, since Denmark Street was laid out straight across its site. The White House next door was also demolished sometime in the decades after Lady Dudley's death, when it had apparently become ramshackle. Thus disappeared, piecemeal, the remaining buildings of the long-standing leper hospital, out of which St Giles parish itself was created.

Denmark Street was named for the husband of the future Queen Anne, Prince George of Denmark, and a generation later was still regarded (by Strype, who revised yet again Stow's seminal work) as 'a fair broad street with good houses, well inhabited by the gentry'. Eight of these houses survive today, and are among the few terraced houses in London that are well over three hundred years old, older than most of those in Spitalfields. For many years in the late twentieth century their ground floors have been occupied by guitar sellers, and their upper and lower regions by studios and the organisers of music festivals. Here, names such as Jimi Hendrix and the Rolling Stones recorded, Elton John worked, the Sex Pistols are said to have lived 'for a week', and in several offices key music papers were produced. A whole world of ad hoc music-making used to be evident in the small notices that, till the end of 2014, papered the wall of the covered passage alongside an ancient shopfront at 27 Denmark Street. This leads into the alley, one-time Dudley Court, later called Denmark Place, that runs behind St Giles High Street, turning a corner to emerge from another tunnel through York & Clifton Mansions. The hidden place, full of ex-stables, small workshops and a smithy, has long been an evocative survival of

St Giles's past – not the distant, grand past of the lady who left her name there, but the obscure urban past of the eighteenth and nineteenth centuries.

However, it is fatally close to the new plaza of what will be the reconfigured Tottenham Court Road station. As I write, Denmark Place is being rebuilt, with the preservation of a few façades, to house a conference centre and 'event space'. Even if the shape of the old alley is conserved, it seems too much to hope that its distinctive character and uses will survive.

At the same time that Denmark Street was being laid out in the late seventeenth century, a grand new gate into the churchyard was erected.

The entrance to Denmark Place, 2014

It had brick pillars, then the latest fashion, and a wood engraving on top said to be a copy of Michelangelo's *Last Judgement* in the Sistine Chapel: hence its name of Resurrection Gate. It was moved to the side entrance off Flitcroft Street two centuries later, and the carving was redone in Portland stone, as it stands today (see p. 271).

For the time being, many of the additions to the ex-village were, like the grandiose gate, designed for a population 'of rank'. Montagu House, described in its time as the most beautiful private house in London, which stood where the British Museum stands today, was burnt down in 1686 but rebuilt again in style with the employment of

Huguenot craftsmen. Southampton House, almost as big and grand, lay a little way to the east of it. Meanwhile, Great Russell Street had been laid out in front of these and was described as 'very spacious and handsome': Sir Christopher Wren had a house there, designed by himself. There was also Bedford House whose owners would eventually develop much of northern Bloomsbury. Fields would for some time remain there, but in the part adjacent to St Giles the new district was developing. Nearer to the church – in fact, opposite across the High Street – on land that had once been the orchard of the leper hospital, there was built in 1672 a double-fronted gentleman's house that was occupied by the family whose name is still preserved in Dyott Street. Huge modernist blocks with metal grids in yellow, red and orange stand there today, far out of scale with the complex and ancient architecture on the other side of the street.

The most ill-fated development in the area in the generation after Lady Dudley's death was that at Seven Dials, on Cock and Pye Fields just south of the church. This was also called the Marshland, which gives one some idea as to why it had not been built on before. Part of the land had probably been used, unofficially, as a plague pit, and then a laystall (dung and general refuse heap) had been established on top. The rest of the Fields were, as they had been for centuries, 'noted for assemblages of dissolute and idle personages', so, as an urban improvement, the building project seemed promising. The plans, put in by a developer and lottery entrepreneur called Neale (remembered today in Neal's Yard), were approved by Sir Christopher Wren in his role as Surveyor General. After considerable delay, and the arching over of a ditch that was regarded as a public nuisance, the agreed pattern began to be constructed, with six fairly narrow streets (not then seven, in spite of the name) all centring on one crossroads where a pillar adorned with seven – or six – faces was to be erected. The houses were intended for well-to-do tenants and for a while it was believed that their arrival had 'completely metamorphosed this sink of filth and iniquity'. Strype, writing in 1720 when, after many further delays, the houses had finally gone up, described the area as being 'of late built into several handsome streets, with a dyall placed in the midst'.

Yet almost from the first the standing of Seven Dials was not quite what the builders had hoped for, and within a few years the area was descending into that social trough in which it remained, more or less, for well over two hundred years. What went wrong? Possibly the very name had created an impression of a slightly sinister self-contained quarter, difficult for outsiders to find their way around. A glance at the scrupulously surveyed map compiled by William Morgan in 1682 shows that this plot of ground was the last unbuilt oasis left at the top of St Martin's Lane before meeting the already-built cross-streets of St Giles, and Neale seems to have been too greedy in what he hoped to get out of it – an attitude identifiable in developers today. The streets he laid out were probably too narrow, and thus too reminiscent of old London, to attract the kind of highly respectable residents who were beginning to occupy the more regular grid-pattern streets of Soho and the other brand-new fashionable quarter of St James's. This fate of houses being built with one class of people in mind but soon descending the social scale to shelter tenants with fewer aspirations may have been relatively new then, but the ongoing development of London over the next two centuries can produce countless examples.

Already the streets east of St Giles parish, which had come up during the previous century around Hatton Garden, had their share of prostitutes, 'cryers of oranges and oysters', and 'indolent and drunken fellows' (Boghurst). So did the crowded alleys off St Martin's Lane to the south, and off the no-longer smart or exclusive Drury Lane. The Dial itself became a natural meeting point for exactly those 'dissolute persons and idle persons' who it was hoped had been disposed of by the new houses. There were simply too many people flooding into St Giles parish, especially immigrants, seeking not to set themselves up in style but simply to lodge themselves acceptably. By the second decade of the eighteenth century the parish, which had been said to number perhaps two thousand souls a century before, had grown exponentially. A count made by the Vestry of the male inhabitants in 1711 came up with:

269 Gentlemen, 1923 Tradesmen and 807 poor housekeepers and we do believe that there are about seven persons in each house

one with another which makes the whole about . . . Twenty
Thousand Inhabitants.

Ten years later the estimate was over thirty thousand. No wonder
the Vestry described the parish as 'very large and over-burdened with
poor', and complained also because its one-time village High Street had
inexorably become 'the great thoroughfare for all persons who travel
the Oxford and Hampstead roads'. This, in itself, was advanced as one
of the reasons for another rebuilding of the church which fronted the
High Street, and which was, till that time, the only Anglican place of
worship – though a 'French church', several Nonconformist chapels
and one for the Roman Catholic Irish had appeared.

In addition, though it was less than one hundred years since the
place had been rebuilt in the previous century, and had been hope-
fully adorned by Lady Dudley, the church was said to be ruinous and
damp:

the ground about it being higher, the floor or body of the church
lower than the street by eight feet . . . Therebye (and by the great
number of burials within it) is become very damp and unwhole-
some, as well as inconvenient to the gentry and others.

A generation earlier, at the time of the plague, the apothecary Boghurst
had been of the opinion that 'dead bodies lying unburied and putri-
fying, churchyards crammed too full', all contributed more to disease
than did God's wrath. General opinion was now agreeing with him.

This was at the period when Parliament had decided that London
needed fifty new churches, many of them on green-field sites to serve
the newly expanded population, and there was much competition
among interested parties to acquire the funding for these. One that
was built, not by Hawksmoor but under his direction, was St George's
Bloomsbury, to serve the growing and still-elegant population on that
side of old St Giles parish. After considerable lobbying and arguing, the
Vestry of the now-reduced but still very big St Giles parish managed to
get the rebuilding of their own dilapidated church counted as another

of the fifty. It was designed in the Palladian style by Henry Flitcroft, a gifted young man of working-class origin whose talent had been spotted by a rich patron while he was still a joiner: the narrow pedestrian way by the church, a relic of the old London of courts and alleys, remembers his name.

By the mid-1730s both the new church and the rebuilt one were open and functioning independently, though, being only a few minutes' walk one from another, they were supposed to cooperate. From then on, endemic tension between the two Vestries (then the only source of local government) becomes apparent. The Vestrymen of the Bloomsbury church tended to be considerably richer and grander than those of old St Giles – far more Vestrymen with 'Esq.' after their names, no doubt a higher proportion of frogged coats and full periwigs round the table – but St Giles still had its share of 'nobility and gentry', some of them from Lincoln's Inn, and they did not like being classified as poor relations. Did they not have a fine new Vestry-room now built separately in the churchyard to accommodate meetings? Their minutes of the eighteenth century make curious reading. There are the usual preoccupations with how much the most distinguished parishioners should pay for the best pews in church, and the suitable fees for marriage and burial, the usual concerns about the state of properties left to the parish 'in perpetuity', about investments (in South Sea securities or other), the usual rows about whether the sexton is doing his job properly and whether or not the graveyard is once again in a bad state. There is also a good deal of discussion about paving and lighting and the running of the poorhouse. In addition, there is a protracted wrangle about the system ('Open' or 'Select') by which the members of the Vestry were elected, a disagreement not helped by the long absences of the vicar supposed to be in charge.

But on the actual state of the parish and the precipitant social decline of some of its streets and courts there is not a direct word and very little to be inferred. Apart from complaints about cattle being driven past the church *even on the Lord's Day*, and leaving aside the occasional irascible mention of 'Barrows and Baskets with fruit and other things' being parked in the church doorways or along the walls, you might almost think you were reading the minutes of some staid country-town parish well away from the pressures of the metropolis.

Perhaps one of the habitual baskets belonged to the girl seller of fruit who, in the late 1740s, was married in the church to an orphaned workhouse boy, Thomas Wilford. He had somehow managed to save up 12 shillings before taking this step, which would suggest a serious and well-intentioned youngster – yet one evening in Dyott Street he got very drunk, assaulted his wife and accidentally killed her. In due course, via a detour through the courts and Newgate, he made the journey west to Tyburn. He was very repentant, lamenting his fate, and was particularly distressed by the fact that, under a new Act of 1752, his body would be handed over to the surgeons for dissection in order to add to his punishment 'further Terror and a peculiar mark of infamy'.

Of this, and other cases in St Giles parish, not a word of reflection appears in the Vestry records.

Yet the fact is, by the mid-eighteenth century, certain parts of what had been St Giles village only a few minutes' walk from the church had become notorious all over London. This was the work of the painter and printmaker William Hogarth, who lent his talents to the campaign to curb the unrestrained gin-drinking that was felt to be overwhelming working-class urban society. Anyone was allowed to distil gin, if they could set up the apparatus, and anyone did: still more, there was no restriction or licensing system on the sale of it. After several abortive attempts to control this, effectual legislation did finally come in the year 1751, after which the notoriously low retail prices ('drunk for a penny') went up and consumption went down. Hogarth's famous print *Gin Lane*, along with its much less well-known companion piece *Beer Lane* which shows peaceful and prosperous working people swilling beer, were published as propaganda in the run-up to the Act.

Gin Lane's depiction of assorted neglect, cruelty, poverty and physical dereliction of both people and buildings imprinted itself on the mind of the public at the time and remains there to this day – as if it were a literal documentary rather than what it actually is: a satirist's piece of justified special pleading. Rather in the way that many readers today will take a realistic novel to be a barely veiled version of a specific true story, so the eighteenth-century public seized on the fact that the spire of St George's church in Bloomsbury is visible in the background to *Gin Lane* and concluded that what was depicted in the foreground must be one actual street near at hand. In reality, though the general reference is clearly to the St Giles district, and one could argue, from the viewpoint, that what was shown was the particularly insalubrious Tom-all-Alone's area that would be pulled down a hundred years later, no street there had that configuration of steep steps in the middle of it. By the same error, you might as well conclude, from the fact of the spire of St Martin-in-the-Fields being in the background to *Beer Lane*, that St Martin's Lane (which ran up as far as Seven Dials) was a gin-free haven of traditional ale-drinking: an unlikely supposition.

The fact is that Hogarth (who was born in Smithfield, by Bartholomew the Great) was living in the 1740s in Leicester Fields, today's Leicester Square, just a few minutes' walk from views of both churches.

Undoubtedly there were by then pockets in St Giles parish, including part of Seven Dials and the Dyott Street area of interlocking court-yards north of the church, that had indeed descended into what were called 'rookeries'. In the back courts cellar-living was common, and beds could be had at 2d a night. A number of small streets were known to be centres for prostitution (convenient, perhaps, for gentlemen from wealthy Soho immediately to the west) and also for receiving stolen goods (convenient for those who went pickpocketing in richer districts). It was said that you could hire a baby or a small child in some places for 4d a day, to go begging with. But statements that have been made in subsequent popular histories, and even sometimes in serious ones, that 'over a quarter of all residences' – or alternatively, 'more than one in six of all houses' – in the whole of St Giles parish were gin shops are not credible. The parish could still summon up its own 'nobility and gentry' to run it (including one lord), and most streets were home to a mass of perfectly ordinary businesses from breweries and smithies to the butchers, bakers and candlestick-makers of the traditional rhyme. It is an irony that the very propaganda that aimed, with some success, to clean up places like St Giles ended up by creating

Views in the Rookery, St Giles, mid-nineteenth century – by which time in fact the famous slums were passing into folklore

its own mythology of the district as some sort of mini City of Dreadful Night.

There is little doubt, however, that the respectable householders who sat on the Vestry had by this time to some extent been overtaken by events. They were still trying to run their parish in the manner set up hundreds of years before for small, cohesive communities: they were not equal to the challenge. In particular, the church had received several donations of property from moneyed citizens in previous centuries, to provide income in perpetuity for 'the poor' or for a similar good cause, and such properties, unless carefully looked after and managed, tended to decline into ramshackle liabilities. The one-time gentleman's house on the corner of Dyott Street had become a low tavern, the Rats' Castle. The last – incompetent – Dyott trustee did not die till 1796, having apparently failed in his duties for decades, and it is clear from many references in the Vestry minutes that there had been no coherent policy on such properties, whether within the parish or elsewhere: problems had accumulated. Dickens's ironic and obsessional remark on Tom-all-Alone's in the next century – 'This desirable property is in Chancery, of course' – had some truth in it.

By the death of the last Dyott, all the names that had been on the Vestry twenty years before had disappeared, and there were twelve vacancies. On one occasion when the Bishop of Chichester himself turned up to chair a meeting (late-eighteenth-century rectors and vicars were notorious for absenteeism), even then the assembly was not quorate. Some further ratepayers were induced to serve and the system struggled on. But in spite of well-intentioned collections to make provision for opposing 'the inordinate ambition and implacable animosity of France in case of invasion' (February 1798), and also a subscription for the purchase of coals to be sold at a reduced rate 'to the industrious poor', and even a long-delayed decision about the need for an out-of-town graveyard, it is clear that St Giles had by this time descended into that social no man's land in which it was to remain, in spite of occasional sweeping Improvements, till the second half of the twentieth century.

CHAPTER IX

'The Imperious Demands of Public Necessity and Convenience'

Our Crossrail journey so far has brought us circuitously back to the time of John Thomas Pocock, the boy who walked all over London and beyond on errands for his father, the failing builder of Kilburn. Only in 1829, very near the end of John's youth as a Londoner, when he was already visiting the brand-new City dock at St Katharine's from which he was shortly to sail across the world, do we find the mention in his diary: 'Rode home in a Paddington omnibus.' The service from the Bank to the Yorkshire Stingo, a public house and tea-garden where Lisson Grove is now, had begun that year. But the price of the ride, with a free newspaper thrown in, put it in the category of minor luxury well above the everyday means of most working men or indeed of the Kilburn family in their straitened circumstances. (By this point John Thomas's father had died, and his uncle, the successful coal-merchant at a wharf near St Bride's, seems to have stepped in to help.)

In trying, for a while with success, to make his fortune by building houses in the fields around London, George Pocock, John's father, was following in the family tradition. His own great-grandfather, Charles Pocock, who had what one must suppose was a successful life as a 'maltster' (brewer) in the Berkshire countryside, in 1740 made the classic move to the big city.[1] Thereafter his son, grandson and great-grandson formed a dynasty of what would now be called 'developers' but were then simply styled 'builders'. It was George who, at the height of his good fortune, moved the family out from the edge of the City to Kilburn, to:

> the best and largest house in the Priory [as the new estate was named] – a perfect triumph of architecture, and one of his own design. Built expressly for himself . . . Excited the envy of many of our neighbours.[2]

This is where the family continued to live, in reducing circumstances, till George's untimely death when John was only fifteen. But up to then the Pocock dynasty seems to have been faithful to Shoreditch, which, in spite of building activity creeping north into Hoxton, did remain a semi-rural area. It will be remembered that on one of John's long walks with his friend Josiah Wright they passed by 'Shoreditch church',[3] and John noted that it was where two very young sisters of his had been buried shortly before his own birth. By the time George died, John had six younger siblings including a newborn baby.

The vicinity of Shoreditch, in fact, was where the Wright family still lived – or to which they had returned, though to a different address closer to the City. At one point in his diary John Pocock has difficulty in locating their house, which seems to have been also their place of business. He had a note that it was in 'Liverpool St, Bishopsgate Street' and walked about in the rain looking for it: 'Liverpool Street' was the then brand-new name for the lane, just widened, which up to that time been called 'Old Bedlam'. There was some long-term work connection between Mr Pocock and Mr Wright, but it is not clear what. The Wrights also had a house in Hastings, then a rapidly growing sea-port, for it was there that George Pocock went to stay when he was ill and his son walked seventy miles to see him. Later again the widowed Mrs Pocock and Mrs Wright quarrelled: possibly the Wrights were felt to have been insufficiently sympathetic to George Pocock's pecuniary embarrassment.

Although Josiah Wright was some five years older than John Pocock, they were the best of friends, each making the trek right across London to call on the other. But their friendship, too, was destined to be cut short, though for a different reason. Just before Christmas 1828, John recorded:

> Left home in the morning according to appointment to see Josiah Wright, & met him (very poorly) with his Mother in Finsbury Square on the way to a chemist at Hoxton. I walked there with them & stayed with Josiah at home all day coming home after tea.

Ten days later, on New Year's Eve, he wrote:

> Left home early, went to see Josiah who is very ill indeed, stayed some time with him; he is not however confined to his room.

It was to be the last time the boys met. Errands for his father, then still living, claimed John and then, in early February, when he 'called at Mr Wright's to see Josiah who is still very ill', he was apparently not invited in. He does not say so in the diary, but years later he wrote:

> the exceeding cold and uncivil reception I met with from the other inmates of the house when I called & the denial of his Father's clerk, when I wished to see him . . . burst my pride, I felt piqued at being refused to visit him for whom I had the warmest affection & esteem, & who I am sure liked me equally well.[4]

In fact he discovered afterwards that Josiah, very feverish, had been repeatedly asking for him.

A week later John received a little note from Josiah's father telling him that his son was dead, and inviting him to come and view the body if he wished. (He did.) The previously tall, strong young man had died of typhus, and was buried in 'Bishopsgate churchyard' (St Botolph's) a few minute's walk from his home, 'close to the side of the Church & very near the active thoroughfare of noisy Bishopsgate Street. I could have wished a more sequestered spot.'

Typhus was still not uncommon in London at that time. Variously known also as 'camp fever', 'gaol fever' or 'putrid fever', from its tendency to break out in crowded places with poor general hygiene, it is not readily infectious from one person to another. Presumably this was generally recognised, since Josiah was not 'confined to his room'. It is passed on via the bite of a flea, louse or other insect: the person bitten scratches the itching spot, and the poison from the insect's faeces thus enters the bloodstream. The fact that Josiah died of this while living just off Bishopsgate does not convey a very favourable view of the state of the housing in that by-then very populous and socially mixed neighbourhood. The Wrights were at quite a good address, since the newly widened Liverpool Street led towards the also recent Finsbury Circus development of elegant houses, but immediately to the north now lay a district of squalid by-lanes with open drains.

Apart from an excursion in Chapter VII to the Old Bedlam graveyard, and to the destruction of a whole swathe of the district by the arrival of two railway stations in the 1860s and 1870s, we last visited Bishopsgate when Paul Pindar's grand timbered Elizabethan house was new and Bishopsgate Without was a pleasant suburb complete with gardens, 'airy and fashionable' if, to sophisticated tastes, 'a little too much in the country'.

Almost the same words could have been used about the village of St Giles-in-the-Fields when Lady Dudley settled there at the same period. Or, indeed, about Stepney where, also at that time, well-to-do merchants were colonising the original Green just off the Mile End Road. There is a rhythm, a progress of rise and decline, observable in townscape as in a living organism. Places, too, are mortal, as are the human beings who create, inhabit, embellish, change and finally destroy them.

Typically, this cycle takes several centuries. From the time when a gallows was first set up for Sir John Oldcastle beside the isolated village of St Giles outside London, through the place's post-Reformation era as an elegant address for distinguished people, to the period when it acquired many new streets and a permanent reputation for harbouring the dissolute and drunken poor, well over three hundred years elapsed. The same is true of Stepney. The pastures and orchards that surrounded the Great Houses of the Colets and Thomas Cromwell, or the later generation of aristocratic schemers, did not abruptly vanish under streets of back-to-back houses as some local histories tend to suggest. The social evolution of Stepney parish into what we would now recognise as 'London's East End', with all that that implies, had some of its roots in the seventeenth century, yet the obvious transformation had barely begun in the early nineteenth century, when Richard Horwood published a finely detailed map in stages near the beginning of the Napoleonic Wars. This was five centuries after Henry Waleys had received Edward I at his Stepney mansion in 1299.

But in exceptional cases, what a pioneer of urban history[5] has called 'the full declension – meadowland to slum' can occur in a single generation.

Paul Pindar died, very old, in 1650. Long before that his brother, Ralph, had built twenty-three smaller houses on land between there and the old Bishop's Gate itself. He also owned a brewery there. The Artillery Ground was now the 'old Artillery Garden' and a new ground was established further north, where space was still available. The open spaces of upper and lower Moorfields survived, but they were much reduced in size and laid out as 'a pleasurable place of sweet ayres for citizens to walk in'. Pepys, in 1661, describes in his diary watching a wrestling championship there, which hardly seems in the category of a genteel walk. During the Commonwealth little further building took place, indeed the fabric of London was generally neglected, so after the Restoration the pace of construction naturally quickened again. But what really put pressure on this district immediately adjacent to the City was the Great Fire of 1666, effecting changes in a few years that otherwise might have taken much longer to materialise.

Wenceslaus Hollar's detailed plan cum bird's-eye view of London after the Fire, which the King commissioned when the burnt ground was still hot beneath the feet in mid-September and which Hollar managed to produce in a matter of weeks, shows clearly the arbitrary nature of the devastation. During the four days at the beginning of the month that the Fire raged, a strong wind had been blowing from the east: this meant that, from Pudding Lane where it started, the flames went in the opposite direction. Thus a narrow swathe of the City within the walls to the east and running to Bishopsgate and Moorfields in the north escaped destruction – about seventy-five acres. Conversely, the fire roared across the entire centre of the City, from the Thames right up to Aldersgate, only just missing Smithfield which was beyond the walls, and continued its course inexorably westward. It was hoped that the Fleet would create a natural fire break, and two days into the blaze there were urgent plans to pull down houses along it to widen the gap, but before this could be achieved the fire 'rushed like a torrent down Ludgate Hill' and took hold of the lower end of Fleet Street and the area round St Bride's church, only narrowly missing the Temple because the wind at last dropped. Some 436 acres had been totally consumed, a vista of roofless ruins of blackened bricks, charred timbers, and the great mounds of ashes which were what was left of people's entire worldly goods and livelihoods.

The dispossessed citizens took themselves in great crowds to the nearest unburnt areas, and in particular to Bishopsgate. There they camped, with such possessions as they had been able to salvage, on the convenient open areas – Moorfields' gardens 'for citizens to walk in' were covered in great piles of stuff and in hastily erected cloth shelters and shanties; so were the remaining tenter grounds, the Artillery Ground and Finsbury Fields. Gradually, as the shockwaves subsided, Londoners trudged further out, colonised Hoxton, Hackney and Islington, or betook themselves to relatives living further away. The ones with more resources and aspirations by and by moved westwards – to new houses erected in the fields of St Giles and St Martin, along the Strand and to the developing areas of Soho and St James's. But many of the craftsmen and artisans, who were dependent on City contacts for their trades, stayed very much where they found themselves. It is from this time that the area beyond London Wall, running up Bishopsgate Without towards Shoreditch, rapidly ceased to be an airy suburb and became subsumed, within a decade, into the metropolis, becoming a de facto part of the City. (Today the formal northern boundary of the City is part way up Shoreditch High Street.) The year after the Fire, Pepys wrote:

> Into Moor-fields, and did find houses built two storeys high, and like to stand; and must become a place of great trade till the City be built; and the street is already paved as London streets used to be.

The map of a decade later shows clearly what happened. Earlier, although there had long been a nest of small alleys and tenements around Old Bedlam, further up the road the ribbon development was mainly of substantial houses with the back land still as gardens. But by ten years after the Fire a great deal of infilling with smaller houses had taken place, and there was a whole line of narrow lanes running off the high road on both sides occupying one-time garden ground. Clearly, pressures on land here had been too great for any authority to resist them. Defoe's account[6] of a plague pit being dug in what was then 'a green field' off Bishopsgate comes to mind. Within a very few years of 1664, that is, not long after the Fire, a 'large fair house' was allowed to be built on the site with its own entry 'as wide as a street'. This was followed shortly after by a row of more ordinary houses, and the digging of their foundations exposed the not-yet-rotted bodies of the plague victims. After a public row, the bodies were reburied, packed together, in a new, deep pit a little way off which, it was understood, was not to be built on. It wasn't, but it became yet another alleyway, this one leading into a Meeting House.

Such a transition from fine gentleman's seat to Meeting House seems typical of the district's changing nature. Nearby, the house once called Fisher's Folly had been lived in before the Fire by Lord Devonshire's family, but they now moved away, following fashion, to the Strand. What had been its courtyard was surrounded with standard town houses by the developer Nicholas Barbon. Paul Pindar's garden and deer park had gone under buildings, and by the end of the century the Corporation of London had erected its first big poorhouse there. This had only a narrow frontage on Bishopsgate, but extended four hundred feet back, a long barracks that soon housed over three hundred children aged between seven and sixteen. They were taught spinning, weaving and the making of nets for fishing, which at least was skilled work: adult inmates, who were kept apart from the children, were given more menial tasks such as beating hemp and chopping wood.

It is also worth recording (in view of the unrelievedly dark image that poorhouses and workhouses have in today's perspective) that the food ordered for the children by the City fathers who ran the place was quite substantial. Bread and cheese figured daily, as did 'small beer' (perceived to be healthier than the local drinking water), and the weekly menu ranged over such staples as peas-pottage, plum pudding and barley broth made with meat. This was a better diet than would have been enjoyed by most children living in poor families: an inherent dilemma in Poor Law administration becomes apparent. A report of about 1720 records that, as well as learning to make their own clothes and shoes 'to inure them to Labour', both boys and girls were taught to read 'and such as are capable, to write and cast Accounts'. The aim was to rescue orphans, some of them inevitably the progeny of hanged wrongdoers at that time of copious executions, and bring them up in safety and Christian principles to be useful citizens. The concept of Progress and of the perfectibility of human nature, which would characterise much of the thinking of the Enlightenment and pave the way for the world we live in today, was beginning to make itself felt.

It is not surprising that the poorhouse taught weaving, for cloth had for centuries been part of the business of the district (all that dyeing and fulling and drying on the Moor's open fields) and now it became more intensively so. By the time the poorhouse was established, the lanes immediately to the north of it – Dunnings Alley, Sun Street, Skinner Street and Primrose Street – housed many weavers, who had their workshops in their back yards with a network of courts and passages linking them: most of this dense townscape was, like slums in other parts of the world today, entirely pedestrian. The Huguenot weavers in silk, of a rather higher social level, were by this time colonising and building up Spitalfields, to the east of Bishopsgate, with the handsome houses some of which have managed to survive to this day. But essentially the lanes off Bishopsgate on both sides were working class, sprinkled with breweries, stables and one-man manufacturing businesses, some noisy, many of them smelly and smoky.

So the situation was reached which was to become common in London for the next two hundred years or more. The principal streets, in this case Bishopsgate Street (as Bishopsgate Without was now generally known), had a prosperous air. The church of St Botolph's was elegantly rebuilt about 1720; the street stretching north from it as one of the routes out of town had busy coaching inns, and a succession of respectable shops – fishmongers, drapers, boot-makers, confectioners and coffee rooms, like the high street of a thriving country town. Well-to do customers came to Bishopsgate Street from the City, from Spitalfields and from a few good-class developments on that side such as Barbon's Devonshire Square. But all the while the back streets were undrained and dirty. By the mid-eighteenth century Moorfields, with its 'sweet ayres', was considered a place of ill-repute, haunted by prostitutes and dangerous with footpads at night. Further bits of the fields were nibbled away with houses.

New plans were made for what remained of Moorfields by the two powerful George Dances, father and son, who between them held the post of Clerk of the City Works for ninety-one years. Some of these plans were distinctly grandiose: an amphitheatre was envisaged for a while, and at another time ten acres of water as a centrepiece for Upper Moorfields, as if the old marsh was, after all, being allowed to reassert itself. (Eventually the scheme was tamed and reduced into Finsbury Square.) As for Lower Moorfields, after much delay it was at last decided that the large, purpose-built Bethlem Hospital, that had seemed so fine when it went up in the 1670s, but now, a century later, was in a poor state, should be relocated again, this time to Lambeth. But the Dances' dream of turning the remainder of Moorfields into a grander version of Bath came to nothing: the pressures of business London were just too great. George Dance the Younger had to content himself with a couple of well-laid-out streets and with Finsbury Circus – elegant enough in its day, but a sadly small vestige of what had once been Londoners' great, open playground.

Today, a main access shaft for Crossrail has been constructed in Finsbury Circus, and the place has been screened off as a lorry-holding

area for the workings at the nearby Old Bedlam site in Liverpool Street.
In Moorgate, the fifteenth-century way out to the fields, will be sited a
west entrance to the immensely long Crossrail platforms.

After the Dances' developments there was an intellectual element in
the district which may be said to have had its headquarters in Finsbury
Circus. There was built there, in 1815, a grand, Palladian structure
complete with reading rooms and lecture rooms: it was to house the
Institute for the Advancement of Useful Knowledge, which had been
founded some ten years earlier. A generation before the University of
London was born, this Institute was dedicated to making scientific
knowledge widely available to those debarred from attending the older
universities, mainly Dissenters and Jews. There had long been a strong
Dissenting presence in the Moorfields area, as there was in Stepney and
other places, such as Southwark, beyond the jurisdiction of the City.
The Institute specialised in chemistry, and one may be sure that among
those who attended meetings there was Charles Roach Smith, he who
lived round the corner in what became Liverpool Street and whose cat
had been buried in the Old Bedlam graveyard that was by then a derelict garden. He had a chemist's business nearby, but this was the least
of his occupations. He was a Fellow of the Society of Antiquaries, and
of other Societies in England and France. He busied himself with the
study of ancient coins, and was a founder of the British Archaeological
Association. He was interested in gardening, though his enthusiasm
for the possibility of growing fruit trees alongside the new railway
lines did not really inspire others. He was one of the first people to
study methodically, and help to save, the Roman material that came
to light as the City was built and rebuilt, including several remaining
tracts of London Wall that developers were on the point of knocking
down. His personal collection went to form the basis of the Museum
of London. Like John Stow, three and a half centuries before, he was
one of those prodigiously hard-working, passionate, self-effacing citizens of London to whom we owe a huge debt.

Another high-minded and essentially Nonconformist association
established very near to Finsbury Circus was the South Place Ethical

Society. It was earlier known as the Philadelphians, or as the Universalists, or yet again as the Finsbury Unitarian Congregation – the very range of these labels suggests a combination of fervour and openness in its principles. It began in Bishopsgate in the late eighteenth century, moved to a street off Finsbury Circus in 1824, and finally shifted westwards to Bloomsbury (by then the natural home of such progressive, faintly eccentric views) in the early twentieth century. Today, as Humanism, it roosts in Red Lion Square, perhaps very near the secret bones of those earlier radicals, Cromwell, Ireton and Bradshaw.

Meanwhile, the more lowly inhabitants of the Bishopsgate area continued to live, work, procreate and die in the crowded courts where old Bedlam hospital had once been and in those to the north of it. The old City gates had been pulled down about 1760 and sections of the walls soon followed, but the notion of what was within the City and what without still persisted in people's minds. The City proper was now given over more and more to offices and to large-scale trading and the generation of wealth, which left the area north of where the Bishop's Gate had stood as its workshop district, a character it long retained. Leatherwork was still done there, as was the making of buttons and buckles; the skins and bones that were the raw material for this were still, till the mid-nineteenth century, readily available as they always had been in nearby Smithfield. Weaving declined as an occupation in the eighteenth century and was almost extinguished by the end of it: the industrialised mills in the north of England were producing textiles far more cheaply and in far greater abundance than the traditional hand-weavers could. But other trades took their place and flourished, especially light metalwork and furniture-making, probably because of the range of new woods, including veneers, that were now being imported from Canada and the Baltic. The Post Office Directory for 1841 lists umbrella-makers, stay-makers, carpenters, upholsterers, brush-makers, a 'grate maker', feather dressers, wire blind makers, a piano-maker, plumbers, general builders, printers of all sorts and numerous furniture-makers. Hollingshead, writing at the beginning of the 1860s, characterised the district comprehensively, if dismissively, as 'a neighbourhood of Greek merchants, institutions and chapels'.

Petticoat Lane was also now established on the east side of Bishopsgate Street, with a growing influx of Jewish immigrant garment-makers. Already this was T. S. Eliot's brown-fogged world city of the following century, where one might go to meet a Mr Eugenides – a Smyrna merchant with an ill-shaven chin – and where Moorgate figures as a heartless street of obscure angst and exhaustion.

With the building of Broad Street station in the 1860s and Liverpool Street station in the 1870s, the last traces of the original Bedlam were swept away and the lanes immediately to the north of it either disappeared or were transformed into iron gantries crossing railway yards. As the goods yards were further enlarged, Paul Pindar's house, as we know, eventually disappeared too. *The Bishopsgate Almanac*, a self-satisfied little publication mainly devoted to advertising the trade premises of various dignitaries in the locality, wrote:

> However we may regret the removal of so striking an object of antiquarian interest . . . it is impossible to deny that sentiment must give way to the imperious demands of public necessity and convenience.

In fact, several voices had been raised in favour of preserving the façade in situ as a grand side entrance to the new station[7] but this was evidently too imaginative a proposal for public convenience to be impressed.

The land taken by the two stations together was twenty-five acres. Huge numbers of the ordinary public lost their homes,[8] many of them to crowd further east into the already packed districts of Bethnal Green and Whitechapel. But the arrival of the trains seems to have acted as a signal for the wealthier inhabitants, the merchants, lawyers and surgeons of Devonshire Square and Finsbury Square and Circus to depart too, so that for the last part of Victoria's reign Bishopsgate was no longer a residential district. It was a place of arrivals and departures, of armies of City clerks congregating every morning from the suburbs round the North London line and the new Metropolitan line, and from developing districts up the North Eastern main line: a great, black-clad tide coming in and going out again every evening. In the 1830s at the time of the first proper census, the population of St Botolph's parish was twelve thousand souls; by the 1880s it was only five thousand.

It did, however, retain its ancient links to manufacturing well into the twentieth century. Furniture and printing businesses continued to thrive towards Shoreditch. J. B. Priestley's *Angel Pavement*, published in 1930, evokes the area 'from Bunhill Fields to London Wall, or across from Barbican to Broad Street Station':

> The little street [Angel Pavement] is old, and has its fair share of sooty stone and greasy walls, crumbling brick and rotting woodwork.

We are led down a flight of steps, past Chase and Cohen, Carnival Novelties, past the Pavement Dining Rooms, then Dunbury & Co.: Incandescent Gas Fittings, and so, past a tobacconist ('Our own mixture, Cool sweet smoking'), to:

> No. 8, once a four-storey dwelling house where some merchant alderman lived snugly on his East India dividends, is now a little hive of commerce.

There is C. Warstein: Taylors' Trimmings, the Kwik-Work Razor Blade Co., the Universal Hosiery Company, and finally, Twigg and Dersingham's. The unfortunate Mr Dersingham has inherited a business importing fancy wood veneers and inlays, for which trade he has no particular taste or aptitude, and has been targeted by a Baltic trader who is planning to asset-strip him. Meanwhile this plausible newcomer passes the time by making the acquaintance of Mr Dersingham's secretary, Miss Matfield, a bright but frustrated young woman living in a ladies' hostel and wondering if this is all life holds.

Readers of this poignant book today can derive some comfort from the fact that, however great the obscure personal disasters in 1930, ten years on these people will be swept up in a far greater whirlwind which may come to them as a salvation. Mr Dersingham, too old by now to be called up into the army, will discover reserves of courage and initiative in himself as an ARP warden and fire-watcher. Mrs Dersingham, children grown up, will find a purpose for her achingly empty life by working in a WVS canteen dispensing mugs of tea and comfort to Blitz workers and survivors at all hours. Lilian Matfield will find fulfilment as a bossy and competent officer in one of the Women's Services, with plenty of male company on hand.

Angel Pavement, like so many of the streets just north of London Wall, the territory of the one-time great Moor, and all the way to Cripplegate, will be wrecked by German incendiary bombs, a second Fire of London. Bishopsgate, Shoreditch and Spitalfields will get off relatively lightly, but the whole townscape immediately to the west will be more or less destroyed. What is not reduced to rubble then will be so by the post-war generation of urban planners, as the monolithic Barbican development with its three concrete towers cuts one neighbourhood off from another and annihilates complex street patterns that have taken hundreds of years to evolve.

CHAPTER X

A Convenient Spot for the Habitation of Mariners

So, the Crossrail leaves Liverpool Street, swings in a northern arc under Spitalfields and on to coincide with Whitechapel. Going south-east again it crosses under the main eastern route away from the City just after Whitechapel High Street becomes the Mile End Road, and continues its course more or less parallel with Stepney Green (the one-time Mile End Green) till it arrives at White Horse Lane and St Dunstan's church. Here, it divides. The east- and westbound tracks that will make their way to Stratford, the open air, and eventually on an above-ground line all the way to Shenfield in the north-east, run here far down one each side of the ancient church. Here too, on the south side of St Dunstan's, another pair of tracks swings more directly south, staying deep underground to Canary Wharf. The actual division point is under that part of the extensive churchyard that was once used to bury plague victims and where people now walk their dogs, but the lines are much too profound to disturb the unnamed dead, any more than they will disturb the numerous wealthy Stepney citizens of the sixteenth, seventeenth and eighteenth centuries who lie in the older ground nearer to the church, or yet the twenty-one scant remains of Colet infants who, among countless others, once vanished into that endlessly receptive earth.

There is no intermediate station, at Stepney or elsewhere, on the long underground run (a good two and a half miles) between Whitechapel and Canary Wharf. Within London, Crossrail is designed to service only key points, and the old East End finds itself today a hinterland between the City and the new business district that has risen like a second, distant City on what used to be dockland, far from the historic extent of London. Canary Wharf might therefore be considered beyond the geographical limits of my journeying – but in any case it is not possible to examine layers of impacted life and history that lie beneath Canary Wharf's elegant, boat-shaped new station because such layers do not exist.

The river Thames east of the Tower dips a little to the south, creating the ancient harbour front of Wapping, then curves round northwards to make the south-bank bulge of Rotherhithe, a long shoreline that was for generations, like Wapping, given over to shipping. The river then swings south, in a true oxbow bend down to Greenwich and up again, before going on to Woolwich, Erith and finally to Gravesend and the sea. The area within this deepest loop of the river, which now forms a district of glistening glass towers with the tallest of all, Canary Wharf, at its centre, was traditionally known as the Isle of Dogs.

One further loop east again, on the Blackwall reach of the Thames where Bow Creek runs in, there were on the north side, for hundreds of years, shipbuilding yards. Wooden vessels were constructed there long ago, and later iron ones. Sir Walter Raleigh had a timbered house there that was demolished in the late nineteenth century to build the Blackwall Tunnel, and forty years earlier some of the fitting was done there for Brunel's *Great Britain*, the first ocean-going iron-hulled liner. A whole other book could be written about the ships, the skills that created them, the men who sailed in them and the world they gradually discovered – but this is not that book. As for the Isle of Dogs, until the West India Docks were constructed there at the beginning of the nineteenth century, there was almost nothing upon it.

This isle, which was never a true island but was marshy enough to be partly cut off from Limehouse by trickling streams which the dock system later converted into canals, does not figure on any map of London proper before the nineteenth century: it was too remote. The old name for the place was Stepney Marsh, but few Stepney inhabitants would have walked that far unless hiking towards Greenwich. Even allowing for the fact that dock-building would have reconfigured the land considerably, no evidence has been found of early human habitation. Medieval drainage created some land dry enough to be used as pasture; a few farmers were encouraged to settle and a chapel was built for them, but the whole place was flooded again seventy years later and more or less abandoned, except for some windmills, and a gallows for hanging pirates.

The southern end of it was, and is, just across the river from Greenwich, an ancient settlement that became royal and fashionable: there is a persistent tale that the name Isle of Dogs comes from some royal kennels that were once located there. However, there is no real evidence for this, and since the kind of dogs large enough to be sequestered in kennels were commonly called 'hounds' several centuries ago, I think this an unlikely derivation. Horwood's map, c. 1800, shows the new, big docks on the north of the Isle, but in all the southern part there is only a wilderness of uncultivated land with the tiny 'chapel house' isolated in the middle of it beside a pathway leading down to the ferry to Greenwich and Deptford. The place was still as deserted in 1850. It was to be another twenty years before Millwall Docks appeared there, and a few streets of dockers' housing rose round the Isle's edges, but this was one of the briefer transformations in London's long history: the bombs of the Second World War seventy years later obliterated the greater part of the buildings.

Another generation, and the docks were run down and then closed, thus making way for the far more extreme transformation of space and identity that is now known generically by the name of its tallest tower. A child who had wandered in the empty marshland around 1860, gathering frogspawn in the shallow streams, could, in adulthood, have lived in a house built near the same site. By the time he was old that house might have been reduced to smoking rubble, and his great-grandson could now have a job in one of the huge offices that have replaced the rubble, the warehouses, the docks, the marsh waters that fed the docks, and the frogs.

*   *   *

Stepney Green will not have a Crossrail station, but Crossrail is very much present there in the form of a large access and ventilation shaft sited just before the line divides into two. There has been much activity here and an important archaeological excavation, for it is the site of 'King John's Palace' and lies at the heart of the old, grand, rural Stepney of big courtyard houses as described in Chapter VI. Here, over the course of three hundred years, Henry Waleys, the Colets, Thomas Cromwell, Lord Darcy, Sir John Neville, the Harringtons, Lord Morley, Sir Thomas Lake, the Countess of Rutland, the Marquess of Worcester and a number of others lived comfortable, wealthy lives well out of London's smoke. In the last years of Elizabeth's reign the first Marquess of Worcester bought up the old, moated house that later generations attributed to King John and partly rebuilt it, though he retained its early-Tudor gatehouse of diapered brick. A social shift in the district was in fact on its way, as well as an architectural one; but it was a subtle shift, and Stepney remained a desirable address for another two centuries.

In St Giles-in-the-Fields, at the Restoration of Charles II in 1660, the church bells pealed joyfully for three days. Considering what a passionate Royalist and religious traditionalist the rector was, this is hardly surprising. But though Stepney, on the other side of London, with its upper-class residents, was to some extent a mirror image of St Giles, I hardly think that quite the same atmosphere prevailed around Stepney Green. For the Dissenting tradition, which a century later was to become so powerful a force in British culture, had installed itself there under the Commonwealth and it never left.

In these early days, the Nonconformist movement existed *within* the Church of England: the clear separation into 'Church' and 'Chapel' that was eventually to create a guarded truce, and then an established fact of English social segmentation, with 'Chapel' indicating 'lower class', lay far in the future. The man who was Vicar of Stepney in 1642, at the start of the Civil War, was a supporter of the King, and soon got into trouble for calling some of Cromwell's men 'red-headed radicals'. He was imprisoned for being 'a proved prelatical innovator of Romish ceremonies', and his parish was given to a Joshua Hoyle, a prominent divine of the new sort who was opposed to the King's autocratic

henchman, Archbishop Laud, and was one of the instigators of his
execution. However, even Hoyle may not quite have bargained for
what began to happen in Stepney. According to a manuscript history
of the parish written long afterwards by someone closely associated
with local religious affairs,[1] Hoyle was 'too scholastic to please
the parishioners and too weak to keep in check the two lecturers at the
church, William Greenhill and Jeremiah Burroughs'. These two men,
known locally and rather derisively as the Morning and Evening Stars,
took it in turns to deliver Puritan lectures to the uneasy but resigned
population every morning and afternoon.

Described by the Royalist Anthony Wood as 'notorious schismaticks
and Independents', the two were also arguably in the process of breaking away from the established Church, for in 1644, only the year after
Hoyle became vicar, Greenhill had a Protestant Meeting House built
near Worcester House. The following year Worcester House was
seized by the Parliamentarians, and the Marquess himself died soon
afterwords; Greenhill and his allies variously took the big house over.
In spite of his unorthodox activities, the Vestry minutes suggest that
he more or less ran the parish too, and when Hoyle died in 1654 he
became Vicar of Stepney himself. At the Restoration, the manuscript
history tells us:

> the absurdity of his position was forcibly evident, and Greenhill
> had to leave; but he kept his congregation together, in spite of all
> the repressive Acts, and at his death left it in a flourishing condi-
> tion to his successor, Mathew Mead.

Although, after the Restoration, Worcester House was theoretically
restored to the family of the Marquess, they did not come back to live
there. The place had been divided into four separate tenements, in one
of which lived a Maurice Thomson, of a wealthy local Puritan family,
who had recently founded a new chapel in Poplar. In 1663 Matthew
Mead, who had been sacked for Puritanism from a neighbouring parish,
Shadwell, was living in another section as Greenhill's assistant. He
appears to have been there during the Great Plague of London, but he

went into exile in Holland the following year when new rules theoretically forbade Independent chapels within five miles of the City. Mead, however, came from a well-to-do City family with influential contacts, and was soon back again. It seems clear that by the time Greenhill died in 1671 and Mead took over as pastor of the Meeting House, the Nonconformist, Dissenting tendency was now so well entrenched in Stepney that it was tacitly tolerated.

It is also relevant to the theme of toleration that, three years before the Restoration, a burial ground for Spanish and Portuguese Jews was permitted to be laid out in Stepney just north of the Mile End Road. Today, long shut for burial, its modest stones sunk in grass, it is the oldest-known Jewish cemetery in Britain. When Sephardic Jews, banished from England since the Middle Ages, made representations to Oliver Cromwell that they were desirable citizens and opposed to Britain's enemies, he did not exactly give them a charter but he connived at their settlement. No doubt the local evangelical tendency looked tolerantly also on these *echt* Children of Israel.

Thomson sold his part of Worcester House to 'the Stepney Meeting House' in 1675. Mead's congregation was the largest of its kind in London, so a bigger Meeting House was built in the orchard of the big old house. It had fine pillars inside, but externally was designed to look like an ordinary dwelling house so as not to attract attention. It had an attic with a concealed entrance, for use as a hiding place should the bad times return. There was in fact trouble in the period leading up to the Rye House Plot of 1683 against Charles II and his brother James. The Meeting House was invaded, the pulpit broken down, and Mead himself was later brought before the Privy Council for supposed complicity in the plot, but the King ordered him to be released. Half a dozen years later William and Mary were on the throne and a new Bill of Rights assured religious freedom to all forms of Protestantism. It was now Catholics, once again, who were suspect, but the great, bloody struggle between differing religious convictions that had started over two centuries before was at last abating.

Galleries were added to the Meeting House to accommodate yet more people. Mead, who was much loved, tried his best, till his death

in the last year of the century, to draw the various strands of Dissent –
Congregationalist, Presbyterian, Baptist, Quaker and so forth – into
one union. He had a personal interest in this in addition to his religious
conviction, for several of the extensive Mead family were Quakers,
including his own brother William. In 1670 William had been prosecuted
(fruitlessly, in the end) for Unlawful Assembly, along with William Penn,
the future founder of Pennsylvania. Needless to say, Matthew Mead's
plea for unity was without success. A tendency to break into contentious smaller factions, each one believing itself to be more truly funda-
mentalist than the next, has always dogged Nonconformist groups.

Meanwhile Mead and his City associates had not been idle in worldly
matters either. Leases had been issued, and the street frontages adjoining Worcester House, as well at the ones encircling its old gardens
and orchard, were beginning to have houses built along them. Mead
owned the old house as well as the Meeting House by this time, and
the property was inherited by his son, Richard, who lived and worked
on the premises as a well-known pioneering physician. The surviving
ancient gatehouse and tower at that time contained Richard Mead's
valuable collection of medical treatises and illustrations.

It is difficult to get a clear mental picture of what the Great Place
looked like by this stage in its fragmented history. Gascoyne's 1703 map
(which refers to it as 'St John's Court') shows that other houses had
been inserted beside it along the northern side, facing Mile End Green,
but on Rocque's 1747 map the old courtyard shape is still apparent. In
1740 Richard Mead sold the whole estate to a Captain James Winter, a
fellow Nonconformist; twenty-four years later Winter sold it to a relative with similar sympathies, Samuel Jones, who later passed it on to his
widow, Susanna. As the eighteenth century progressed, a charity school
was built on the southern part of the site, near the Meeting House, and
it has been said that the Meeting House acquired its own graveyard in
1779 although on the site no physical trace of this has been found.

By the 1790s, however, Daniel Lysons, the indefatigable author of *The
Environs of London*, could write: 'The site of Worcester house is now
the property of Berington Marsh Esq.' He was in fact the nephew of
Susanna Jones,[2] and this accords with a deed of 1786 in which Berrington

or Barrington Marsh was letting the place on an annual basis to half a dozen different people. This suggests that by this time much of the old house had been demolished or adapted out of recognition. Indeed, on Horwood's early-nineteenth-century map the courtyard shape has disappeared and beside the tiny inscription 'King John's Palace' only one building is evident, set back from the road. A new street, Garden Street, was just being developed across the western part of the site.

A 'Stratford College' was established on the estate in 1826, and in 1844 Gliddon, the author of the manuscript history of Stepney, wrote:

> The site of Worcester House has been purchased by certain persons in trust for the purpose of establishing an academy for the education of young men intended for the ministry among the Baptists.

This Baptist college had originally been founded elsewhere in 1810, and it is my guess, from various clues in the manuscript, that Gliddon was professionally involved with it. A print of about 1840 shows the gatehouse still complete, with the tower absorbed into the college buildings, and, a few yards further along, a new Baptist chapel with a similar pointed arch framed in mock-pillared stone. In between these two structures is a short run of decent-looking Georgian terraced houses, several storeys high, with some slightly later ones continuing the terrace on the far side of the gatehouse. Genteel people with top hats and crinolines parade in the street, as they commonly do in such prints.

So the Tudor gatehouse and the chapel with its mock-Tudor doorway did coexist for a while, but in 1858 the gatehouse was disgracefully sacrificed to further buildings. The Baptists had moved on three years before; the chapel was taken over successively by other Nonconformist congregations and thrived. It was burnt out in the Blitz of eighty-odd years later. Its doorway with the stone surround remains, and is often supposed by passers-by to be a genuine remnant of the original gatehouse to Worcester House. I have even seen a photograph of it in a local newspaper describing it as a last relic of 'King John's Palace', such is the force of legend.

King John's Gate and the Baptist Chapel, *c.* 1840

Further demolitions took place when the gatehouse was destroyed, to build streets of more modest houses in and around the site, for Stepney was now undergoing a profound change. The lane past the church which had, for centuries, been a countrified place, well away from the relative busyness of Mile End New Town up on the road from London, had been renamed Stepney High Street and was now lined with shops and small businesses. The North London Railway and the Blackwall Railway had joined forces to cross the district, and the fields were receding rapidly at Limehouse and Bow. Mead's Meeting House survived in these transformed surroundings, though Stanford's map of 1864 confusingly shows it as a 'Wesleyan chapel' on this parcel of land to the south of the site, while the section on the north facing Mile End Green, where the Baptist college was, is marked 'Presbyterian church'. A grandiose mock-Gothic Congregationalist church finally appeared beside the Meeting House in 1882, and the old place was then demolished. The impression is of the assorted Nonconformist cults all competing on the same site, but in practice the Baptist college and its successors had taken over the land on which Worcester House itself had sat, while the Congregationalist church on the one-time garden land took over from the Meeting House in catering for the needs of the local populace. The area never housed that classic late-Victorian phenomenon, 'a mission to the slums', a training ground for enthusiastic young men looking to bring light into the poverty and attendant sin for which crowded Stepney was now a byword, but it clearly remained, as it had two centuries before, a focus for Nonconformity and piety.

Recent archaeological work on the site for Crossrail has revealed a medley of remains as disjointed as the house's history. Some ancient ones were discernible on excavation – the shape of the moat of the late-medieval manor house and a still-older drainage ditch containing pottery dated from between the twelfth and fifteenth centuries – while other better-documented buildings, such as the seventeenth-century Meeting House, were found to have been obliterated by later constructions. In the part of the plot which is today the Stepney City Farm, among the free-ranging chickens and piled-up logs and seed-boxes there is a ruined stone-faced wall with a pointed arch in it that is a relic of the late-nineteenth-century Congregationalist church: like the chapel on the other side of the site, this was a victim of the Second World War bombing. Only sixty years elapsed between its proud building and its destruction, yet the vagaries of time, chance and the effects of the weather have been such that one might well imagine this fragment to be a survivor of a much older construction, perhaps even of a moated manor house.

Apart from a Tudor bowling ball made of wood brought from the then newly discovered South America, and some scraps of exquisite Venetian glass probably dating from Lord Darcy's time, most of the items found at the Crossrail dig dated from the nineteenth-century housing. These included a chamber pot with a giant eye painted inside it, and the inscription: 'What I see I will not tell'. I doubt if the long-ago aristocratic inhabitants of rural Stepney would have found this as funny as someone evidently did in a Victorian two-up, two-down.

* * *

Let us go back to the late seventeenth century, when Stepney did not even figure on London maps, although already at the Restoration a few fine new houses of brick and stone were appearing up Mile End Green. Something else significant besides Dissent was happening in Stepney and in the other Tower Hamlets that were still part of St Dunstan's parish. Sir Christopher Wren, who was soon to be appointed Surveyor General to the City of London and to redesign so much that had been destroyed in the Great Fire, including St Paul's, expressed the opinion that Stepney 'was a convenient spot for the habitation of mariners and manufacturers who supplied the shipping'. That indeed was what was taking place. Perhaps Wren knew of the old tradition that any British subject born on the high seas could lay claim to being a parishioner of Stepney, which was an important consideration in the centuries when all Poor Relief depended on which parish the person concerned came from. Already, in the early sixteenth century, a sea captain of the parish had founded the Deptford Mariners' Guild of the Holy Trinity, which became Trinity House and is still in charge of lighthouses and piloting to this day. By the seventeenth century the link between spread-out Stepney and the sea lanes of the world was becoming more pronounced. Before the Civil War and the Commonwealth, the seagoing Stepney family called Thomson had made a fortune importing tobacco from the new colony of Virginia. In 1647 Maurice Thomson was a member of St Dunstan's Vestry and it was he who became the owner of part of Worcester House. There was also the Garland family (see Chapter VI) who, in 1651, acquired the old courtyard house and gardens just north-east of the church that had earlier belonged to grand families including the Herberts. On the deed of sale Roger Garland is simply down as 'mariner', a term of fairly wide social application, and he signed his name with self-conscious elaborateness like someone not used to much writing; but his son of the same name who took over his father's house, and also his place on the Vestry in 1654 and for many years after, was styled 'Captain Roger Garland'.

The turbulent seventeenth century is one of those many periods in British history of which 'the rise of the middle classes' is said to have been a feature; certainly the Thomsons and the Garlands seem classic examples of ordinary trading families adopting the houses that aristocrats were now abandoning for districts to the west of London, and setting up as gentry in their place. But in any case, given that St Dunstan's four outlying hamlets were on or very near the Thames, by the end of the century the graveyard and church were full of memorials for mariners and sea captains and also for shipwrights and ship's chandlers. One of 1696, for a Captain John Dunch, read:

> Tho' Boreas Blasts and Neptune's Waves
>> Have tost me to and fro;
> In Spight of both, by God's Decree,
>> I harbour here below.
> Where I do now at Anchor ride,
>> With many of our Fleet:
> Yet once again I must set Sail,
>> Our Admiral Christ to meet.

The inscription has now disappeared, but it is quoted by Strype, himself a Stepney inhabitant and the third person to take over Stow's great London work of over a hundred years earlier and add to it once again. Writing about 1720, he refers to the recent splitting-up of the parish into separate parishes for the different hamlets, and remarks that now 'Stepney may be esteemed rather a Province than a Parish, especially if we add that it contains in it both City and Country'. He comments on the pastures, woods and marshes on the northern side, then adds:

> Towards the south Parts, where it lies along the river Thames for a great Way, by *Limehouse*, *Poplar* and *Radcliff*, to *Wapping*, it is furnished with every Thing . . . of a great Town; Populousness, Traffic, Commerce, Havens, Shipping, Manufacture, Plenty, and Wealth . . . And, among other Places of Remark, at *Blackwall* is a wet Dock belonging to the *East-India* Company, of sufficient Bigness to contain ships.

Strype could not have known just how pregnant with implications for the future this paragraph was. The small dock at Blackwall, and another he does not mention that had recently been built by the Russell family on those same marshes of Rotherhithe, were the harbingers of what, by the early nineteenth century, would become the huge and far-flung acreage of the East End's docklands, shining wetly up at the smoke-darkened sky and creating a special 'East End light'. It was the docks, and their attendant commerce and industry, that would, in the fifty years after 1800, transform the heart of Stepney from semi-country into a crowded and predominantly working-class urban district.

But for the whole of the eighteenth century the central area round St Dunstan's church was less busy and commercial than the riverside hamlets. Apart from 'rope walks' where the rigging for ships was made, which appeared in the pastures east of the church, there was no manufacture near there except for a brewery up on the Mile End Road. Stepney Green (then still known as Mile End Green) was a pretty garden suburb for those whose business took them both to the City and to the riverside. Strype's mention of the East India Company is, in itself, significant. This oldest of trading corporations (it received its charter in 1600) was the source of many of the family incomes that supported a comfortable lifestyle in Stepney. Jewels, ivory, silver, silks, muslins, alpaca, cotton, jute, spices and pepper made fortunes. So did the associated trades in porcelain and opium from further east in China. The other enterprise that brought wealth into Stepney, increasingly as the eighteenth century went by, was the Hudson's Bay Company, which had been founded in 1670 and traded with the newly explored regions of northern Canada, bringing in quantities of valuable furs and, later, timber. The two prominent and related families who occupied the remains of Worcester House in succession for much of the following century, the Winters and the Joneses, were directors, respectively, of the East India Company and the Hudson's Bay Company. At one point Jones loaned the Hudson's Bay Company the then-enormous sum of £2,000 to get it out of trouble, but clearly this was a successful move as, when Jones had joined his forefathers in the churchyard, his wife Susanna was said to be the wealthiest widow in a district that had plenty of them, due to the hazardous nature of foreign merchant venturing.

Moreover, the general wealth was increasing. In 1693 Stepney had just over one hundred citizens rich enough to pay tax; by 1727 this had risen to three hundred and thirty, and then to nearly four hundred in 1741. In the two years before, the Vestry included Captain John Redman (after whom a new street leading down from Mile End Road to join with Stepney Green was later named), Martin Leake who was the son of one of Queen Anne's admirals and became Garter King at Arms, Captain William Snelgrove who was a slave-trader (West India connection), Captain Clark, Captain Posford, Captain Bonham, Captain Brooks, and two brewers called Newell and Burr representing another very prosperous local trade. Nor were these people unthinking nouveaux riches. They built charity schools and endowed almshouses. Prominent among them was William Bancroft, who was born in Stepney parish and grew up to be the Lord Mayor's Officer and a wealthy member of the Drapers' Company. He was so much disliked, apparently for officious summonses and for taking bribes, that at his funeral in 1727 people cheered,[3] but he left thousands of pounds for the establishment of a set of almshouses near Mile End. (The extensive buildings of Queen Mary's College have now swallowed the site, which has its echo in Bancroft Road.) Trinity Almshouses, which stand to this day on the north side of Mile End Road,

complete with miniature ships on the four pillars of the front lodges, had already been founded in 1695 for 'decayed Masters and Commanders of ships and their widows'. In 1750 one of the principal supporters was Francis Cockayne, Merchant Adventurer and Mayor of London in that year. So was James Winter, he of the East India Company and of Worcester House.

At Trinity Almshouses

A little further along the road there is still a handsome Queen Anne brick house, on whose wrought-iron gates one can see the monogram of the Gayer family. Sir John Gayer was an early governor of Bombay in the contentious pre-Raj days, and he died there. His widow bought the house in 1714, and forty years later it seems to have been taken over by another East India Company family, providentially with the same initial – the Gibsons. On the south side of the road was a third house belonging to a Company family, the FitzHughs, who were the cadet branch of an enterprising dynasty: their cousins were busy making a fortune of their own in Virginia. William FitzHugh died in Calcutta, a notoriously unhealthy place, in 1731, but his widow had built for herself and their five children a home of such grandeur that it was valued at twice the rate of any other in the parish.

This house was not sold for over a hundred years, by which time the family had moved into the equally lucrative business of iron manufacture on the Welsh borders.[4] Soon after, in 1849, part of Jubilee Street, full of small houses, was built on the site. This date may represent the ultimate tipping point after which Stepney became irretrievably a working-class district. The later, notorious poverty of the East End has distorted our view. We tend to see Stepney through the prism of the late nineteenth century, all pawnshops, street markets and grubby children at play. Earlier, it was quite otherwise.

And yet even at the time of its prosperity there was a perception elsewhere in London that the whole area east of Aldgate was somehow socially and materially inferior. John Noorthouck, who published *A New History of London* in 1773, wrote that 'these parishes, which are chiefly inhabited by seafaring persons and those whose business depends upon shipping in various capacities, are in general close and ill-built'. Whitechapel was indeed very congested by this time and full of industries, with the London Hospital replacing a large dunghill and rubbish tip that had stood on the south side of the high road, but Stepney with its run of private gardens did not please Noorthouck any better. He said that it 'was now considered as a straggling appendage to this great metropolis'. Possibly he also disapproved of the fact that the

The Gayer house, later Gibson, Mile End Road

old, timbered house to the south-west of the church which had once belonged to Henry Colet and then to his widow, and for a while in the seventeenth century had been the headquarters of Trinity House, was now, according to Lysons, 'Spring Gardens coffee house'. Today, a school stands approximately on the site, and the city farm with pigs, geese and shaggy cattle occupies a nearby spot.

But what Noorthouck really meant was that, however wealthy some of the citizens were, this was not the inherited wealth of the landed gentry who had now colonised the St James area and the Grosvenor estate in what would become the West End. Nor, in spite of having a few large houses on Mile End Road and Stepney Green that were filled with spoils from around the world, did Stepney have any pillared mansion comparable with the Montagu, Southampton or Bedford Houses in Bloomsbury. Stepney was solid, middle-class comfort, such as used to be found in prosperous provincial trading cities like Bristol, Norwich and Portsmouth, rather than in fashionable London; but comfort there was. It has been calculated[5] that in the 1760s over half the inhabitants of the parish would have considered themselves 'of the middling sort' – that is, they had an income of at least £50 a year and often much more: they could afford a servant, or several. In 1780 about twenty-five households had manservants, usually in towns a sign of a well-to-do establishment. The wealthy Widow Jones in Worcester House paid tax for no less than three male servants, in addition, one must suppose, to several untaxed maids. In a few households these male servants were black, an indication of trade interests with the West Indies.

Even those living on a more modest scale, in the smaller terraced houses that began to be built in the later decades of the century, were gentlemen; they were fully literate, they educated their sons, and to some extent their daughters; they had miniature portraits painted, they purchased elegant wallpapers and elaborate tea-caddies; meat appeared regularly on their tables; they invested in good clothes. And yet, one understands what lay behind Noorthouck's condescending remarks. These were, for the most part, men who had lived and made their money in the tough seagoing world, where there were great opportunities but also great risks, financial as well as personal. Many of them would have started adult life as shipboard midshipmen at fourteen or fifteen, exposed to extraordinary hardships and dangers, ranging from assault and capture by pirates to death from drowning, scrofula or 'the bloody flux' (Asiatic cholera). They had acquired a wide range of specialised skills, and even if they no longer went to sea themselves in later life their fortunes were intimately bound up with those who did. Most of them would have had no personal taste for the elegances, extravagances, the clubs, theatres and gambling of the fashionable world, and – given the nature of Stepney – a number of them must have held the slightly puritanical, no-nonsense views that tended to go with religious Nonconformity.

Remarkable among them, and yet in a way typical also, was James Cook the explorer who first, and literally, began to put Australia and New Zealand onto the still-cloudy world map. In 1764 Cook bought a sixty-one-year lease on an unpretentious but brand-new, eight-roomed house on the south side of Mile End Road, near to the FitzHugh house and not far from Mile End Green. He was then thirty-six and had been based before in Shadwell by the river, with his young wife and their first child, a son who had been born while he was away on a long exploratory voyage round Newfoundland. Four years and three more children later, when preparing the first of his great scientific journeys to the Pacific, he insured the Mile End Road house for £250, his household goods for another £200, the family's clothing for £50, the plate (silverware and cutlery) for £25 and a timber shed and its contents in the back garden for £10. Taking into account that £50 a year was then a sufficient income for a modestly genteel lifestyle, these sums were not inconsiderable. Cook was now fairly embarked on his illustrious career as a ship's master and would soon become a captain; he was well known to the Admiralty, and was a trusted confidant of members of the Royal Society.

But he had not been born into this world. He was a Yorkshire boy, of a father who had come south from the borders as an agricultural labourer and had risen to become a farm foreman. The farmer's wife taught James Cook his letters and, seeing how bright he was, arranged for him to go to a charity school. Later, when he was apprenticed to a shopkeeper in a small fishing port, the shopkeeper noticed the same thing and got him a three-year apprenticeship with a Quaker shipmaster in Whitby. After that, via a spell as an ordinary seaman and experience in a brief war with France, his career of obsessional hard work and visionary conviction unrolled without a backward glance. The voyage he set out on in 1768 did not bring him back to the house in Mile End Road till 1771. He was off again from 1772 to 1775, and again from 1776 to 1780, which was the journey that finally carried him to an inglorious death off Hawaii where he had, untypically, antagonised the local natives. His wife did not get the news of his death till the following year. She inherited the house and all its contents and received a pension for life from the King of £200 a year. She was thirty-eight and had had six children, three of whom had already died – her eldest boy, who was by then a teenage midshipman, was tragically drowned in the same year that his father's life ended on the other side of the world. Both her other surviving sons died young, one in a violent robbery and another of fever, and her only daughter also died. Deeply distressed by these repeated blows of fate, she nevertheless lived on for decades, till the age of ninety-three, apparently sustained by a fervent Nonconformist faith now in the form of Methodism. She did not remarry. She must have been as resilient in her own way as James Cook was in his.

At the time of her death she had long moved away, to still-rural Clapham, from Stepney that was rapidly filling up with houses. Later in the nineteenth century, when the one-time prominent inhabitants were a forgotten memory, the Cook house, along with neighbouring ones, had a shop built out on the ground floor. In the early twentieth century, with a new tide of East End life and immigration, this became a women's clothes shop, and then a kosher butcher. An LCC blue plaque commemorating the fact that Cook had lived there was put on the house in 1907, yet this did not prevent it from being demolished in 1958, at the height of post-war ideological destructiveness, on the pretext of a need to widen a narrow lane alongside which then led to a brewery. In practice, the lane never got widened; its cobbles are there today, as is the rest of the terrace. The pointless brick wall that has replaced the house was given a different commemorative plaque in the 1970s, by which time the enlarged local authority of Tower Hamlets had acquired some notion of respect for the past – but not sufficient, it seems, to rebuild the house as it had been, or to construct anything worthwhile on the puddled parking lot that has replaced it.

In the summer of 1963, five years after Cook's house was destroyed, a girl is walking round Stepney with a pack of index cards in the little basket she uses as a handbag.

She wears a checked cotton dress she has made herself, and flat sandals. Her plait of hair is pinned up. Young and energetic, she can walk several miles a day through the streets without effort, but she does not always have her mind entirely on what she is supposed to be doing. She is incidentally exploring the East End for the first time, and there is so much to take in. From the Charrington's Anchor brewery near Trinity Almshouses a pungent scent of hops envelops a long stretch of the Mile End Road, and sometimes a dray pulled by huge shire horses comes sonorously past and turns in at the great gates. The sight, with jingling harness and the rhythmic clopping of heavy, whiskered hooves, is an assertion of a long tradition that in a few more years will have become extinct, but the girl doesn't know that. Nor can she guess the nature of the secret orchard that seems to lie at the end of a cul-de-sac of small houses with front plots that are like a forgotten fragment of a village, reached through an archway off the road near Stepney Green Underground station. One day, when there is no one around to tell her not to, she manages to climb up on one of the garden walls to look over into the orchard. Among the lushly overgrown grass, and a light scattering of rubbish, she glimpses worn, flat stones, laid out in lines, and understands that here are a colony of the long-dead. She does not know, till she is older and develops a lifelong relationship with outdated maps, that this is the oldest Jewish cemetery in Britain still in existence, the Velho Sephardi ground. Nor does she discover at the time that adjoining this cemetery, and still more hidden away from the surrounding streets behind high walls, is an Ashkenazi Jewish burial ground that is almost as old. Some of the local descendants of those who lie there are people she has recently met.

She is employed by the Stepney Old People's Welfare Association, on a casual basis, to check up on the names and addresses she has on the dog-eared index cards. How many of the old ladies, and a smaller number of old men, are still at their recorded addresses, and what state are they in? And, indeed, what state are the houses in – still tremulously there, or swept away by the Greater London Plan that is designed to change the old parish of Stepney beyond recognition?

It is not that the girl isn't interested in the old people. She is. Many, though by no means all, seem to be ageing representatives of the great immigrant Jewish influx from Eastern Europe of the 1890s and 1900s. Their children, she discovers, have usually moved to London's

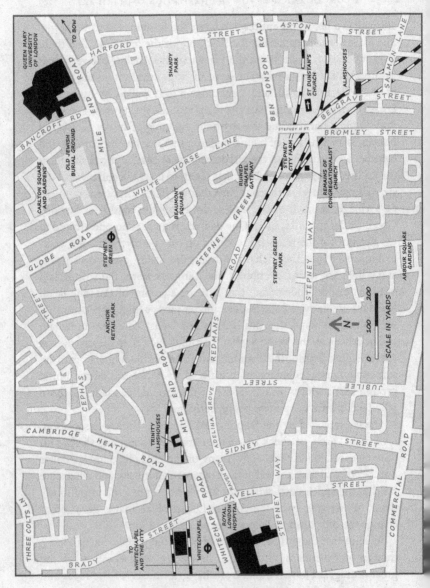

Stepney today, with Crossrail

northern suburbs – or have been 'relocated' more recently under the Greater London Plan. The old people's cards mostly show birth dates in the 1880s, some even in the 1870s. Some of them try to detain her with sagas of ancient achievements or griefs, to which she listens with a guilty awareness that she has many more names to visit in the next two hours. Today, over fifty years later, she would dearly like to have these garrulous old people back, even for one afternoon.

She likes the mantlepieces in their front rooms, some of them dressed with the bobbled chenille runners of the previous century, with symmetric china dogs or vases at each end, some with a photo of a husband or son who never came back from the First World War. She likes it when they tell her of happy times past, of 'nice shops' and good markets and distant celebrations, and she has even learnt to swallow the strong tea that is offered and to which very sweet, tinned milk is automatically added. She allows herself to be taken to see the place in the cracked wall of the kitchen or the upstairs bedroom where 'you can see the daylight through it, darlin', can't you?', and the privy in the back yard with the perennially leaking roof: 'It isn't very nice, you see, 'specially when it rains. My husband, he could have fixed that, but now I'm on me owney-oh . . .'

The girl speciously promises that the Old People's Welfare will try to do something about these things. She has not yet discovered the extent to which the forces of bureaucracy are preventing such simple, ad hoc improvements from being carried out. A few years earlier, Stepney Council specifically refused permission to the landlord of three houses in White Horse Road, which runs from Mile End Road down to Stepney church, to make good the war damage, on the grounds that:

> the carrying out of substantial works of repair to this old and obsolete type of property would seriously prejudice the Council planning proposals for the redevelopment for residential purposes of this part of Stepney and Poplar Reconstruction Area.[6]

These post-war plans were not dreamed up by Stepney Council on its own: the Greater London Plan was imposed by the LCC, but the local council had adopted its assumptions with enthusiasm. As early as 1946 a few warning local voices had been raised, especially about the way the envisaged Brave New Stepney of high-rise blocks set in 'green spaces' did not seem to allow any place for the small businesses that had long been the lifeblood of the East End. In fact, Labour thinking in those years had an absolute aversion to small businesses. And so carried away were the council by the prospect of reducing the borough's population substantially by moving half of them out of London (a key element of the Plan that was somehow presented as a moral obligation, though it was based upon a totally antiquated notion of public health) that the views of the inhabitants themselves counted little for many years. An enthusiastic contemporary description of these plans in a popular illustrated magazine[7] staggers the reader of today by its Stalinist disregard for the population's own preferences:

A New East End for London . . . will create a new and better London, of town planning on scientific lines . . . [It] will make a clean sweep of two-thirds of Stepney and one-third of the neighbouring borough of Poplar . . . More than 1,960 acres will be transformed . . . 3½ miles long and 1½ miles wide.

Then comes a complacent admission:

There may be heartbreaks in store for some before they can return to their new homes. The grocer who catered for his customers in the dark days must leave his shop in the dilapidated house on the corner; the pub where men lift their glasses of ale must be pulled down; neighbours who discuss the week's events outside their doorways on Sunday mornings will have to be parted.

The article further mentions that most of the people living in houses that had 'escaped the blitz' (to the regret, one feels, of the writer) say they do not actually want to be moved into flats, often well out of their old neighbourhoods, but this is brushed aside as a piece of incorrect thinking. Meanwhile, the houses must not be repaired nor the bomb debris properly cleared away, as that would simply encourage people in their quaint attachment to the recent past.

The girl, as she goes on her well-intentioned way among the witnesses of this past, knows nothing of the struggle that has been going on for almost two decades now between planners who regard themselves as an enlightened elite and those who are becoming increasingly critical of the new townscape that is being imposed. She does notice, however, that the mantra of almost all the old people she visits, whether in snug little houses that only need the roof mended and a bathroom added to the back, or in multi-occupied, once-elegant terraces or in serviceable Victorian dwelling blocks, is: 'Oh, it's all going to come down round here, dear.' She can tell that though they are acquiescent they are not enthusiastic about the prospect. They mind, even dread, the much-heralded change; they feel hurt at a profound, inarticulate level by what is being done. For what impresses itself on the girl's mind and memory, sowing the seeds of a lifetime's interest in the landscape of people's lives, is the awful state Stepney is in. It becomes clear to her that something terrible is happening there, a social and organic destruction that goes far beyond the results of the generally blamed Blitz.

She – or, I should say, I, for of course that is who she is – walks down into Stepney Green. Round St Dunstan's church and especially to the east of it, is a scene of wartime devastation: that much is true. The bombs of the Second World War did arrive here in battalions, aiming at the gas-holders and the docks, although the church itself was hardly touched. But the war has been over for eighteen years, so why is the place still a wilderness reminiscent of Ypres just after the First World War? On the west side of the church, on what must once have been a street corner, the remains of a shoeshop stand, apparently untouched since it was set alight by an incendiary bomb some night in 1941 or 1942, maybe the same night that the Baptist chapel or the Congregationalist church was destroyed. Burnt shoes still litter the dank interior of the shop, among other rain-sodden rubbish. But then who is there to clear it, since the grid of small streets adjoining it are in the process of being abolished? Some contain houses which seem still solid, liveable homes but they have all been boarded up. Others have already been supplanted by two long fences of corrugated iron, with just the occasional public house left isolated on a corner with no one to go to it. (Was this an empty concession to the criticism the Plan was now attracting?)

What had happened here, I could see, was not bomb damage but something worse: a wholesale assault on a neighbourhood, reducing to worthlessness in the eyes of the dispossessed inhabitants what had been the fabric of their existence, creating dereliction where it need not exist. *All coming down* – people's memories, their sense of self-worth, the meaning of their lives.

I walked back up Stepney Green and here, seeing a few runs of substantial old houses still standing in a battered state among overgrown bushes, I dreaded that next time I came past the iron screens would have taken over here too. In fact, this did not happen. Stepney Green was saved in the nick of time and rehabilitated. Unknown to me in that summer of 1963, a rebellious conservation movement was beginning to grind into effective action. Post-war doctrines about the state knowing what was best for its citizens were at last being questioned, on the political Left as well as the Right. The obsession, which originated in the second half of the nineteenth century, with the need to destroy the decor of the past in order to eradicate the poverty of that past, as if the streets themselves were somehow the source of urban ills, was at last perceived to be false. By the 1970s articles in illustrated magazines were not about a future of radiant towers but had titles such as 'An Indictment of Bad Planning'. Many of the new developments were on the way to becoming slums that were as bad, in their way, and far more threatening, than the old ones. Stepney, as one distinguished commentator[8] put it, had not been destroyed by the war but had been 'broken on the planners' wheel'.

For the conservation movement came too late for much of the borough. Off the Mile End Road and the Whitechapel Road in the 1960s small side streets still ran, but only to end after a dozen yards in wildernesses of deliberately created space on which tall blocks unrelated to the original townscape were beginning to rise. Other great tracts

Gloomy Sunday, 1960s Stepney under redevelopment, by John Claridge

of land that had been genuinely emptied by the Blitz, and could readily have been turned into parks and sports grounds, were 'scheduled' for similar development, or sometimes for the far higher tower blocks that for a disastrous few years captured the municipal imagination. This happened to the district to the east of St Dunstan's church. Meanwhile, whole neighbourhoods of houses that had survived the bombs more or less unscathed, such as the small streets to the west of the church, were perversely knocked down as late as 1969 to create other 'open space' where the Plan said it should be. That is the origin of the present-day displaced (and not much used) 'Stepney Green Park', and also of the city farm: the farm was started by a handful of surviving local inhabitants on the wasteland that had been arbitrarily created.

The bizarre result is that the immediate surroundings of the church, the original heart of the parish – which in the seventeenth and eighteenth centuries were a secluded residential area compared with the busyness of Mile End Road, and then became a thriving urban centre in the nineteenth and up to the Second World War – are now once again something of a grassy no man's land. At least this has provided useful scope for Crossrail's necessary shafts and caverns. It has also made possible its extensive excavation into the distant past.

Meanwhile on the original Stepney Green, the curving road with a linear park lined with old trees down the middle of it, the Georgian houses have been saved and restored. It is today, as it was over two hundred years ago, a place of carefully tended prosperity. If you approach this oasis from the Mile End Road, down the small cobbled turning called Hayfield Passage that is opposite the one-time brewery (now 'Anchor Retail Park'), you could believe you were entering some desirable enclave in Hampstead or Canonbury. It sits a little oddly with the heavily Bangladeshi community that now occupies the surrounding territory, living of necessity in the extensive housing estates which were built with a quite other population in mind. The old East Enders are scattered far and wide, to Dagenham and Stevenage and a long way out into London's north-eastern hinterland. It is they, or their children's children, whom Crossrail will carry in to jobs in central London, running without pause from Stratford to the edge of the City, bypassing Stepney as if the place had never existed.

CHAPTER XI

Favoured Slums

The eastward or westward journey from the countryside in and out of London town was gradually, with the passing centuries, transformed into a journey between two great urban regions, the East End and the West End.

Mythologies have accreted around these two terms, so that each carries its fixed load of social assumption. Today, as one hundred years ago, you still go 'up west' from anywhere east of Ludgate Hill, while those living westwards still 'go down' to Shoreditch, Whitechapel and further points east such as Stepney and Wapping, just as John Thomas Pocock did. The prepositions do not make much sense geographically, since much of the old West End is not significantly higher than the East: Whitechapel is well above the marshy areas of Rotherhithe and the Lee valley, and Westminster Abbey itself was built on an island in a one-time marsh. Nor do 'up' and 'down' entirely make sense socially, since Stepney was still a pleasant place to live when St Giles-in-the-Fields, in spite of its proximity to new and grand developments, was in florid decline. The social connotations that still persist today derive from the second half of the nineteenth century, by which time the East End had, within a generation, ceased to be separate hamlets and had become a vast agglomeration of streets to house workers connected with the docks and with attendant industries. At the same period, the West End was spreading out further and further, swallowing lonely Tyburn as if it had never been, colonising Knightsbridge and then the wide fields of Chelsea and Kensington with houses for an ever-expanding upper middle class of the commercially and professionally prosperous.

In reality the location of what are generally considered the Bad Lands, no-go areas, 'the slums', 'the rookeries', 'the black streets' and other terms at other periods, has moved back and forth. Parts of Farringdon Without, the City's first suburb, which ran down and across the Fleet, were becoming crowded and of ill-repute by the seventeenth century and did not improve over the next two hundred years. The market at Smithfield, with its perpetual slaughter of animals on the hoof that spread out into adjacent streets towards Newgate, did not make for a totally salubrious neighbourhood, in spite of the presence of some grand houses and institutions. In addition, the annual Bartholomew Fair was now an occasion not just for trading but for sports and amusements as well. There were jugglers, acrobats, card sharps and cockfights, and there was another fair each May.

And then there had long been the prisons down the line of the Fleet: the several-times rebuilt Newgate, the notoriously brutal Fleet prison and the ex-palace-turned-prison of Bridewell, none of which improved the tone of the district. But the central problem was the Fleet itself and the perennial human tendency, in the absence of proper drains, to use any convenient waterway as a sewer. Already, by the thirteenth century, there were complaints that its lower reaches smelt awful, and in spite of periodic efforts at dredging and 'cleansing' the problem always reappeared. By 1652 the one-time river was said to be

impassable for boats, by reason of the many encroachments thereon made, by the throwing of offal and other garbage by butchers, saucemen and others and by reason of the many houses of office [latrines] standing over upon it.

When the Fire of London had burnt out everything along the Fleet below Holborn Bridge this was regarded as a great opportunity for improvement. With a dream of Venice in mind, Christopher Wren and Robert Hooke between them redesigned the whole length of it from Holborn to the Thames as a ship canal with wharves on each side, and thus it proudly appears on the Restoration maps. However, ships did not much use it, wharves filled up with ramshackle buildings and

refuse dumps – and more latrines – and in the 1730s defeat was generally admitted. The same fate overcame the Fleet that had befallen the
smaller Wallbrook river centuries before. In several stages, the lower
part of the river, which had become nothing but a large open drain,
was covered over, and in the middle of the eighteenth century a new
arcaded market, the Fleet Market, designed by George Dance the
Elder, was built on top of it. But parts of the higher reaches, through
crowded Clerkenwell, remained open to the sky between overshadow-
ing buildings, and the charges of filth and disreputableness now displaced themselves to there.

It is probably no coincidence, however, that at just the same period
when part of the Fleet and its squalid surroundings were disappearing, the complaints began about the St Giles-in-the-Fields area, and
grew louder as the eighteenth century went by. London had expanded
enormously, and predominantly towards the west. Great urban centres tend to need slums, both for the practical purpose of housing
the poorer, more transient and less respectable part of the population, and also as part of urban mythology. St Giles, now surrounded
by the spread of the metropolis, with its old and mortgaged buildings
going unrepaired, its new but gimcrack estate of narrow streets round
Seven Dials, and its equally new but rapidly expanding population of
Huguenot refugees and Irish, fitted neatly into the role. Being so close
to the respectable area of Soho and the positively grand developments
in Marylebone and Piccadilly, it was highly visible (in a way that
Whitechapel, say, was not), and thus became for many Londoners the
iconic slum to which they could all knowledgeably refer.

And so it remained. By the end of the eighteenth century, when Soho
itself had declined into the slightly melancholy and shabby-genteel
district depicted in Dickens's period novel *A Tale of Two Cities*, and
wealthier society had taken itself northwards to the newly developed
Bedford Estate in Bloomsbury, St Giles and its 'rookeries' were
firmly fixed in the popular consciousness. The parish figured as
the permanent embodiment of Hogarth's *Gin Lane*, no matter what
changes occurred elsewhere. Dickens spent some time nearby in his

early childhood, and then again as a very young man, living north of Oxford Street, a short walk away from St Giles. He had relatives at other addresses in the same area. St Giles, or more particularly Seven Dials, figures specifically in his earliest work, *Sketches by Boz*, which was first published anonymously as a series of articles in a magazine in the early 1830s when he himself was just twenty-one:

> The inexperienced wayfarer . . . traverses streets of dirty, straggling houses, with now and then an unexpected court composed of buildings as ill-proportioned and deformed as the half-naked children that wallow in the kennels. Here and there, a little dark chandler's shop, with a cracked bell hung up behind the door . . . others, as if for support, lean against some hand-some lofty building, which usurps the place of a low, dingy public house; long rows of broken and patched windows expose plants that may have flourished when 'the Dials' were built, in vessels as dirty as 'the Dials' themselves; and shops for the purchase of rags, bones, old iron and kitchen-stuff, vie in cleanliness with the bird-fanciers and rabbit-dealers.

Having passed by 'announcements of day-schools, penny theatres, petition-writers, mangles, and music for balls or routs', and by cheer-fully quarrelling women and permanently lounging men, Dickens finally moves in on Monmouth Street. It had by then become a centre for the sale of old clothes, in a period when (as in most times before the present) many clothes were so elaborately made and costly that ordinary working people never thought of buying an overcoat or a Sunday dress new. Monmouth Street – where Dickens fantasises the whole lifetime of a boy and his relations by observing the various suits up for sale – is clearly quieter than some of the others that make up the Dials, but is similarly overpopulated:

> The inhabitants of Monmouth Street are a distinct class; a peace-able and retiring race, who immure themselves, for the most part, in deep cellars or small back-parlours, and who seldom come

forth into the world, except in the dusk and coolness of evening, when they may be seen seated in chairs on the pavement,
smoking their pipes, or watching the gambols of their engaging
children as they revel in the gutter, a happy group of infantine
scavengers.

It was just at the period when Dickens was writing this that the first
cholera epidemic hit London in 1832, followed by other outbreaks. In
practice, cholera killed fewer people than typhus still did, but its dra-
matic symptoms, the speed with which it could bring death, and the
way outbreaks seemed to target specific districts, all alarmed both
the public and the government. The theory that sickness was produced by foul air, ill-ventilated rooms and such evils still held sway.
Bad smells in themselves, it was thought, actually generated disease.
Not for twenty-two years after the first outbreak and several intervening ones would Chadwick's associate, John Snow, prove, by putting a
particular pump out of action in Soho, that cholera was waterborne. It
was several years more before the lethal role of the polluted Thames
as a source of drinking water was identified as the prime cause, but the
agitation about the need to clean up parts of London did, in a general
way, some good. Wheels turned, speeches were made, and by the mid-
1840s it was decided that one notorious 'rookery' must be demolished.

Where? Why, in St Giles of course, so uncomfortably close to politer
districts. Conveniently, this would also make it possible to cut a modern
road through from the east end of Oxford Street to High Holborn. For
the first time in over seven hundred years St Giles High Street would
no longer be a main highway into London. Ten years later John Timbs,
a Victorian commentator on London life who, like Dickens, lived long
enough to see much of the city of his youth swept away, wrote with
gusto in his book *Curiosities of London* (1855):

The 'Rookery' was a triangular space bounded by Bainbridge,
George, and High Streets: it was one dense mass of houses,
through which curved narrow tortuous lanes from which again
diverged close courts – one great maze, as if the houses had

originally been one block of stone, eaten by slugs into numerous small chambers and connecting passages. The lanes were thronged with loiterers; and stagnant gutters and piles of garbage and filth infested the air. In the windows wisps of straw, old hats, and lumps of bed tick or brown paper, alternated with shivered panes of broken glass; the walls were the colour of bleached soot, and doors fell from their hinges and worm-eaten posts. Many of the windows announced, 'Lodging at 3d. a night', where the wild wanderers from town to town held their revels.

Bainbridge Street ran off the north side of St Giles High Street approximately along the line that the much-wider New Oxford Street would take. George Street ran into Dyott Street, and was joined by Church Lane, another notorious alley that formed the section generally supposed to be Hogarth's Gin Lane of a hundred years before, and is the most identifiable locus of Tom-all-Alone's. By 1847, the new street that replaced part of this slum was open to traffic. Another cholera epidemic occurred the following year, and a year later again a rather different complexion is cast upon Timbs's 'wild wanderers of the night' in a letter written from adjacent Church Lane and Carrier Street, with goodness knows what effort, and published in *The Times* on 5 July 1849:

Sir – May we beg and beseach your proteckshion and power. We are Sur, as it may be, livin in a Wilderniss, so far as the rest of London knows anything of us, or as the rich and great people care about. We live in muck and filthe. We aint got no priviz, no dust bins, no drains. No water-splies, and no drain or suer in the hole place. The Suer Company, in Greek Street, Soho Square, all great, rich and powerful men, take no notice whatsomever of our complaints. The Stenches of a Gully-hole is disgustin. We all of us suffur, and numbers are ill, and if the Colera comes Lord help us.

Some gentlemans comed yesterday, and we thought they was comishoners from the Suer Company, but they was complaining of the noosance and stenche our lanes and corts was to them in New

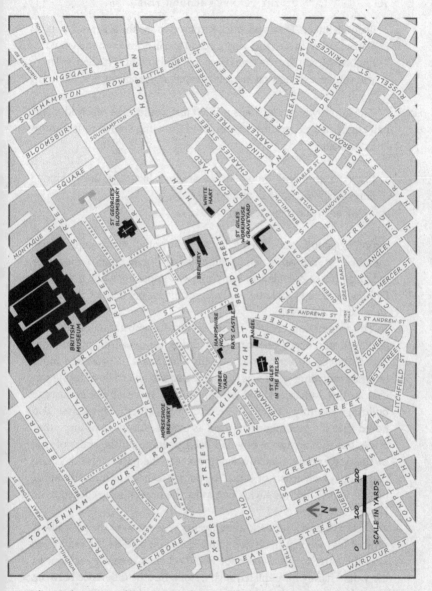

St Giles High Street and Seven Dials district, *c.* 1840. The dotted road indicates New Oxford Street, cut through small streets in the mid-1840s

Oxforde Street. They was much surprised to see the seller in No. 12 Carrier Street, in our lane, where a child was ill from fever, and would not beleave that Sixty persons sleep in it every night. This here seller you couldent swing a cat in it, and the rent is five shilling a week.

The letter, which *The Times* printed just as they had received it and had confirmed as genuine, continues in the same vein for a few more lines, and ends:

Praye Sir com and see us, for we are livin like piggs and it aint faire we should be so ill treated.
    We are your respectful servants . . .

Fifty-four people had signed it, mostly but not all male, some clearly members of the same family. Although Church Lane, famous for lodging houses crowded to bursting, was popularly known as Little Dublin, or 'The Holy Land', only about fifteen per cent of the names were obviously Irish.

The impression created by the letter was substantially different from the stereotype of a drunken, dishonest, layabout population, that had been current for a good hundred years. It provoked more letters confirming what was said, and also a long article pointing out that all this squalor existed 'within twenty yards of the handsome buildings recently erected in New Oxford Street'. The writer also noted that the landings were used as privies, for want of any other place, but that a strange boy had been sleeping on the stairs of one of the desperately overcrowded houses for the past twelve days and had been 'given crusts of bread' by people as poor as himself, out of pity. Evidently he was such a one as Jo, the crossing-sweeper in *Bleak House*.

Dickens's novel, set back some twenty years or so to the pre-railway time of his own youth, came out in instalments a couple of years or so after the letter to *The Times* appeared: Dickens's keen eye for London life would hardly have missed such a story. But the difference between his early years and the mid-century was that public opinion was now astir, in a mixture of civic awareness, moral alarm and cholera-fearing self-interest, in a way it had not been in pre-Victorian days. Poor people had been living huddled together in old houses without drains or privies, in one part of town or another, since medieval times and no doubt before: only now was this considered scandalous. The creation of New Oxford Street, which had already demolished part of the old rookery, was a sign of the times. So was the establishment in 1855 of the Metropolitan Board of Works, the first London-wide municipal authority, and the decision in the same decade that London must have proper sewers. (The 'comishoners of Suers' referred to in the impassioned letter were too local for their efforts to be efficient.) Other Improvements followed: in 1864 the editor of *The Builder*, Geoffrey Godwin, could write:

> In the once notorious St Giles, model lodging-houses, churches, chapels, fine school rooms, and other useful buildings have taken the place of former dens.

More fundamental changes came in the 1870s, in the form of Charing Cross Road, relieving the crowded St Martin's Lane which lost itself in Seven Dials, and Shaftesbury Avenue as a new east–west route, once again bypassing St Giles, from High Holborn to Piccadilly.

One gets the impression that St Giles had become everyone's pet project. With that mixture of confident religious fervour and genuine compassion for the destitute that came to characterise the Victorian era, assorted missionaries (the volunteer social workers of the time) descended in flocks upon St Giles and competed for who could claim (or 'rescue') the largest number of souls, sometimes inadvertently bribing the poor with handouts to attend this or that favoured chapel or revival meeting. Edward C. W. Grey, cleric and teacher, who worked in St Giles parish for all the last thirty years of the nineteenth century, and whose book on the history of the district (*St Giles of the Lepers*, 1905) was only published after his death, wrote:

> There can be no manner of doubt that on account of its proximity to the West End, the district has been considerably pauperised

by dole givers in the streets. It is so hard to refuse a whining beg-
gar and so much easier to give him a coin to get rid of him . . .
Besides this, St Giles's has been the happy hunting ground of
empirics in philanthropy, whose schemes are too often crude
and immature, and it also became the battlefield of religious
sects.

By the time Grey was writing, he could comment on how much the
district had been transformed geographically, and therefore socially,
since his earlier days there. It no longer figured as London's Famous
Slum: indeed, assaulted by Metropolitan works, it had ceased to do so
by the time Dickens was writing his last books. In *Our Mutual Friend*
(1864–65) there is Mr Venus's 'little dark greasy shop' of antiquities
and junk, including an articulated skeleton. Dickens places this in
Clerkenwell, but he confided to an associate in a letter of 1864 that
the real-life original of the shop he had in his mind had been in
the St Giles area, and there is documentary evidence of him being
seen in that place at the height of his fame.[1] Evidently, by the 1860s,
Clerkenwell presented itself as a more resonant location for quaint,
old-fashioned squalor.

Of course the Clerkenwell–Farringdon area, with its proximity both to
Smithfield and the Fleet, had had its slums for centuries, and Dickens
himself had made much of them in *Oliver Twist* (1837–39) for the location of Fagin's thieves' kitchen.

> Near to the spot on which Snow Hill and Holborn Hill meet,
> there opens, upon the right hand as you come out of the City, a
> narrow and dismal alley leading to Saffron Hill. In its filthy shops
> are exposed for sale huge numbers of second-hand silk handker-
> chiefs of all sizes and patterns; for here reside the traders who
> purchase them from pick-pockets.

This alley is named as Field Lane, one of those country paths that Stow
had complained was becoming built up three hundred years before.

But in addition to commonplace thieving – although those who shuddered enjoyably over the supposed iniquities of Seven Dials were probably unaware of this – other small streets in Farringdon held a much darker secret than any to be found in St Giles parish.

Here, just north of Snow Hill, near the junction of Giltspur Street and Cock Lane, was Pye Corner, where the Fire of London was stopped on its north-west course by the remains of the City Wall. At Pye Corner was a naked pygmy figure called the Golden Boy, which had been erected to commemorate the stopping of the Fire, and behind it stood a public house called the Fortunes of War.[2] This pub, ostensibly just like many other watering holes around the edge of the City, was notorious

Field Lane about 1840, with Dickensian names

in certain circles by the early nineteenth century. It was the main house north of the river to which Resurrection Men, those stealers of bodies from graveyards on which surgeons depended for their anatomy studies, used to bring their booty before passing it on to their contacts in the main hospitals.

The readiness of even the most respectable and prestigious surgeons to receive bodies that they must have known, or strongly suspected, were illicitly taken from graves shocks us now. Presumably they justified it to themselves in terms of what they were learning from dissection and the contribution to the greater good of humanity. The Act of 1752, popularly called the Murder Act, which allowed surgeons the hanged bodies of what were judged the worst offenders as an extra post-mortem punishment, only provided a few bodies each year and anyway was much resisted by the relations and friends of the condemned: they did their utmost to carry the bodies off for secret burial and often succeeded. This was why, in the late eighteenth and early nineteenth centuries, the business of grave-robbing flourished, with the occasional Burke-and-Hare-style seizure and murder of a living person if the practice of digging up fresh graves in churchyards at dead of night was being made too difficult.[3] This notorious situation eventually brought about the Anatomy Act of 1832, under which anyone who died in the workhouse or a similar institution, and whose body was not claimed within seven days, could legally be sent for dissection. This did provide a supply of bodies, and the Resurrection Men, along by and by with the old, squalid inner-London burial grounds, became a thing of the past. But the new Act added an extra dimension of distress and shame for those dying in poverty without family, knowing that they would not lie after death in any ground, however crowded and insecure, and that no prayer would be said over them. Those who ended up interred in the pauper burial ground of St Sepulchre's Workhouse were by comparison the lucky ones.

This ground lay immediately to the south of the street called Cowcross. As we know, the ground and its maze of surrounding alleys, courts and 'rents' was destined to be swept away at the beginning of the 1860s, when the Metropolitan line came down alongside the Fleet.

Farringdon station was established at Cowcross, and a great swathe of shunting lines curved down into Smithfield Market, displacing everything in their way, the living and the dead. Today, Farringdon's new Crossrail and overground station on the south side of Cowcross occupies a space that, before the railway arrived, had for centuries been resonant with life and death.

The westward journey of the condemned from the Tower of London or Newgate, initially to St Giles and later, for several centuries, on to Tyburn at the far end of the Oxford road, became an integral part of the death sentence. The phrase 'to ride up Holborn Hill' carried a profound extra meaning: mass executions took place several times a year, and often, if one or more of the condemned were a well-known personality, a handsome highwayman or such, their last ride in a cart resembled not so much a solemn and terrible occasion as a bank holiday revel. Some of those due to die took care to dress as if for a wedding, in fine white clothes, so as to 'go off gamely', exchanging jokes with the crowd; alternatively, the occasional one repented so loudly of his or her sins, exhorting the crowd to repent of theirs, that the procession 'was more like a revival meeting than a hanging match'. But by the late eighteenth century (an era extraordinarily free with its use of capital punishment) it was evidently felt that the undisciplined crowds tramping through what was now west London had become too large and unmanageable. Tyburn was no longer the isolated spot it had earlier been, and from 1783 onwards public executions took place, instead, immediately in front of Newgate gaol, next to St Sepulchre church, overlooking Snow Hill and the Fleet valley.

A good deal of enjoyable ceremony, however, still attended the event. In the early seventeenth century a donation of £50 had been given that St Sepulchre's bell, 'the bells of Old Bailey', might be tolled by the sexton, in perpetuity, for each condemned felon on the morning of his death, and the practice continued with enthusiasm when Newgate itself became the site of that death. On a hanging day the bells of other City churches also were rung, but muffled. The streets around resounded with the cries of hawkers selling ballads and 'Last Dying

Speeches'. A service was held in the prison chapel, attended by the condemned and by those able to tip the gaoler, and after that the prisoners' chains were struck off in the press yard in front of friends and relations and the heaving crowd looking in at the prison gate. Then the condemned were brought out to the scaffold.

The return of the gallows site to the vicinity of Smithfield had the incidental effect of recreating the ancient synthesis between the slaughter of beasts and that of man. By the eighteenth century, with London's growth, more animals were being killed at Smithfield than ever. In 1725 Londoners were consuming sixty thousand beef cattle, seventy thousand sheep and two hundred and thirty-nine thousand pigs in a year, and some of these were driven on the hoof from as far away as Wales and Scotland. Turkeys and geese were marched from Norfolk and Suffolk, sometimes with their delicate feet wrapped in cloth 'shoes' to protect them on the journey.[4] A hundred years later, with London much expanded again, the figure was one hundred and fifty thousand cattle and one and a half million sheep. Smithfield was also trading all the year round now, since, with the cultivation of new winter feeds, the old practice of wholesale slaughter before the onset of winter had been abandoned. By the mid-century the annual numbers were substantially higher again – but by now Victorian public opinion was taking hold of the situation: complaints of crowding, noise, dirt, quarrelling drovers, confusion and casual cruelty were beginning to be loudly heard. In Dickens's *Great Expectations* (a late novel, written at the beginning of the 1860s, but, once again, set back in time to the author's youth) the young Pip comes across the market district and refers to it as 'the shameful place, being all asmear with filth and fat and blood and foam, [which] seemed to stick to me'.

In August 1849 – one can imagine how bad the market smelt in hot weather – *The Builder* carried a long article on the need to move Smithfield somewhere else, describing the vast area of pens full of bleating and mooing creatures, and undrained old streets around which were to be found the sellers of poultry, the private knackers' yards, the tripe-boilers and fat-melters and similar noxious trades. Among all this

The Last Day of Old Smithfield Market, June 1855

children ran about, arguably becoming habituated to blood, guts and violent death. With a classic appeal to the fear of The Mob that had been aroused in the British breast by the French Revolution sixty years before, and by subsequent lesser ones, the article claimed:

> Should any great political convulsion upset the elaborate artificial system of our society, and drag us through the horrors of a revolution, it is among [these children] that the future Dantons will seek the instruments willing and able to commit the crimes and butcheries they may order.

More prosaically, a parliamentary inquiry into the possibility of moving the market on grounds of space and hygiene was already under way, and a site was selected by 1851 in the fields between Islington and Kentish Town.

The establishment of this Metropolitan Cattle Market as the main slaughterhouse, together with the fact that the railways now made it possible to bring in overnight meat that had been freshly killed in its place of origin, meant that the pens at Smithfield full of terrified beasts were at last on their way into history, but the 'dead meat market' in the lanes to the south of Smithfield was more extensive than ever. Towards 1860 John Hollingshead wrote of the 'Newgate Market . . . seeping round the black prison in Paternoster Row and Ave Maria Lane, up Ludgate Hill', creating traffic jams – 'meat blocks'. He spoke longingly of plans by then afoot to 'transform Smithfield into a great central market for flesh, fish and fowl . . . a light, airy structure, well ventilated at the top'.

This was what was eventually constructed. The new market, still in partial use today, was designed by Horace Jones and opened in 1868 – another of the transformations that decade wrought on this very ancient quarter so close to the City. For the previous twenty years commentators had busied themselves with London-as-she-might-be plans for the market. In 1851 an entire short book, *What Shall We Do with Smithfield?*, was published by 'An Old Sanitary Reformer'. After a glance at the place's earlier history as a site of martyrdom and execution of 'the best and most sincerely devout of our race' (which appears to mean the Protestant section of the executed), the writer remarked that it could not be left empty or it would become a dunghill (perhaps a rather outdated fear) and that selling it off might be hazardous in case 'Papal gold' should build a church there for 'aliens'. He called for a city park – the need for greenery, purer air and so forth – and envisaged arches, galleries, fountains, a roof garden *with soil from elsewhere, not London soil*. He also suggested, on the model of the Crystal Palace of the Great Exhibition the same year, that acme of enlightened thinking, a 'crystal pavilion'. At just the same time Charles Pearson, the visionary progenitor of the Metropolitan Railway, was launching his early scheme for it to run in a 'crystal way'. Glass was the new purity, and there was glass in plenty in the upper layers of the new market.

A degree of public revulsion at the sight of animals being killed wholesale on the streets undoubtedly contributed to the market's move, though one could say that the new refinement of the Victorian era simply wanted the slaughter out of sight. A comparable evolution in public feeling, at exactly the same period, overtook the slaughter of human beings. Informed and liberal opinion was beginning to turn against the idea that public executions had any moral effect. (Dickens disapproved of them on the grounds that such a spectacle visibly debauched and degraded those who watched it, though he showed some eagerness to witness these degrading sights himself.) After 1868, executions at Newgate, which were now confined to murderers rather than the assortment of unlucky thieves, chancers and other petty criminals who had been hanged so readily in earlier times, took place within the walls.

The following year Holborn Viaduct was finally opened nearby, after six years' work, complete with uplifting bronze statues of Science, Agriculture, Commerce and Fine Art. This new, great iron carriageway across the valley of the Fleet, replacing Holborn Bridge, transformed for good the old, bumpy and slippery route down into the valley and up again, which had been described by Dickens in *Nicholas Nickleby* as:

> that particular part of Snow Hill where omnibus horses going eastwards seriously think of falling down on purpose, and where horses in hackney cabriolets going westwards not infrequently fall by accident.

The viaduct, together with the construction of the railway line and the completion of Farringdon Road, sent Fagin's London into history.

Yet if we go back a hundred years earlier, or even fifty, this same district had been enjoying a golden last era. Such was the complexity of London by the late eighteenth and early nineteenth centuries, that even though the Farringdon area was widely regarded as a shocking slum it had become, along with Holborn on the other side of the Fleet valley, an epicentre for the prosperous and ever-growing coaching trade. The good network of gravel roads, turnpikes and others, that now extended all over southern England and to many key places in the north, enabled more and faster coaches. Journeys that, well within living memory, had taken several days were now accomplished in a non-stop twenty-four to thirty-six hours, with a whole panoply of inns, staging posts, ostlers at the ready to change the horses with expert speed like today's motor-race attendants, and fervent competitive spirit between the various companies. Naturally, many of the journeys began or ended in London, and the old galleried inns just outside the confines of the City became significant headquarters. Like today's airport hotels, they received travellers at any hour, and also their horses: fed, watered, warmed and bedded them down, man and beast. Coaching inns, in the seventy or eighty years before their sudden demise with the arrival of the railways, were a huge and profitable industry.

It was logical that Dickens, in his first-ever literary work, *The Pickwick Papers*, should make one of his key characters, the archetypal Londoner Sam Weller, a child of the inns. Weller is the son of a coachman who becomes an employee of the Belle Sauvage. This galleried inn, south of the Fleet prison, near the foot of Ludgate Hill, was probably first constructed in the fourteenth century by a William Savage. Four hundred years later, it had coaches leaving daily for Bath, Bristol, Plymouth, Oxford, Cambridge, Coventry, Manchester and Carlisle. At this time it had forty rooms for travellers and stable space for a hundred horses. Parson Woodforde from East Anglia, paying one of his occasional trips to

London in June 1786, recorded in his diary that he and his accompanying servants had first arrived at another inn, the Swan with Two Necks, which he describes as off Aldersgate, but which was actually in St John's Street, just north of Smithfield:

> where we had some rum and water . . . After staying some little
> time in Lad Lane we had a coach and went with our luggage to our
> old inn the Belle Savage at Ludgate Hill where we supped and slept.

He ended up, however, somewhat irritated because his companions (a trusted manservant and a maidservant) 'walked out in the evening by themselves', and that later, after a supper for which they had wanted a bottle of wine, went straight to bed (whether together or not is not clear) and left the parson to drink most of the wine on his own. London must have been an exciting place to visit, for country people.

There was another very well-known inn, the Saracen's Head, at the top of Snow Hill right by St Sepulchre, which dated from the twelfth century. It had a galleried yard and a great door with a carved 'saracen's

The yard of the Belle Sauvage inn, early nineteenth century

head' on either side, harking back to the time of crusades to the Holy Land. Stow called it 'a large and fair inn' when it was four hundred years old already, and by the late eighteenth century it was the starting point for coaches to the north as well as other places. It figures in *Nicholas Nickleby* as the inn where Nicholas meets Wackford Squeers, the headmaster of a bleak and exploitative boarding school in faraway, snowy Yorkshire: Squeers already has three downtrodden small boys with him, and doesn't hesitate to offer Nicholas a minimally paid job.

The Saracen's Head was pulled down in 1868 for the building of Holborn Viaduct, though some part of it lingered on into the twentieth century as cheap dining rooms for City workers. An office block now bears its name. By the 1860s the Swan with Two Necks had already been demolished and the Belle Sauvage would shortly disappear too. It is sad that these historic and distinctive buildings became redundant before regard for the venerable buildings of Old London got properly into gear. In 1860, when the railways were well established and the big stations were building new, modern hotels for a new time, John Hollingshead wrote an evocative piece about arriving by night, in what must have been the early 1850s, on 'the Last Stagecoach' at an imaginary Old Dragon Inn in Smithfield. The gates were standing wide open because they were rotten, and there was a single 'old, palsied ostler'.

> The principal entrance – a long passage lined with what were formerly stables – was now turned into a narrow street of small, dirty, cattle-smelling houses, let out in tenements, and decorated with festoons of ragged, yellow clothes that danced upon clotheslines . . . Several pools of liquorice-coloured water were in the yard, presided over by rotten wooden pumps. The stones were saffron-coloured, broken and uneven.

The inn no longer had a prosperous clientele, but lodged cattle drovers, and currently a collection of 'jugglers, horse-riders, tumblers and fair-people' – for Bartholomew Fair, which was finally abolished in 1855. There were rotten planks giving way in the galleries, a derelict mail-coach in one yard and a van in which people were sleeping.

The fixed nineteenth-century perception, which persisted well into the first half of the twentieth, was that, if constant vigilance were not exercised, slums would grow organically: one can see that the notion did have some kernel of truth in it. Or did it depend, rather, in which direction the commentator was looking? It is noticeable that, though Whitechapel and Shoreditch had long been extremely overcrowded, agitation about their being classic examples of 'Darkest London' did not really begin till St Giles was cleaned up and new roads and Metropolitan Board of Works industrial dwelling blocks were eviscerating Clerkenwell. The hysteria that would arise about Whitechapel and the Ripper murders in 1888 was due only in part to the repeated and brutal nature of the murders. It also owed a certain amount to a generalised fear of 'the masses', and to the needs of respectable London to have a district to hold – at a safe distance – in disapproval and dread.

A hundred and seventy years have passed since the extinction of the stagecoaches' glorious last era, which had turned the inns of old London into central clearing stations for countrywide travel and also for the start of foreign journeys via Dover, Plymouth or Harwich. Over one hundred and fifty years have passed since Charles Pearson was frustrated in his attempt to build a central railway station for London linking the various existing main lines, and had to content himself with bringing his new Metropolitan line to Farringdon. For most of the twentieth century this central London section of the Metropolitan and District line languished, outclassed by the newer, deeper tube lines. The tunnel south from Farringdon under Snow Hill, that had been constructed in the late 1860s to link the Metropolitan with the London, Chatham, and Dover line, fell out of passenger use during the First World War. Buses and trams had taken over for cross-London journeys. Farringdon was seen as an old-fashioned backwater of a station known only to City workers, especially in the two decades after the Second World War when it lost its freight lines into Smithfield Market. The North London and various other overground lines were so neglected too, and so little advertised, as to be on the brink of closure. Not till the Thameslink service was established in 1988, running over some of

Ludgate Hill with the planned new railway bridge across it, 1860s

these old lines and reopening Snow Hill tunnel, to link Bedford in the north with Brighton in the south via King's Cross and Farringdon, did Farringdon begin to revive from its shabby obscurity.

How different is its standing today. The old station is still there, but below ground has been doubled in size, with a new entry on the opposite side of Cowcross and enormously long platforms. When Crossrail is open, Farringdon will become the only city-centre station in the world to be a gateway to five different international airports. It is already, via Thameslink, connected to Luton in the north and Gatwick in the south. With Crossrail's opening, it will be linked, via Liverpool Street, with the Stansted Express, and with London City airport which is a short bus- or taxi-ride from Canary Wharf, also directly with Heathrow in the opposite direction. In a new form that he could never have predicted, Charles Pearson's dream is at last coming true.

CHAPTER XII

From the End of the World to Pickled Onions

The removal of the Hangman's Tree from Tyburn back to Newgate in 1783 has taken our attention off that haunted road west from St Giles High Street, variously described on maps of the time as 'the way to Uxbridge', 'the way to Oxford' or, simply, 'Tyburn way', and, much nearer the present time, as 'Oxford Street'.

What had been happening to it during the hundred years before the removal of the gallows, while St Giles at its eastern end was still a good address though becoming ominously crowded, and Soho was being laid out on the south side? During that Restoration period, Piccadilly, further south, began to be built up on both sides with fine, detached properties – Burlington House, Albermarle and Berkeley. In the usual traditions of ribbon development, the road to Oxford too, you might think, would attract a sprinkling of houses along its length.

It did not. By the beginning of the eighteenth century, although the first side streets off Piccadilly were beginning to develop between the mansions, in the direction of the Oxford road all building petered out. Where New Bond Street now lies, close to the planned Crossrail station, was a field called Conduit Mead, after that medieval conduit system which conveyed Tyburn water to the City and of which we have heard before. Roughly where Regent Street now runs north from Piccadilly was an old path called Swallow Lane (a suppressed fragment of it still exists today) and the narrow streets of Soho were established to the east of it, but westward development stopped there. Swallow Lane

The execution site at Tyburn (with viewing platform), mid-eighteenth century

or Street (according to Walford, the indefatigable nineteenth-century author of *Old and New London*) was:

> a long, ugly and irregular thoroughfare. The tradition is that it
> bore a reputation by no means good, and contained, among its
> other houses, a certain livery stable which in the last century was
> a noted house-of-call for highwaymen.

Appropriate, one might say, for the highwaymen to call there, when they would eventually make their final appearance at Tyburn just a few hundred yards along the Oxford road. Most highwaymen, even the successful and glamorous, ended up on Tyburn Tree, from Claude Duval in 1670 to 'Sixteen String Jack' in 1774, and finally John Austin in 1783, who was the last person to be hanged at that spot. But going northwards up Swallow Street buildings were few, and it was said by another later commentator[1] that in Claude Duval's time and even afterwards:

> He who then rambled to what is now the gayest and most crowded part of Regent Street, found himself in a solitude, and was sometimes so fortunate as to have a shot at a woodcock.

The old hunting tradition, for which a lodge had been built in the thirteenth century near the reservoir, was clearly not quite extinct in that unfrequented district (near the Oxford Circus of today). As for the northern, Marylebone side of the Oxford road, for a long time it remained almost without buildings for its entire length. Fanny Burney, the writer, who lived in Poland Street, Soho, in her childhood around 1760, wrote later: 'Oxford-road . . . into which Poland Street terminated, had little on its further side but fields, gardeners' grounds, or uncultivated suburbs'.

Walford described the road at this period as having been: 'deep and hollow . . . full of sloughs, with here and there a ragged house, the lurking place of cut-throats'.

Just the thing for a highway leading to a gallows.

Change, however, was inevitably coming, gallows or no gallows. The very clearly drawn mid-eighteenth-century map by Rocque shows almost all the land to the south of what we will now call Oxford Street fairly developed by the Grosvenor estate (Mayfair). Yet the last hundred yards or so, beyond North Audley Street, is still indicated as rough ground, with a turnpike at the top of what we know as Park Lane but is still marked at that point as 'Tiburn Lane'. A very little further along on the opposite side is the junction with the Edgware Road, with 'Tiburn House' on the corner (today, a large cinema occupies the site). There, in the middle of the road junction, is drawn a three-cornered gallows to accommodate several bodies at a time. Just below this graphic indication: more or less on the spot where Marble Arch stands today, is the daunting inscription: 'Where soldiers are shot'. Immediately to the south lies Hyde Park, as it does today.

On the north side of Oxford Street, developers had been busy too, with Cavendish Square and its surroundings beginning to take shape – but no Portman Square as yet, for the buildings stopped short at Marylebone Lane. It seems likely that the stream that runs on the map alongside Marylebone Lane, on a slantwise route into Mayfair – Tyburn brook itself – discouraged speculators from risking their money on marshy ground, though the stream had already been accommodated on the south side by the construction of South Molton Street, which follows its line to this day. Further accommodation with the persistent stream has had its place in the Crossrail workings for Bond Street station.

It may be, rather, that there was a general, unspoken recoil from constructing terraces of houses right up to the gallows ground. This end-of-our-world place for thousands over the course of the hanging centuries was also regarded definitively as the end of town, however much the slow but relentless westward expansion of London might have indicated otherwise. The Elizabethan map takes in St Giles and the beginning of 'the way to Uxbridge' but no more: the Restoration maps hardly get even that far, though Soho, Piccadilly and St James's districts were then burgeoning. Rocque's plan of 1747 gets just to the gallows site but no further, the Edgware Road at once disappearing off at an angle. No question of the tiny village of Paddington appearing half a mile or so up the road: Paddington, entirely surrounded by pastures and with only a small, scattered and entirely farming population, was definitely not London. Even Horwood's plan, some fifty-odd years later, goes no more than a couple of hundred yards further west of the Edgware Road junction, where an overflow burial ground had been established in 1767 for St George's of Hanover Square, as if in further confirmation that this was territory only fit for the dead.[2] The plan does not reach north as far as the new canal or yet Paddington church and green; indeed, the very name Paddington seems to have been still generally applied to a rural district rather than to its insignificant centre. When the poet William Blake wrote famously of 'Albion's Fatal Tree' – the

gallows – and associated it with 'mournful, ever-weeping Paddington' he was evoking an image not so much of a place as of empty,
rainswept fields.

The hamlet of Paddington, unlike St Giles-in-the-Fields, seems to
have had oddly little history – which is one reason, among several,
why this book does not deal with the site of the Crossrail works
at Paddington station. The settlement does not appear in the
Domesday Book. The land for miles around belonged for centuries
to the Abbot of Westminster, and later the Bishop of London, who
let it to cow-keepers. No religious house was established there, nor
yet a grand mansion. The vicar in charge of the spread-out parish
got little remuneration. No prominent or well-to-do sixteenth- or
seventeenth-century inhabitants are recorded: no Colets, no rich
merchants, no Lady Dudleys; the district was simply too far from
town. Stow does not mention it, nor did it appear in the edition of
his work revised and augmented in the eighteenth century by Strype.
Neither John Evelyn nor Pepys ever seem to have visited Paddington,
for why should they? Someone[3] – who did actually write *Paddington
Past and Present* in the mid-nineteenth century, by which time the
arrival of the railway had changed everything, including the perception of what the name 'Paddington' indicated – remarked of the
recent past that:

> although the people of Paddington lived at so short a distance
> from the two rich cathedral marts of London and Westminster,
> they made apparently no greater advances in civilisation than
> did those who lived in the most remote villages in the English
> shires.

By the end of the eighteenth century just a few moneyed people had
settled in newly built houses round the pretty Green with its cows and
milkmaids (as in the song 'Pretty Polly Perkins of Paddington Green').
These included Charles Greville, the founder of the Royal Horticultural

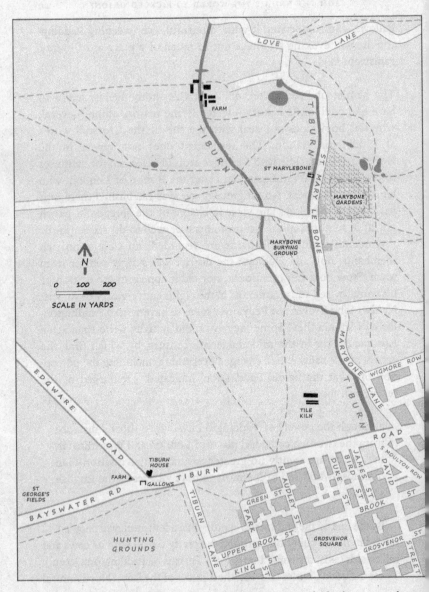

'The way to Oxford' through the Tyburn crossroads, *c.* 1750, the built–up area shown in darker grey

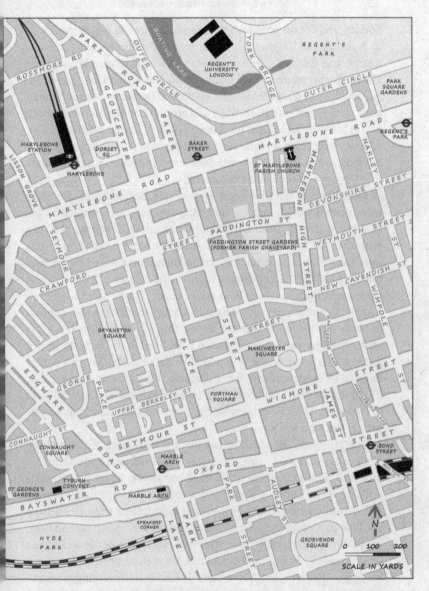

Oxford Street, Marble Arch and Marylebone districts today, with Crossrail

Society, and his supposed niece Emma who was to achieve celebrity as Nelson's Lady Hamilton. There were other renowned gardeners nearby, and the actress Sarah Siddons was a neighbour at Westbourne Green, further north by the Harrow Road. But these mild signs of civilisation did not place Paddington on any of Dickens's boyhood itineraries, those great tramps through and around London and its outlying parts that were to inform his later work. It is hardly surprising that, when George Pocock made his unwise decision in the 1820s to acquire building lots in a still-more remote location further up the Edgware Road, the speculation failed to take off.

But although the Horwood map of the beginning of the nineteenth century stops short at including Paddington, it is full of signs of coming change. Portman Square was completed in 1784, the very year after the gallows had been definitively removed, and, as if this removal were a sign of release, streets then soon covered all the land on the north of Oxford Street right to the Edgware Road. By 1815 Connaught Place had been built on the corner near where the gallows had been, and where previously had stood a small farm that appears in some old prints of Tyburn. When this was demolished, a great quantity of human bones is said to have been found beneath it. My guess is that most of these would have dated from Tyburn's earlier days as an execution site, when Catholic martyrs in particular met brutal deaths there. Today, nearby, in the middle of Hyde Park Place, in a convent labelled 'Tyburn Shrine' over the door, nuns pray in perpetuity for their souls.

The Horwood map also shows just the beginning of this terrace along what was to become the Bayswater Road, and a sprinkling of individual houses running north in ribbon development up the western side of the Edgware Road, with a collection of apparent cottages called Tomlins New Town. However, it is noticeable from other maps the best part of twenty years later that not much progress had been made in the intervening time. This may have been partly due to the lull in building during the Napoleonic Wars that in many places was made good soon after, but a Revd J. Richardson, writing a generation later in the mid-nineteenth century (*Recollections*, 1856), was of the opinion that people continued to be wary of the place's former associations:

Ragged fields stretched across scores of acres of ground . . . In fact, this part was a blank in the improvements of London for years after other suburbs had been built upon; and it was not until comparatively recent date that the tea-gardens, and other similar low haunts of debauchery, gave way to the elegant and stately buildings with which it is now covered.

It is reassuring to know that low haunts of debauchery, even of a modest tea-garden kind, found a place here, on land that had till then been so empty but was now the significant edge of town. It may have been a mistake to try to market the proposed new estate as 'Tyburnia' (a name which has now entirely disappeared) but eventually development did get going. Thackeray, who lived in one of the new streets as a young man in the late 1830s, wrote in middle age:

What a change in a century; nay, in a few years! Within a few yards of that gate[4] the fields began . . . behind the hedges of which highwaymen lurked and robbed. A great and wealthy city has now grown over those meadows.

He also noted that, if a hanging were to be carried out there by the time he was writing:

The windows would be closed, and the inhabitants would keep to their houses in sickening horror. A hundred years ago people crowded there to see the last act of a highwayman's life, and made jokes on it.

Victorian refinement was in the ascendant. The preferred term for the whole new district was now 'North Kensington', though it never acquired quite the cachet of Kensington proper which developed on the far side of the park. A celebrated later-nineteenth-century *Punch* cartoon showed one fashionably dressed Kensington matron telling another: 'No, I don't know the lady. She lives in one of the wildest parts of Bayswater.'

In practice, the railway that arrived not far from Paddington church and Green in the late 1830s, hijacking their old name for itself, and making that district a part of London town for the first time, also put paid to the idea that Paddington would ever rival Mayfair, Belgravia or the elegant estates north of Oxford Street. The writer cited by Walford in 1853 could waffle on about 'a city of palaces, sprung up here within twenty years' and how this was due to 'a road of iron, with steeds of steam' that had brought Paddington into the metropolis, but in practice railways tended to lower the social tone of an area, and a big station attracted (and attracts today) that same 'debauchery' that the Revd Richardson complained about. There tends to be a trade-off between convenience and exclusiveness: Pearson's choice of Paddington station as the western terminus for his Metropolitan Railway in the 1860s simply confirmed the surrounding district's non-aristocratic status. Praed Street, running along the south of the station, is hardly a select area even today; and although the adjoining terraces now attract wealthy tenants, for decades in the mid-twentieth century they were notorious for a kind of louche poverty, complete with prostitutes and corrupt, rack-renting landlords.

Had Brunel been able to carry his Great Western line further into town, to link up with the London and Birmingham at Euston (as he originally hoped and planned), then the whole of London west of the Edgware Road might have grown up differently. The eventual tube map would have taken another form, the Circle line might be a north–south oval rather than an east–west one, and Crossrail would not now be routed through Paddington.

As it is, Crossrail continues its journey west from Bond Street, running just south of the old route westwards which the Central line follows. Crossing near the top of Park Lane, it runs under a segment of the park, and then swings northwards at the level of Victoria Gate and Hyde Park Gardens. Just near Victoria Gate is a long-standing pet cemetery. It was originally the back garden of the late-nineteenth-century gatekeeper in Victoria Lodge, who endeared himself to local children by selling lollipops and ginger beer. One April, in 1881, a well-to-do family whose children regularly played in the park asked if they might bury a beloved Maltese terrier in his garden, and the gatekeeper agreed. The following year the garden received the body of a small dog from Mayfair belonging to the Duchess of Cambridge, and after that many other local families made requests concerning dogs, and also cats, which were regularly granted. The gatekeeper seems to have made a modest business of it, seeing to the burials himself and taking orders for uniformly styled headstones, till the entire garden resembled a Lilliputian Highgate or Kensal Green. It was shut, quite full, in 1903, but survives today, and can be visited by special appointment with the Royal Parks.

On the first detailed plans that were produced of Crossrail's trajectory, complete with proposed new buildings on the surface and areas that were to be used as work sites and storage places for vehicles, it looked as if part of this cemetery would be appropriated for a ventilation and access shaft. By 2012, however, when the works had begun, the plans had been slightly changed and engineering techniques were modified: the pet cemetery, its inmates and their loving inscriptions remain undisturbed. Since the present account has come upon bones of many kinds, from those dead of long-extinct plagues, those savagely hacked and dispersed in the interests of True Faith, those packed many deep into sanctified if foetid churchyards, those whisked away by railways in the cause of Progress, and those (like Roach Smith's cat) illicitly tucked into already overburdened earth, it seems right to record the rescue from oblivion of this most peculiarly English of resting places.

Oxford Street runs for well over a mile. While the section between Bond Street and our present-day Marble Arch was taking a long time to be appropriated as part of London, much of the rest of it was already a flourishing shopping place. In 1786, only three years after the removal of the gallows at the far end but when the section west of Marylebone Lane was being laid out with smart terraces, a German visitor, Sophie von La Roche, wrote in her journal:

We strolled up and down lovely Oxford Street this evening, for some goods look more attractive by artificial light. Just imagine, dear children, a street taking half an hour to cover from end to end, with double rows of brightly shining lamps, in the middle of which stands an equally long row of beautifully lacquered coaches, and on either side of these there is room for two coaches to pass one another; and the pavement inlaid with flagstones, can stand six people deep and allows one to gaze at the splendidly lit shop fronts in comfort. First one passes a watch-maker's, then a silk or fan store, now a silversmiths, a china or glass shop. The spirit booths are particularly tempting, for the English are in any case fond of strong drink. Here crystal flasks of every shape and form are exhibited: each one has a light behind it which makes all the different coloured spirits sparkle. Just as alluring are the confectioners and fruiterers, where, behind the handsome glass windows, pyramids of pineapples, figs, grapes, oranges and all manner of fruits are on show.[5]

Clearly this had now become London's smartest place for commerce, helped along by street lighting from the lavish use of oil lamps (a luxury before centrally organised gas lighting began to creep into London in the next century) and by the recent importation of a method of obtaining fair-sized sheets of window glass: the old-fashioned shop windows of the City and Holborn had had tiny, leaded panes often marked by glass-blowing distortion. But even as the nexus of fashion and wealth moved westwards along Oxford Street, the eastern end was beginning to decline. In 1772 there had been opened on the south side a grand Assembly Rooms designed by James Wyatt, which were intended to be the kind of venue for smart evening amusements that were provided in the summer in gardens such as Ranelagh. With its rotunda said to be based on that of Hagia Sophia in Constantinople and its elegant decorations and lofty pillars, the building was much admired and was christened the Pantheon. However, by 1780 its moment of high fashion had apparently passed, for entrance fees were lowered and the entertainments on offer were less select. It became a theatre but changed hands a number of times, was burnt out and rebuilt, failed to get a certificate from the Lord Chamberlain as an opera house, and by the 1830s had become a bazaar, before sinking to further indignity as a storage warehouse for wine later in the century.[6]

Adjoining Soho, too, had long gone into gradual decline. The owners of the very grand houses, such as seventeenth-century Monmouth House and Falconberg House which had been the beginning of Soho Square, and the elegant one of the same vintage that still graces the corner of the square with Greek Street, had moved off to Piccadilly, Belgravia or Mayfair. So had the rich gentry who had populated Greek, Dean and Frith Streets from the early eighteenth century. In their place was a substantial colony of refugees from France and their descendants, respectable but hardly aristocratic. Assorted foreign legations were sited there, and doctors, lawyers, auctioneers and moneylenders plied their trades in front rooms.

We have a perfect image of this kind of occupation, and of what appears to be the very corner house in the first years of the nineteenth century, when it was briefly the refuge of a boy of seventeen who would go on to earn some celebrity as a writer. Thomas De Quincey, who grew up mainly in the Manchester area, had already lost the sympathy of his family (and a promised guinea a week allowance) by setting off to tramp round Wales and failing to keep in touch. He borrowed some money to get to London and, once there, tried to get some more from a lender whom he believed, rightly or wrongly, was in a position to obtain it from a dubious lawyer. The lawyer did not share this view but, when De Quincey reached the point of destitution, allowed him to sleep at night in the business premises. This house is described as being 'at the . . . corner of Greek Street, being the house on that side the street nearest to Soho Square'.[7] The lawyer himself spent every night at a different address, apparently from fear of arrest: 'Of his whole strange composition I ought to forget everything,' De Quincey wrote long after, 'but that towards me he was obliging, and, to the extent of his power, generous.' This was the house in the winter of 1803:

The house was not in itself, supposing that its face had been washed now and then, at all disrespectable. But it wore an unhappy countenance of gloom and unsocial fretfulness, due in reality to the long neglect of painting, cleansing, and in some instances of repairing.

The place appeared desolate enough to be uninhabited, but in fact 'it already had tenants through the day, though of a noiseless order, and was destined soon to increase them'.[8] De Quincey moved in, and discovered that there was already another informal lodger, possibly a servant of some kind:

a poor, friendless child, apparently ten years old; but she seemed hunger bitten; and sufferings of that sort often make children look older than they are. From this forlorn child I learned that she had slept and lived there alone for some time before I came; and great joy the poor creature expressed when she found that I was in future to be her companion through the hours of darkness.

The two of them had a cloak to cover them, and 'an old sofa-cover, a small piece of rug, and some fragments of other articles' and took to sleeping huddled together for warmth.

De Quincey's principal companion in his homelessness, however, was nearer to his own age:

Being myself, at that time, of necessity a peripatetic, or a walker of the streets, I naturally fell in more frequently with those female peripatetics who are technically called street-walkers.

One, called Ann, a year or so younger than himself, became a particular friend:

For many weeks I had walked, at nights, with this poor friendless girl up and down Oxford Street, or had rested with her on steps or under the shelter of porticos.

He learnt her sad and typical story of seduction, false promises and abandonment, and tried without success to get her to seek recourse from a magistrate. When he was ill, and fainted, she rushed off and:

> in less time than could be imagined, returned to me with a glass of port-wine and spices, that acted upon my empty stomach . . . with an instantaneous power of restoration; and for this glass the generous girl, without a murmur, paid out of her own humble purse.

He yearned to do good by her, and when at last family wheels turned, and his own affairs began to sort themselves out, he made plans to help her. He needed to leave London for what he thought would be a brief period.

> She who was parting with one who had little means of serving her, except by kindness and brotherly treatment, was overcome by sorrow, so that, when I kissed her at our final farewell, she put her arms about my neck, and wept without speaking a word.

De Quincey believed he would be back in a week but he was detained much longer, so Ann's evident forebodings were justified. Having missed a series of carefully arranged meetings with her on consecutive evenings, he never found her again.

> If she lived, doubtless we must have been sometimes in search of each other, at the very same moment, through the mighty labyrinths of London . . . During some years I hoped that she *did* live . . . I must have looked into many myriads of female faces, in the hope of meeting Ann. I should know her again amongst a thousand . . . Now I wish to see her no longer, but think of her, more gladly, as one long since laid in the grave . . . taken away before injury and cruelty had blotted out and transfigured her ingenuous nature, or the brutalities of ruffians had completed the ruin they had begun.[9]

De Quincey's time of trial was now over.

So then, Oxford Street, stony-hearted stepmother, thou that listenest to the signs of orphans, and drinkest the tears of children, at length I was dismissed from thee!

Five years later, he was on friendly terms with Wordsworth, Coleridge and Leigh Hunt, and moved into Wordsworth's old cottage in the Lake District. But his boyhood ordeal in London had one permanent consequence. It was there that he started taking the opium that was later to play a dominating part in his life and work. He claimed that a college acquaintance had recommended it to him as a remedy for toothache, and that it had been readily obtainable from a chemist in Oxford Street near to the Pantheon.

He recounts in *Confessions of an English Opium-Eater*, which ironically has become his best-loved and best-remembered work, that he revisited Soho Square many years later, and found that the old house where he had spent his nights:

is now in the occupation of some family, apparently respectable. The windows are no longer coated by a paste composed of ancient soot and superannuated rain; and the whole exterior no longer wears an aspect of gloom. By the lights in the front drawing room, I observed a domestic party, assembled, perhaps, at tea, and apparently cheerful and gay.

That actual building became the headquarters for the Westminster Commissioners for Sewers (the same gentlemen who visited the inhabitants of Church Lane, St Giles, in 1849), then a Metropolitan Board of Works office used by Sir Joseph Bazalgette when he was constructing the Embankment, then a hostel for destitute women called the House of Charity. Today, known as the House of St Barnabas, it is both the headquarters of a charity for the homeless and the premises of a successful club which subsidises this. Since the new Crossrail line runs directly under the house, its seventeenth-century foundations and the fine plaster mouldings that were installed by an eighteenth-century resident have been extremely closely monitored.

A passage from the concluding paragraph on 'Ann of Oxford Street' runs:

> Successors too many to myself and Ann have, doubtless, since then trodden in our footsteps, inheritors of our calamities. Other orphans than Ann have sighed; tears have been shed by other children; and thou, Oxford Street, hast since those days echoed to the groans of innumerable hearts.

The homeless street-sleepers, whom De Quincey so nearly had to join in his own time of destitution, virtually disappeared from the capital for much of the twentieth century, but since the 1980s have materialised again, like figures from a past that had been comfortably imagined to be over. Today – or rather, tonight – some of the shop doorways of this famous shopping street, which still draws foreign visitors as it did Sophie von La Roche when it was new and shiny, will hold human forms huddled in quilts, lying on pieces of newspaper or cardboard.

De Quincey's view of the quarter of London in which he arrived as a complete stranger and in which he suffered is inevitably imbued with his own sense of alienation. Other evidence from the same period, however, suggests a more humdrum and cheerful district, though one already subsumed into the restless commercial heart of London. There is also the fact that Regent Street, with its elegant colonnades, began to be laid out from 1813, and this, as was intended, gave greater form and definition to a West End that had been developing rather haphazardly. The creation of Oxford Circus (then called Regent Circus) at the point where the new, fine street intersected with Oxford Street probably helped to raise Oxford Street's sagging tone.

Early in the Napoleonic Wars three houses on the north side of Soho Square, between Charles Street and Dean Street, had been reconstructed by a supplier to the army as a storage warehouse – one of the long Crossrail platforms, that will link the main underground ticket

Trix at the Bazaar

hall with the new west hall alongside Dean Street, now runs under a corner of the site. After the war the now-wealthy army supplier converted the warehouse into the Soho Bazaar. Sellers of jewellery, millinery, gloves, lace, baby clothes, toys, lamp shades and the like could rent stalls by the day to display their wares. The stalls were originally intended for the widows and daughters of officers who had died in the great battles with Napoleon, and much of the merchandise was handmade. One can imagine the atmosphere of brave gentility that pervaded the place. Later, however, when this Bazaar had become a much-loved fixture of Victorian London, it seems to have been more representative of the unprecedented buying power of the comfortably-off middle classes. It figures in a popular children's book of the time,[10] *A Six-Years' Darling, or Trix in Town* (1880):

> When Mr Western led Trix by the hand into the Soho Bazaar, the child thought herself in fairyland . . . It was all like a wonderful dream. There were dolls almost as big as herself, and enormous rocking-horses, dolls' houses and butchers' and grocers' shops. There were pretty Swiss clocks, in which, when the hour struck, a little trap-door opened and out came a tiny bird that nodded and said 'Cuckoo!' in quite a friendly manner, and there were boxes that wound up and played a number of pretty tunes. There were mice that ran round a table, and rabbits that beat on drums.

Rather earlier, Charles Dickens, whose father was, notoriously, in and out of debtors' prison like poor George Pocock, had relatives established near the Soho Bazaar. His uncle ran a coffee shop at 35 Oxford Street, close to Charles Street, and his grandmother spent her last years there. A cousin had a draper's shop directly opposite, by Rathbone Place; and Charles himself spent two periods of his young life living near at hand just up Newman Street in what was then called Norfolk Street.[11] He was a child of Rochester and Chatham but also of the old Marylebone that, by the time of his birth, was covered in streets and with an infiltration of light industry. Furniture-making was a speciality of the area, and so of course were dressmaking and millinery, to supply all those well-lit Oxford Street shops. In *Nicholas Nickleby* the Mantalinis' pretentious dressmaking establishment, where Kate is sent to work, appears to be in or just off Oxford Street. So are the lodgings that the respectable John Jarndyce takes for his young relatives for extended periods in *Bleak House*, but one may suppose that these are rather further west in what was then (and still is) the most prestigious section of the street.

By the mid-nineteenth century Soho was becoming still less of a residential quarter: it was infected perhaps by St Giles, so nearby across a narrow road that was not yet the divider that Charing Cross Road would eventually become. St Giles, with its big working-class population, was a centre for minor ironwork and also for brewing. There was a huge brewery just to the north-west of the High Street, on the corner where the Dominion cinema now stands – from which a vast beer flood had surged in 1814 when the iron hoops holding the vats together began to give way in chain reaction. The vats may have been manufactured locally, for later nineteenth-century insurance maps show a mass of small industries in the immediate area: barrel-making, tin-box making, printing, frame-making, bedsteads, billiard table covers . . . There was also a bacon-curing business almost directly opposite the church, which must, like the brewery with its hops, have been rather smelly, but this was not the only trade of this kind in the immediate district. In the 1850s Crosse & Blackwell, the pickle manufacturers, established offices and a bottling works on the east side of Soho Square, where Falconberg House had once stood, and extended the premises in the 1880s.

Crosse & Blackwell were still there in the early twentieth century, but by the time Crossrail was being planned – and Soho was associated rather with restaurants, sexual services and the film industry – their presence had long been forgotten. But the Crossrail engineers, excavating a deep basement near the site of the Astoria theatre, found it full of Crosse & Blackwell pots and jars. Some of them are said to have been still tightly lidded with their preserves intact inside them, which may be something of a new urban myth, though one would like it to be true. Of all the things hidden in London earth that have briefly seen the light of day once more due to Crossrail – numerous human remains, a medieval reservoir, Roman horses' sandals, skates made of bones, Venetian glass, part of a comic chamber pot – pots of fish paste and pickled onions that are still good to eat are surely among the strangest.

CHAPTER XIII

The Mind's Eye

Forget the spreading of the hideous town;
... And dream of London, small, and white, and clean,
The clear Thames bordered by its gardens green.

So wrote William Morris who, among his many other concerns
with traditional arts and crafts, founded in 1877 the Society for the
Protection of Ancient Buildings. One may wonder if London was ever
quite as 'white and clean' as he envisaged, in a medieval world where
large dungheaps, like crippled beggars, were a fact of daily life, but it is
indisputable that certainly up to the late seventeenth century 'gardens
green' ran from large houses on the Strand down to a river Thames
that was still vibrant with edible fish, and the City itself still contained
garden plots behind some of the houses. And although, by the same
period, anxieties were already being raised about the amount of smoke
London was generating and its likely effect on gardens and orchards,
well over a hundred years later Wordsworth could still write[1] – on
what one must suppose was an early Sunday morning in summer, with
no soap-boilers or breweries at work:

This City now doth, like a garment, wear
The beauty of the morning; silent, bare,
Ships, towers, domes, theatres and temples lie
Open unto the fields, and to the sky;
All bright and glittering in the smokeless air.

Over the following century the smokeless air was progressively
dimmed and tainted as the fields receded, giving way to further and
yet further building developments as far as the eye could see and much
further. By the late-Victorian era the population of London had
expanded from rather less than one million to almost seven times
as many, as outlying hamlets such as Chelsea, Fulham, Paddington,
Kilburn, Kentish Town, Hackney and Bow were swallowed whole and
the urban bandwagon pushed relentlessly on into country districts till
then unknown to London map-makers or cab-drivers. The sheer volume of smoke emitted by such an accumulation of traditionally English
open domestic hearths burning bituminous coal, not to mention all the
railway lines, shunting yards and minor industries pouring their own
soot-laden clouds into the air, created a polluted atmosphere unique in
the world. From the mid-century on, references to the famous fogs of
London, usually derogatory but sometimes even admiring as if the fog
were a function of London's special role as world metropolis, become
frequent in fiction. The early example which became the prototype of
these is the famous passage from the opening paragraph of *Bleak House*
(1852–53), located in the lawyer-land of Holborn Hill, in which the fog
and attendant dirt are real in themselves but also symbolic of the evils
of urban life in general and of financial and legal dealings in particular:

> Smoke lowering down from chimney-pots, making a soft black
> drizzle with flakes of soot in it as big as full-grown snowflakes –
> gone into mourning, one might imagine, for the death of the sun.
> Dogs, indistinguishable in mire. Horses, scarcely better; splashed
> to their very blinkers. Foot passengers, jostling one another's
> umbrellas, in a general infection of ill temper, and losing their
> foot-hold at street-corners, where tens of thousands of other foot
> passengers have been slipping and sliding since the day broke (if
> this day ever broke), adding new deposits to the crust upon crust
> of mud, sticking at those points tenaciously to the pavement, and
> accumulating at compound interest.
>
> Fog everywhere. Fog up the river, where it flows among green
> aits and meadows; fog down the river, where it rolls defiled

among the tiers of shipping, and the waterside pollutions of a great (and dirty) city.

Seventy years later, this same theme of the inherent physical and spiritual dirtiness and dimness of a still-vaster London is taken up in T. S. Eliot's *The Waste Land*. The city is rendered 'unreal' by 'the brown fog of a winter dawn' which has become, some pages later, the brown fog 'of a winter noon'. Over the intervening decades, artists as eminent as Whistler and Monet had rather revelled in the visual effects produced by London's murk. The French photographer Camille Silvy, who set up shop in London in the mid-century, arrived expecting interesting effects of gloom and achieved them. His famously evocative photograph of a man and a boy in a foggy twilight under a street lamp was in fact

Twilight, 1859, by Camille Silvy

carefully constructed from several different negatives. The sinister literary concept of London as 'vast, immense . . . rain-sodden, smelling of heated iron and soot, smoking continuously into the foggy air . . . in a perpetual twilight'[2] became fixed in the minds even of writers who had never visited the place. Meanwhile, late-nineteenth-century novelists who did know London well harped on the badness of its weather and the noisiness of its traffic – though there is no objective evidence that either had become worse than it had been earlier in the century. Jane, the wife of Thomas Carlyle, was complaining about deafening traffic noise already by the 1830s. In *The Nether World* (1889), George Gissing was writing of a Clerkenwell that had, by then, been extensively Improved, with numerous slum alleys obliterated, Holborn Viaduct cutting across the Fleet valley, the Fleet itself imprisoned in pipes, and broad Metropolitan Board of Works streets such as Clerkenwell Road driven across the ancient geography of the district. The lot of the poor was also considerably better, by and large, than it had been at the start of Victoria's long reign. Yet Gissing's description is – as the book's title suggests – of some daemonic underworld of the spirit peculiar to London's unique size:

> It was the hour of the unyoking of men. In the highways and byways of Clerkenwell there was a thronging of released toilers, of young and old, male and female. Forth they streamed from factories and workrooms, anxious to make the most of the few hours during which they might live for themselves . . . Along the main thoroughfares the wheel-track was clangorous; every omnibus that clattered by was heavily laden with passengers; tarpaulins gleamed over the knees of those who sat outside. This way and that the lights were blurred into a misty radiance; overhead was mere blackness, whence descended the lashing rain. There was a ceaseless scattering of mud; there were blocks in the traffic, attended with rough jest or angry curse; there was jostling on the crowded pavement. Public houses began to brighten up, to bestir themselves for the evening's business. Streets that had been hives of activity since early morning were being abandoned to silence and darkness and the sweeping wind.

You may feel that Gissing, a lover of traditional literature, could have reflected that 'the wind and the rain' of life were hardly peculiar to London and had been lamented centuries before by Shakespeare. But H. G. Wells, a writer of far more elastic imagination than Gissing, had a similar view of the:

> huge dingy immensity of London . . . something disproportionately large, something morbidly expanded, without plan or intention, dark and sinister. (*Tono-Bungay*, 1909)

Arnold Bennett, at the same period, in spite of coming from a heavily industrial area of England himself, had a similarly apocalyptic view of the great metropolis – which, by this date, had an army of what we would call commuters pouring in and out of it each day:

> Often [the train] ran level with the roofs of vague, far-stretching acres of houses – houses vile and frowsty, and smoking like pyres in the dark air.

A dozen years, and a Great War later, Bennett's specifically London novel, *Riceyman Steps* (1923), still harps on the theme of London's noise, dirt and general inhumanity:

> Below him and straight in front he saw a cobbled section of Kings Cross Road – a hell of noise and dust and dirt, with the County of London tramcars, and motor-lorries and heavy horse-drawn vans sweeping north and south in a vast clangour of iron thudding and grating on iron and granite, beneath the bedroom windows of a defenceless populace.

* * *

I am not the first person to point out that, by some odd twist of the collective consciousness, the post-First World War view of England in general, and London in particular, seems to have become tainted by that war. It is almost as if the mud, cold, fear and pessimism that were experienced by those fighting in Flanders had transferred something of their essence back home. Inter-war novelists as disparate as George Orwell, Graham Greene, J. B. Priestley and Patrick Hamilton all denigrated London, as if there were some moral imperative to do so. We are very far here from the cheerful sense of being at ease when going about a large city that infuses the boyhood diaries of John Thomas Pocock a hundred years before. In the ladies' hostel where the frustrated secretary in Priestley's *Angel Pavement* lives, it is a standard conversational habit for the inmates to agree that life is 'foul', the weather 'revolting' and their own presence in London somehow an unfair imposition on them.

Hamilton (1904–62) emerges as the classic novelist of the London he perceived as the 'vast, thronged, unknown, hooting, electric-lit, dark, rumbling metropolis' (*Twopence Coloured*, 1928). In addition (and like George Gissing, a forerunner whose work he admired) there is a touch of the apocalyptic in his view, a suggestion that some End of Days is surely on its way:

> In the murky dusk of evening, it was a turbulent and terrifying spectacle which met her eyes and smote her ears. She had never seen so many desperate buses, and blocked cars, and swarming people, in her life. In all the teeming, roaring, grinding, belching, hooting, anxious-faced world of cement and wheels around her it really seemed as though things had gone too far . . . that these days were certainly the last days of London, and that other dusks must soon gleam upon the broken chaos which must replace it.

The novel from which this comes is the third of Hamilton's semi-autobiographical trilogy *Twenty Thousand Streets Under the Sky*. Published in 1934, its title is *The Plains of Cement*, though the editors had wanted to call it *Off Tottenham Court Road*, a name which would have been more to the point and, for any Londoner, more resonant. We are back here, once again, in the territory of

St Giles High Street, Seven Dials, Oxford Street and Soho, the present-day centre of London and of Crossrail's major future junction.

The 'she' of the extract is Ella, a barmaid, and the 'broken chaos' that is to come is not a prediction of the London Blitz, which still lay half a dozen years in the future, but rather a hint of the inherent inner chaos of Hamilton's own alcohol-fuelled life: a slightly later book was entitled *Hangover Square*. The major female character in the trilogy is Jenny, a servant girl with an appetite for fun who turns to prostitution – we have been here before, in this same network of streets. Prostitution characterised St Giles in the eighteenth century; by the beginning of the nineteenth Thomas De Quincey was wandering nightly in the side lanes of Oxford Street with his street-walker friend Ann. George Gissing, after his first disastrous marriage with a prostitute, made a barely more suitable one with a working-class girl he picked up at the Oxford Theatre, which was a music hall on the corner of Oxford Street and Tottenham Court Road.

Hamilton seems to have had something of a lifetime preoccupation with what, in youth, he liked to refer to quaintly as 'mixing with low-life courtesans . . . It's been my ambition to write about harlots. I have two first rate novels'.

Long after, describing the London of the late 1920s, he wrote:

Prostitution, in fact, was just then approaching its heyday – the collapse of the 1926 strike having put the working class into a mood of dejection, apathy and submissiveness . . . more women upon the West End streets than perhaps, ever before.[3]

There may have been an element of romanticism and wishful thinking here, for Hamilton had already invented his fictional Jenny before he actually met her real-life prototype in the form of a good-time girl called Lily Connally (whom he shared with a couple of other literary men). But the sense of the same kind of human encounter being enacted through the generations and even the centuries in the same streets, the same pavements tramped again and again, is a powerful one. When I was in my teens, before the Street Offences Act of 1959, ladies in very high heels, more or less respectably dressed but with a cigarette always cocked between their fingers, still loitered in ones and twos after dark in the doorways of Charing Cross Road and in the Soho and Seven Dials side streets off Shaftesbury Avenue. It was unwise to dawdle there yourself, or you would be taken for one of the same kind and propositioned by some furtive would-be customer.

But the image of London that progressively darkened from the late nineteenth century till well after the Second World War bred, in turn, its own redemptive visions. The spreading 'hideous town' identified by the early Socialist Morris was taken up by other dreamers, movers and shakers, more specifically by the Fabian Society. Since literature lasts longer than theory, much of what the Fabians thought is now dust, but their dream as enshrined by the children's writer E. Nesbit[4] in her time-travelling *The Story of the Amulet* (1906) speaks to us across a century with a rueful poignancy. In this book the four indomitable children, who have already appeared in previous tales, travel mainly into the distant past to seek a lost talisman, but on one occasion they go into a future that cannot be more than forty years ahead at most. They leave behind in their own time a day on which:

> the sky was grey, the street was foggy, a dismal organ-grinder was standing opposite the door, a beggar and a man who sold matches were quarrelling at the edge of the pavement on whose greasy black surface people hurried along.

By the power of their magic amulet, they find themselves inside the nearby and recognisable British Museum. This is merely 'lighter and brighter somehow' than the museum they are used to, but when they emerge:

> They blinked at the sudden glory of sunlight and blue sky. The houses opposite the Museum were gone. Instead there was a big

garden with trees and flowers and smooth green lawns . . . There
were comfortable seats all about and arbours covered with roses.

The idyllic description continues, replete with white statues, plashing
fountains, silvery-clean pigeons and Japanese lamps among the trees.
People are hatless, and wear clothes of:

bright, soft colours and all beautifully and very simply made . . .
Men, as well as women, seemed to be in charge of the babies and
were playing with them.
   The streets were wide and hard and very clean. There were
no horses, but a sort of motor carriage that made no noise.
The Thames flowed between green banks, and there were trees
at the edge, and people sat under them, fishing, for the stream
was clear as crystal . . . There was no smoke.

The William Morris dream incarnate. On the hatlessness, the motor
carriages, the lack of smoke as such and also on some degree of social
levelling and participant fatherhood, one has to say that Nesbit got it
right. But when you think what the area near the British Museum – the
south part of Bloomsbury close to New Oxford Street – was actually
like forty years on from her book, and what London and its inhabitants had then recently undergone, the heart quails. 1946 . . . Only the
flowers, that sprang up surprisingly quickly on the rubble-piled bomb
sites behind St Giles church, reddish rosebay willowherb and yellow
yarrow, would reflect, as if in mockery, Nesbit's improbably peaceful
rose-gardens.

But in the mind's eye even the prosaic urban landscape of greater
London could be transformed. Cities do not, in practice, kill the heart
and the imagination as they are sometimes said to, but provide in
themselves the kinetic energy to transcend dingy reality. Already,
in the mid-seventeenth century, in a London battered by the effects of
the Civil War and visited by plague, the mystic cleric Thomas Traherne
could write:

The Dust and Stones of the Street were as precious as GOLD: the Gates were at first the End of the World . . . And young Men Glittering and Sparkling Angels, and Maids strange Seraphic Pieces of Life and Beauty! Boys and Girls Tumbling in the street, and playing, were moving Jewels. I knew not that they were Born or should Die; But all things abided Eternally.

A hundred years later another visionary, William Blake, famously claimed that 'if the doors of perception were cleansed then everything would appear to man as it is, Infinite'. While excoriating 'each dirty street / Near where the dirty Thames does flow' Blake could conjure up an extraordinary mirage of the then-outskirts of expanding London as a quintessential Albion, a new Jerusalem:

The fields from Islington to Marybone,
To Primrose Hill and Saint John's Wood,
Were builded over with pillars of gold,
And there Jerusalem's pillars stood.

Pancrass & Kentish-towne repose
Among her golden pillars high,
Among her golden arches which
Shine upon starry sky.

Needless to say, however, given Blake's apocalyptic view, Jerusalem falls – 'from Lambeth Vale / Down thro' Poplar & Old Bow' as death and woe supervene. What would he have made of post-Second World War Stepney?

During much of the nineteenth century, as the engines of Progress whirled ever more noisily, the visionary tradition in London seems to have gone underground. But it surfaces again with an odd and appealing figure, Arthur Machen, who was born in Wales in 1863, the son of an ill-paid clergyman, and who developed a fervent belief in seeing beyond the prosaic with 'unsealed eyes'. He settled in London, leading a hand-to-mouth existence as a freelance writer, moved in Bohemian and literary circles, dabbled in Celtic Christianity and Grail legends, and was for a while a journalist on the *Evening News*. Finally he achieved his one great popular success with a short story, 'The Bowman', which was the fictional original of the enduring Angels of Mons myth in which British troops were helped by phantom archers from the Battle of Agincourt. A generation ago, when there were old soldiers of the First World War still alive, you could find some who would swear that they had themselves witnessed figures in the clouds above the battle-field of Mons, so perhaps the unsealed eyes are indeed a reality if they seem so to the beholder.

Not Machen's best-known work, but one of the most interesting, was written when he was already in his seventies. It is a novella which he called simply *N* and which recounts the apparently magical trans-formation of a dull piece of London townscape: it is a story within a story. The narrator says that he has found – on a bookstall in the Farringdon Road – a book by a mid-nineteenth-century clergyman called 'Meditations in the Streets of the Metropolis'. In this supposed account, the clergyman tells how he has visited a reclusive devotee of mystical philosophy in the then-distant suburb of Stoke Newington. Asked to look out of the window of the mystic's rooms he sees 'exactly what I had expected to see' – the terrace of similar houses opposite. But when asked to look again he finds to his amazement:

> a panorama of unearthly, of astounding beauty. In deep dells, bowered by over-hanging trees, there bloomed flowers . . . I saw well-shaded walks that went down to green hollows bordered with thyme . . . bubbling wells . . . architecture of fantastic and unaccustomed beauty.

He rushes excitedly out into the street – only to find that the row of houses is back again and the street trees leafless in the cold March air. The mystic turns out to have escaped from a private lunatic asylum.

In the story, the narrator tries to replicate the clergyman's experi-ence but without success. The tale ends with deliberate inconclu-siveness. Is the suggestion that the (invented) clergyman might have glimpsed through the veil of time one of those Great Houses that once sat in the countryside north of the City and would have been familiar to Thomas Cromwell, to Lord Mayor Thomas Roe, to the Gunpowder plotters and to Paul Pindar?

(I should so very much like to be crossing Bishopsgate or St Giles High Street at some unaccustomed hour, at dead of night perhaps or unnaturally early one summer morning, and suddenly catch sight, however fleetingly, of a fine, timbered house, and hear a clop of hooves towards it. Or even a thatch-roofed hovel, with a donkey cart at the door, and a passing whiff of woodsmoke, old oyster shells and dirty straw . . .)

But perhaps the vision described by Machen is simply a might-have-been, and he wanted to suggest that the capacities of human perception, once 'cleansed' in Blake's words, are limitless? Like De Quincey, he himself believed that on long rambles through London he had sometimes found streets that did not exist on any map. Today, he is regarded as one of the founders of psycho-geography. The only nagging flaw in N is that Machen seems to have envisaged the district of Stoke Newington as it was by the early twentieth century, shabby and grey. Yet if the clergyman was supposedly writing in the 1850s, apparently of an experience that took place still earlier, Stoke Newington was then still a flowery village where one might indeed glimpse in reality a big old garden.

There have been many twentieth-century urban dreams, townscapes which did not not get created, but lingered long on the drawing boards and in the ambitions of architects, town planners and politicians. Many of these took to heart – too much – the stereotype of London as dirty, dismal, dark, mean, rain-sodden, smoke-polluted, traffic-jammed, sinister, tawdry, hideous (add adjectives at will) and were determined to build a Brave New World. The concept of Blake's New Jerusalem was indeed never far from the minds, and sometimes even the lips, of those who fantasised about gleaming white towers set in green expanses, kept firmly apart from all those nasty but essential cars (for whom huge and elaborate road-systems must of course be built) and inhabited by a grateful populace. *'We have not an abiding city, but we seek after the city that is to come.'*

The truth that the white towers, once created, soon lost their gleam and revealed themselves as inconvenient and unnatural places to live, that green spaces without a designated use degenerated into littered and dangerous no man's lands, and that Londoners began to rise up in furious demonstrations against having their familiar townscape carved up and wrecked by motorways – these facts are too well known today, seventy years on from the Greater London Plan, to need labouring. The disasters and near-miss disasters of post-war planning have intermittently haunted this book. I have already mentioned the systematic destruction of Stepney, along with a whole way of life that had been sheltered there. A similar huge mistake occurred south of the river, where the bomb-battered but still-living quarter of the Elephant and Castle was turned into little but a series of traffic roundabouts. A comparable fate was initially planned for the Angel, Islington; but fortunately, by the time the 'Motorway Box' that was a key part of the scheme began to be drawn on London maps, public opinion was running so strongly against such destructive reshaping that all but a small section of the intended ring road – today's Westway – was abandoned.

Which brings us back once again to St Giles-in-the-Fields and the genesis of Centre Point, that anomaly of a skyscraper on thirty-four floors sitting in a part of London that, however built-up, has otherwise retained a human and traditional scale. Centre Point, too, owes its existence to an aborted traffic scheme, though with the going-on of time few commentators seem to realise this.

Briefly, the Second World War brought an abrupt fall in the notional value of land in London. Bizarre as it now seems, the idea that even land in many parts of central London, let alone buildings, was not actually worth very much persisted for years after the bombs had ceased to fall. A number of obscure businessmen were canny enough to take advantage of this. By the 1950s Harry Hyams, son of a bookie, who had joined an estate agent's, was quietly buying up properties in that corner of London and doing deals with other new-style developers.

The fact that the LCC's Plan was to create a roundabout at the bottom of Tottenham Court Road – which then, like nearly all London roads, carried two-way traffic – gave Hyams his big chance. Much of the property around St Giles had been bought up already by rival developers called Pearlberg. The LCC tried to buy it from them for its road scheme, but the Pearlberg family refused because the valuation on the buildings had been set at pre-war rates and now, in the mid-1950s, with post-war planning restrictions being at last lifted, true property values were rising. Hyams at this point stepped in. He proposed to the LCC that he would himself acquire the Pearlberg properties, and others as necessary, and then, out of this composite holding, donate land to the LCC for their roundabout – on condition, naturally, that they would give him planning permission for what he wanted to build. With what seems today remarkable ease, the LCC agreed to this, and even allowed the area covered by the planned road system to be included in the height-to-plot-size ratio for permitted building. This is how Hyams, and his architect Seifert, ended up with permission to build something exactly twice as high as would otherwise, under prevailing regulations, have been permitted.

Because the LCC were so fixated on the supposed need for a roundabout, the whole business seems to have been conducted with considerable discretion and latitude. A knowledgeable commentator on planning matters,[5] writing almost as the building was completed, remarked:

> Hyams' extreme aversion to publicity has paid big dividends in terms of his business. Had he spilt the beans, it is doubtful whether Centre Point . . . would ever have been built.

Extraordinary as it may now seem, purchasers of properties were not then required to reveal their intentions for the site to the owners who were selling them, though legislation to remedy this came in very shortly afterwards. Many of the old buildings round St Giles were bought when permission to redevelop had already been given, but the owners were not made aware of this. Nor were Londoners in general, and nor even were the Royal Fine Arts Commission. This body was supposed to be consulted by the LCC in respect of any substantial building or one planned for a significant location. Centre Point would obviously qualify on both counts, but the Commission heard nothing about it during the crucial period when objections could have been raised – probably because council officers guessed what the Commission would think of a skyscraper next to St Giles church. Many indignant protests were made when half St Giles High Street began to be knocked down, but they came too late.

The building of Centre Point progressed slowly, owing to the cramped unsuitability of the site. By the time it was finished in 1967 concepts of traffic management had moved on, and the new Minister of Transport had changed the road layout to a one-way scheme. The roundabout which had been Centre Point's entire justification was

St Giles 'Resurrection' Gate, Centre Point behind, 2015

now useless. For the past fifty years the roadway around it has had no purpose except as a stand for buses and – recently – a parking place for Crossrail vehicles. A local-authority notion of reinstating Tottenham Court Road for two-way traffic seems to be in abeyance as I write, but may surface again.

For many years after its completion the skyscraper was notoriously left un-let while its value went up and up with London's continuing property boom, and thus a tax-free gain accrued to the owner. Various urban-conspiracy myths about it circulated, including one about the government paying Hyams a hefty subsidy to keep it empty for possible use during a nuclear attack. What use a skyscraper, even an air-conditioned one, would be in such circumstances was never clear. It was occupied by squatters at one point (they are said to have subverted the security men) and this created useful publicity for a separate organisation for the homeless calling itself Centrepoint but based in Soho. Eventually some sections of the tower were let to various commercial organisations and to the Confederation of British Industry; and more recently a private club has been run on the top three floors. In late 2014 a deal was negotiated, attended by a certain amount of acrimony, that the entire block should become 'luxury flats'.

That the Brave New World visions of the mid-century town planners should now be embodied in what has been called 'a monument to planning incoherence and greed' is a sad irony. The only positive thing to be said about it is that the semi-destruction of the line of ancient St Giles High Street was one of a number of factors that put the nascent conservation movement on its guard against other re-development plans – in particular the government-sponsored scheme c. 1970 to demolish ninety-six acres of historic Covent Garden. This was defeated by popular campaigning, and – further irony – Covent Garden's preserved market buildings are now the commercial success story of London.

Harry Hyams was still alive while this book was in preparation. In retirement he occupied a Stuart mansion in Wiltshire that was built about the time that Lady Dudley was living in the old Master's house near St Giles church. He still appeared averse to publicity, but near the beginning of 2015 he surfaced momentarily into newsprint objecting to a country neighbour, a fellow millionaire, building a nine-bedroomed house on land over which he, Hyams, claimed shooting rights. His objection did not appear to have been successful, and one may hope that his death at the end of the year has brought closure to the matter.

Visions come in different forms with the changing times. The London vision of the last few years has been Crossrail.

The dream had an origin of a kind all of seventy years ago, when rail tunnels through the centre of London were envisaged as part of the London Plan by its principal creator, Sir Patrick Abercrombie. This idea harked back to Charles Pearson's unfulfilled dream of a central London rail terminus where the various railway companies could unite, but the rise of the motor car as mass transport through the 1950s distorted what was left by then of the tattered Plan, and tunnels, except as underpasses on main roads, were out of fashion.

Although tube lines had been lengthened to distant suburbs in the first few decades of the twentieth century, no new tube was constructed through the centre in the fifty years between 1910 and 1960. Then the much-appreciated Victoria line was built, serving such hitherto little-regarded places as Tottenham and Brixton, followed in the 1970s by the Jubilee line. This took over one northern branch of the Bakerloo line, but its extension south-eastwards to Bermondsey and onwards improved another part of London which had been starved of good transport connections. As I write there are plans in the air for a further extension for the Bakerloo line beyond the Elephant and Castle, to reinvigorate parts of south London that have long lost their Victorian train stations. The popular belief is that when the tube map first began to take shape class snobbery was involved, with an idea that trams were good enough for the working classes south of the river – but the fact is that the sandy ground on that side of the Thames is not easy to tunnel. Specialised 'slurry' machines have had to be used for boring the tunnel at the end section of Crossrail that runs down to Woolwich and Abbey Wood, and it was only decided to carry the line this far when the works on the rest of Crossrail were already under way. For a while, the plan was that the line would terminate at Custom House in the rebuilt Docklands area.

The whole question of just where Crossrail should run and even what its prime purpose should be has not been entirely stable. The post-war plans were for some sort of east–west cross trajectory, but numerous alternative routes were proposed at intervals over the years as London reconfigured itself piecemeal, socially and geographically, in ways that the dreamers had not envisaged. The name 'Crossrail' first seems to have been used in a study put out by the Greater London Council and the Department of the Environment in 1974, and by then eyes were being turned towards Paris where the new, deep, fast underground, the RER, was being constructed. However, in London numbers using the Tube actually declined slightly in the 1970s and early 1980s. This was before the capital became the major destination for foreign tourists that it is today, and it was also the period of greatest enthusiasm for American-style commutes by car from distant homes. It was a time of road-widening, of claims that unless this was energetically pursued 'London will become gridlocked by the year 2000', and of solid, decent blocks of flats being demolished in Farringdon Road to create a multistorey car park.

It was not really till 1988, when the Bedford-to-Brighton line was established, utilising the old Metropolitan route through Farringdon and reopening Snow Hill tunnel, that the true value of cross-London routes became apparent to all. Soon after, a Central London Rail Study brought the idea a little more into focus, with both British Rail and London Underground now keen on the project. In 1990–91 the two organisations joined forces to bring a private bill to Parliament for a line from Paddington to Liverpool Street: Crossrail as we see it emerging today was taking its shape. The government rejected the bill on grounds of expense, but made sure the proposed route was safeguarded.

By 2000 the administrative decor had changed; it was now the Strategic Rail Authority and Transport for London who were the bodies concerned, but in the next two years, in the words of someone who had been waiting eagerly on the sidelines, 'the project really came together'. Route options began to be seriously appraised and funding was studied by the Treasury. It is not within the remit of this book to go into the details of this, but it is worth pointing out that Crossrail is the one example, in recent times, of the City of London actually donating a large sum of money towards a project. Cynics have remarked that many of the City names were so hermetically enclosed within their own well-paid carapace that they supposed the main purpose of Crossrail was to carry them and their cronies at Canary Wharf swiftly to Heathrow and back. Indeed a number of Londoners, disgruntled by having to walk round Crossrail diggings and put up with the temporary closure of various changing-points on the Tube, nurse the same grumpy misperception to this day.

But what exactly was the core purpose of Crossrail thought to be, apart from the obvious one of providing an efficient route through central London? The original detailed route-plan as drawn up in 2003 has, a dozen or so years on, a quaint air, like some Victorian fantasy of a never-built railway from Highgate cemetery. At that time, with the rerouting of the Eurostar line from Dover via a non-place christened Ebbsfleet, to Stratford East and thence to St Pancras, there was much focus on international travel: the idea of a line essentially between Ebbsfleet and Heathrow airport seemed likely to find favour. Since at each end of the main London section the Crossrail line is required to split into two (twice as many trains are scheduled to run through the centre as on the outlying sections) the west side needed an alternative destination to Heathrow, and it was thought this should run down to Richmond and Kingston. This proved extremely unpopular, however, with the citizens of that prosperous part of London, who felt no need for it, and the projected usage rates did not justify the expense. So the current plan evolved, that of carrying the western section from Paddington on towards Maidenhead and possibly as far as Reading, with just a spur line from Hayes and Harlington off to Heathrow airport. Thus it has remained, though as this book has been written there has been a running question about a potential new station and further development at Old Oak Common between Paddington and Acton, near Wormwood Scrubs. There are also occasional flurries of fancy about a true alternative westward branch from there towards Watford. Or possibly Aylesbury . . . Other suggested railway lines, still in a notional, ghostly state, hover in the air, including the much disputed High Speed Two (HS2) to Birmingham and points north. Far less spectral and more generally welcomed are the developing plans for a 'Crossrail Two' running north-east to south-west, due to intersect with Crossrail One at Tottenham Court Road. The route for it, including variant possibilities, is already safeguarded – and, needless to say, already giving rise to a few protests. I do not, however, expect to be still writing when, long years ahead, it may become a reality.

The government's own Crossrail bill began to make its tortuous way through both Houses of Parliament in 2005, and finally the Act was passed, in spite of a recent and abrupt downturn, in the national economy in July 2008.[6] Construction began in May 2009, with impressive numbers of workmen from all over the United Kingdom, and has, by and large, proceeded on time and without mishap. Since then, the Crossrail organisation has been putting out on the Internet regular reports full of facts and figures – length, height, depth, tons of earth removed, methods and progress, along with bulletins on the health of the lovingly named, thousand-ton tunnel-boring machines, 'Phyllis' and 'Ada', 'Victoria' and 'Elizabeth'. The four and a half million tons of deep-down London soil that Phyllis and her sisters have gradually cast back behind them have been taken nightly on lorries from Old Oak Common and several other portals. They have been transported out of London by barge – the old methods proving useful once again – then downriver, to a remote spot on the Essex marshes across a creek from Burnham on Crouch, called Wallasea Island. Here, the earth that has supported, far down, so many of the houses, shops, churches, streets, markets, gardens and graveyards that figure in this book will be used to create a wetland bird reserve.

In the meantime, the idea that Crossrail is somehow intrinsically connected with international travel has receded, possibly because it has been noticed that Stratford International station has turned out something of a white elephant. Before the bill reached Parliament, the proposed branch to Ebbsfleet was cut back to Dartford, but that was still felt to be too expensive since it would involve a new river crossing. Finally the plan was settled for an ending at Abbey Wood, with a much-wanted next-to-last station belatedly agreed at Woolwich. Future growth of London may one day cause the original extension to a burgeoning Ebbsfleet to be reinstated. But essentially the concept of passengers on Crossrail travelling from one distant suburb to another destination equally far from the centre of London has been understood to be unrealistic. While some will do this, most will use Crossrail as an efficient way of getting from the outskirts to certain main central destinations, and, within London, as an alternative to the existing tube lines with their frequent stops. The Crossrail trains, or what is now to be called the Elizabeth line, will be about twice as long as the traditional tube trains, and so, correspondingly, will the platforms – which is why the new station at Tottenham Court Road has entrances as far apart as Centre Point in the east and Dean Street off Soho Square in the west. Farringdon station similarly extends to the Barbican, and Liverpool Street to Moorgate. As the population of London continues to grow, and the existing tube trains become noticeably more crowded at most hours of the day and evening, the simple concept of an extra route and congestion relief through central London begin, to seem Crossrail's most solid and pragmatic achievement.

I do not think I can do better, finally, in this account than repeat the words written by John Hollingshead at the end of his book *Underground London*, in which he hailed the arrival of the metropolis's very first buried railway, almost the first in the world, in 1863:

> These works, like all alterations and repairs, will give employment to many, and be a nuisance to others, as long as they are being constructed; but when the mess is cleared up, and the new channels are thrown open, a sense of comfort and relief will be felt throughout the vast general traffic of London.

Notes

Introduction

1. This appeared first in an article, then was incorporated in a book, *Living London*, in 1906.

Chapter I: Coming into London

1. *The Diary of a London Schoolboy 1826–1830*, John Thomas Pocock.
2. The Embankment, placing a barrier between the lanes from Fleet Street and the Thames, would not be built for another generation.
3. Walham Green was where Fulham Broadway now joins North End Road.
4. The present station was not opened till the 1850s.
5. By the Middle Ages, the jurisdiction of the Corporation of London had spread beyond the City walls into the adjoining areas on the Westminster side – the Liberties of London.
6. Named after a wealthy goldsmith, William de Farringdon, who acquired it in 1281 as his personal fief.
7. There is some evidence that a far more ancient, indeed pre-Roman track, between Silchester in Hampshire and Colchester in Essex, ran along this route before London even existed. See W. F. Grimes, *The Excavation of Roman and Medieval London*, 1968.
8. Paddington station marks the limit of the gravel shelf.

Chapter II: The Engines of Progress

1. Simon Winchester, *The Map that Changed the World*, 2001.
2. Charles Kingsley, *The Water Babies*, 1863.
3. Quoted by Richard Altick in *Victorian People and Ideas*, 1974.
4. Christian Wolmar.
5. In the biblically literate nineteenth century, this phrase would at once have evoked Jacob's dream of a ladder between Heaven and Earth. See Genesis 28, v. 10–19.
6. Demolished in 1847.
7. Nicholas Barton, *The Lost Rivers of London*, 1962.
8. This point is made on an impassioned and authoritative website: www.londoncanals.co.uk/rivers/flto2.htm.
9. Plans to extend the line to South Kensington in the west and to Tower Hill in the east, with the idea that the two ends would curve round and meet underneath the new Thames Embankment, were prepared as soon as the first line opened.
10. The full story may be found in *Mr Briggs' Hat* by Kate Colquhoun, 2012.
11. This Dalston, Haggerston and Shoreditch section now, after decades of abandonment, forms part of the much-appreciated East London Overground line, which links with Whitechapel, Wapping and Rotherhithe and thence with a swathe of south-east London.

Chapter III: The Underground in the Mind

1. See *The Journey of Martin Nadaud*, Gillian Tindall, 2000.
2. 'An Underground Tragedy', by C. Hadden Chambers, in *Belgravia: A London Magazine*, December 1886.
3. 'The Mysterious Death on the Underground Railway'.
4. Robert Browning, 'The Pied Piper of Hamelin', 1842.
5. From 'East Coker', in *The Four Quartets*.
6. 'South Kentish Town' in *The Cynthia Asquith Book*, 1948. In recent years this story has become more widely known and has been cited as if it were true. In fact, it is based on a few brief lines about such a mishap that Betjeman saw in a local newspaper, and Mr Basil Green himself and his awful experiences are invented.

7. Translated by Norman Denny as *Fattypuffs and Thinifers* in 1941.
8. Peter Ackroyd, *London Under*, 2011.

Chapter IV: The High Road and the Low Road

1. See Chapter XIII.
2. See Chapter XII.
3. 'Megaproject as Keyhole Surgery, London's Crossrail', in *Built Environment*, vol. 37, No. 1.
4. St Barnabas House. See Chapter XII.
5. Myths tell of him living in a cell or a cave, lame from a royal hunting incident, succoured by the milk of a tame hind, and resisting the invitation of the penitent King to accept more comfortable lodgings.
6. *A Survey of Cornwall*, 1602.
7. Siegfried Sassoon, 'Memorial Tablet', 1918.
8. *A Brief Chronicle Concerning the Examination and Death of Sir John Oldcastle Out of the Books and Writings of those Popish Prelates Which were Present.*
9. The Second Epistle of St Paul to Timothy.
10. The song has been more specifically associated with the Jacobite rebels of 1745, some of whom were hanged in London and whose bodies were exhibited on the road north. But the concept of the fairy route long pre-dates that uprising.

Chapter V: 'No Man may by the Eye discern it'

1. There are varying views on the derivation of the name, but I think this is the most probable.
2. As I write, it is being examined prior to its removal back to its original site.
3. I am indebted both to Stephen Myers and to the archaeologists of the Museum of London for this conclusion.
4. The convention of the bird's-eye view cum street plan, sophisticated and skilled in its way but odd to our modern perception of what a map should be, was to last for another hundred years, only being superseded by two-dimensional, carefully surveyed plans after the Restoration. Ralph Tresswell's meticulous, late-Elizabethan Surveys were of small areas only.

5. Three of the St Botolphs remain today, at Bishopsgate, Aldersgate in the west, and Aldgate in the east. The fourth one, just outside Billingsgate, by the Thames, was destroyed in the Great Fire of London and not rebuilt.

6. When permission was granted for the White Hart's virtual destruction – only a cosmetic sliver of façade grafted onto the side of a modern tower is to be retained – those consulted about this decision somehow failed to register that the inn's original medieval cellars, which had remained much as they were while the other floors were built and rebuilt above them through the centuries, were still intact. They were destroyed in early 2015 by deep piling.

7. Had the wall, in the sixteenth and seventeenth centuries, still been regarded as a truly defensive structure, it would in any case have been rebuilt further out as London expanded, as were the successive walls of old Paris.

Chapter VI: Going East

1. Crossrail's intention at one point was to locate a substantial shaft for the removal of spoil between Hanbury Street and Brick Lane, but equally substantial protest from the Spitalfields Trust and from various influential local residents caused the plan to be modified.

2. I am indebted to Dan Cruickshank and to the Gentle Author of the SpitalfieldsLife blog for this recondite piece of information.

3. Some commentators, not apparently noticing the geographical progression that follows the rhythmic one, have suggested instead St Mary-le-Bow in Cheapside, but this seems to me illogical as a final destination.

4. Latimer was not executed himself for his semi-involvement in the Pilgrimage of Grace, though the risk that he might be was great at one point. He died quite soon afterwards. He was the second husband of Catherine Parr – she who, for her third venture into marriage, became the sixth and last wife of Henry VIII.

5. I am indebted to the East End History Group for this research.

6. Cromwell's only son, Gregory, survived his father by eleven years. Presumably the reason he was not made Cromwell's principal heir was that he had married into the wealthy family of Jane Seymour, Henry's third wife.

7. See Chapter X, Note 1.

8. The almshouses, rebuilt by the Mercers' Company in 1856 as 'Lady Mica's Almshouses', are there on the same plot today, but are in the care of the local authority.

9. According to C. S. Truman, *Mile End Green: Famous Residents and their Association with Historic Events*, the East London History Group, 1968.

10. I am indebted for this to Ian Grimble, *The Harrington Family*.

Chapter VII: 'Man goeth to his long home'

1. I am grateful to Stephen Porter for pointing this out to me.

2. See Chapter II.

3. Quoted in *Broadgate and Liverpool Street Stations*, compiled by Rosehaugh Stanhope.

4. You cannot, of course, get to Liverpool from it, only to east coast sea-ports.

Chapter VIII: St Giles Before the Fall. And After

1. One or two eminent commentators have located Tom-all-Alone's across the river in Southwark. While there were nests of dilapidated houses there too, this identification makes no sense in the novel's geography, either actual or symbolic. In any case, Dickens the novelist is thought to have fed in extra impressions from a slum he knew in his Chatham childhood.

2. *A Mirrour of Christianity, and a miracle of charity; Or, A true and Exact Narrative of the Life and Death of the most Virtuous Lady ALICE, Dutchess DUDDELEY.*

3. Anthony Wood, antiquarian, scholar and herald.

4. See also Michael Harrison, *London Beneath the Pavement*, 1961.

5. Oliver Plunkett, Archbishop of Armagh.

6. Those curious enough to wonder why I think I know exactly where Hollar was living in the 1650s and early 1660s are invited to consult my book *The Man who Drew London*, 2002, and also the *Survey of London*, vol. 5, part II.

7. *Loimographia: an Account of the Great Plague in London in the year 1665.* The original print-run probably went up in flames in the Great Fire of 1666, in the crypt of St Paul's, along with the stocks of most London book and print dealers, but it was finally reprinted for the Epidemiological Society of London in 1894.

Chapter IX: 'The Imperious Demands of Public Necessity and Convenience'

1. See the Introduction by Marjorie Holder to *The Diary of a London Schoolboy*, 1980 edition.
2. Addition made by John Thomas Pocock when he recopied his diary some years later, far from home.
3. St Leonards, to the north of Bishopsgate, is meant.
4. See Note 2.
5. H. J. Dyos.
6. See Chapter VII.
7. I am indebted to the Gentle Author of SpitalfieldsLife for this further piece of information.
8. See Chapter VII.

Chapter X: A Convenient Spot for the Habitation of Mariners

1. Marchant Alexander Gliddon, who lived between 1819 and 1869, and seems to have been associated with the Baptist ministry.
2. I am indebted to Dr David Sankey for revealing this family connection to me.
3. According to Gliddon, *op. cit.*
4. I am indebted for this information to Henry Fitzhugh, a descendant of their American cousins.
5. I am indebted to Derek Morris, of the East London History Society, for this figure.
6. Quoted by Samantha L. Bird, *Stepney: Profile of a London Borough from the Outbreak of the First World War to the Festival of Britain*, Cambridge thesis, 2011.
7. From an unattributed cutting in Bishopsgate Institute Library.
8. Ian Nairn.

Chapter XI: Favoured Slums

1. I am indebted to Ruth Richardson for these details.
2. Today the pub has long gone, but the modern building on the site incorporates a small statue of the Boy on its façade.
3. See *The Italian Boy* by Sarah Wise, 2004, which recounts the murder of a young member of Clerkenwell's immigrant population.
4. I am indebted to Alec Forshaw for these details.

Chapter XII: From the End of the World to Pickled Onions

1. Lord Macaulay.
2. Two hundred years later, town planners and a number of MPs tried to get this now-abandoned graveyard released for flats to be built on the whole of it, but met with such substantial opposition from Bayswater residents and other influential people that they backed down. Today, the remains of 'St George's Fields', still with their old railings, form a decorative garden complete with a fish pool, for the five blocks that did get built behind.
3. A Mr William Robins cited by Walford.
4. Cumberland Gate: the way into Hyde Park. The name is remembered today in the Cumberland Hotel.
5. As quoted in *A London Year*.
6. The name 'Pantheon' survives in the branch of Marks & Spencer now on the site.
7. It is often said that this *is* the house where Dr Manette and his daughter lodge in Dickens's *A Tale of Two Cities*, and the street alongside has been renamed accordingly. However, nothing in the novel links the tale explicitly to the house or to its exact location: it is described as being 'not far from Soho Square' rather than on it, and in the late eighteenth century a number of houses in Soho would still have had 'a courtyard where a plane-tree rustled its green leaves' at the back. A novel, however dependent on realistic touches, is (it should be said) an invented tale.
8. In fact the owner of the house at that location was then a Mr Mowbray, who had acquired it on marrying a widow who had inherited it from her first husband. When he died a few years later, Mrs Mowbray was declared to be 'a lunatic', so it seems doubtful they would have been

living domestically in the house themselves. I am indebted to Catherine Dille for locating these obscure references for me.

9. Cynical readers may feel that it was perhaps just as well De Quincey did not meet poor Ann again. Much later in the century, another sensitive, depressive and talented future writer, George Gissing, became fatally entangled with a young prostitute whom he insisted on marrying in order to 'rescue' her. The consequences were not happy. See *The Born Exile*, Gillian Tindall, 1974.

10. By 'Ismay Thorn', whose real name was Edith Caroline Pollock.

11. I am indebted to Ruth Richardson for establishing these details.

Chapter XIII: The Mind's Eye

1. 'Upon Westminster Bridge', 1802.

2. J. K. Huysmans, *À rebours*, 1883.

3. Quoted in *Patrick Hamilton*, Sean French, 1993.

4. Enid Nesbit, the wife of Hubert Bland, who edited the Fabian Society's journal, was a fervent believer in equality and fairness, and a lifelong friend of H. G. Wells, Sydney and Beatrice Webb and George Bernard Shaw.

5. Oliver Marriott, *The Property Boom*, 1967.

6. It has, alternatively, been suggested to me that the financial crisis of early 2008 actually helped the bill along, as Crossrail was seen by many in government as a means of providing employment and reflating the economy; but one may feel that, by this time, the project was almost decided anyway.

Select Bibliography

It would be difficult to identify all the materials that, in addition to the archival sources listed in the Acknowledgements, have over the years contributed to my knowledge of the districts and people covered in this book. I have made much use of general works of reference, such as the *Oxford Dictionary of National Biography*, various volumes of the *Victoria County History* and *The Survey of London* volumes, and of nineteenth-century back numbers of *The Times*, the *Illustrated London News* and *The Builder*. In addition, the books, articles and a few manuscripts listed below have all made a contribution. So have the regular updates on the progress of construction, posted on the Crossrail website. I have benefited greatly also from the publications of the London Topographical Society, which has, over the years, made available in an accessible form many street plans of different periods, in addition to other London-related materials.

Books

(the place of publication is London unless otherwise stated)

Andrew, Jonathan, and others, *The History of Bethlem*, 1997

Anon., *Broadgate and Liverpool Street Station*, published by Rosehaugh Stanhope Developments and the British Railways Board, 1991

Anon., 'An Old Sanitary Reformer', *What Shall We Do with Smithfield?*, 1851

Arnold, Catharine, *Bedlam: London and its Mad*, 2008

Barber, Peter, *London: A History in Maps*, London Topographical Society with the British Library, 2012

Barton, Nicholas, *The Lost Rivers of London*, Leicester, 1962

Beaglehole, J. C., *The Life of Captain James Cook*, 1974

Bennett, Arnold, *Riceyman Steps*, 1923

Boghurst, William, *Loimographia: An Account of the Great Plague of London in the Year 1665*, ed. Joseph Frank Payn for the Epidemiological Society of London, 1894 (reprinted 1979 and 2013)

Brett-James, Norman, *The Growth of Stuart London*, 1935

Brown, Walter E., *A Short History of St Pancras Cemeteries*, 1896

Burton, Edwin H., *London Streets and Catholic Memories*, 1925

Carroll, Lewis, *Alice's Adventures Under Ground*, 1864, facsimile ed. Dover Publications, NY, 1965

—*Alice's Adventures in Wonderland*, 1865

Colquhoun, Kate, *Mr Briggs' Hat: A Sensational Account of Britain's First Railway Murder*, 2011

Cox, Jane, *London's East End, Life and Traditions*, 1994

Defoe, Daniel, *A Journal of the Plague Year*, 1722, revised edition 1962

Denford, Steve and Hayes, David (eds), *Streets of St Giles: A Survey of Streets, Buildings and Former Residents in a Part of Camden*, Camden History Society, 2012

De Quincey, Thomas, 'Ann of Oxford Street', from *Confessions of an English Opium-Eater*, 1821

Derbyshire, Nick, *Liverpool Street: A Station for the 21st Century*, Granta, 1991

Dickens, Charles, *Bleak House*, 1852–53

—*Dombey and Son*, 1846–48

—*Great Expectations*, 1860–61

—*Nicholas Nickleby*, 1838–39

—*Oliver Twist*, 1837–39

—*Our Mutual Friend*, 1864–65

—*The Pickwick Papers*, 1836

—*Sketches by Boz*, 1836

—*A Tale of Two Cities*, 1859

Dobie, Rowland, *The History of the United Parishes of St Giles in the Fields and St George Bloomsbury*, 1829

Dominik, Mark, *A Shakespearean Anomaly: Shakespeare's Hand in 'Sir John Oldcastle'*, Alioth Press, 1991

Edwards, Percy J., *A History of London Street Improvements 1855–1897*, LCC publication, 1898

Elborough, Travis and Rennison, Nick (compilers), *A London Year: 365 Days of City Life in Diaries, Journals and Letters*, 2013

Eliot, T. S., *The Waste Land*, 1922

Finch, Harold, *The Tower Hamlets Connection: A Biographical Guide*, 1996

Forshaw, Alec and Bergstrom, Theo, *Smithfield Past and Present*, 1990

French, Sean, *Patrick Hamilton: A Life*, 1993

Frere, Walter Howard, *Two Centuries of Stepney History 1480–1680*, 1892

Gissing, George, *In the Year of Jubilee*, 1894

—*The Odd Women*, 1893

—*The Nether World*, 1889

Godwin, George, *Another Blow for Life*, 1864

Grey, E. C. W., *St Giles of the Lepers*, 1905

Grimble, Ian, *The Harrington Family*, 1957

Grimes, W. F., *The Excavation of Roman and Medieval London*, 1968

Hamilton, Patrick, *Twenty Thousand Streets Under the Sky*, 1934

—*Twopence Coloured*, 1928

Harrison, Michael, *London Beneath the Pavement*, 1961

Hay, Douglas, and others, *Albion's Fatal Tree: Crime and Society in England*, 1975

Hebbert, Michael, *More by Fortune than Design*, 1998

Hill, William T., *Buried London*, 1955

Holden, C. H. and W. G., *The City of London: A Record of Destruction and Survival*, Corporation of London and the Architectural Press, 1951

Hollingshead, John, *Odd Journeys*, 1860

—*Underground London*, 1862

Holmes, Mrs Basil, *The London Burial Grounds*, 1896, ed. Kessinger Legacy Reprints, 2010

Hutchings, W. W., *London Town: Past and Present*, 1909

Jones, Nigel, *Through a Glass Darkly: The Life of Patrick Hamilton*, 1991

Jordan, W. K., *The Charities of London, 1480–1660*, 1960

Lysons, Daniel, *The Environs of London*, vol. III, 1795

Mackenzie, Mary L., *Dame Christian Colet: Her Life and Family*, Cambridge, 1923

Marks, Alfred, *Tyburn Tree: Its History and Annals*, 1908

Marriott, Oliver, *The Property Boom*, 1967

Maurois, André, *Patapoufs et Filifers*, 1930, translated by Fritz Wegner as *Fattypuffs and Thinifers*

Mayhew, Henry, *London Labour and the London Poor*, 1851

McKellar, Elizabeth, *Landscapes of London: The City, the Country and the Suburbs 1660–1840*, Paul Mellon Centre and Yale University Press, 2013

Merritt, J. F. (ed.), *Imagining Early Modern London: Perceptions and Portrayals of the City from Stow to Strype*, 2001

Morris, Derek, *Mile End Old Town 1740–1780: A Social History of an Early Modern London Suburb*, East London History Society, 2002

—*Whitechapel 1600–1800: A Social History of an Early Modern London Inner Suburb*, East London History Society, 2011

Myers, Stephen, *Walking on Water: London's Hidden Rivers Revealed*, Amberley Publishing, 2011, revised edition Historical Publications, 2016

Nesbit, E., *The Story of the Amulet*, 1906

Noorthouck, John, *A New History of London*, 1773

O'Donoghue, Edward G., *The Story of Bethlehem Hospital: From its Foundation in 1247*, 1915

Palmer, Christopher, *The Collected Arthur Machen*, 1988

Parton, John, *Some Account of the Hospital and Parish of St Giles in the Fields*, 1822

Penn, Thomas, *The Winter King: the Dawn of Tudor England*, 2011

Pocock, John Thomas, *The Diary of a London Schoolboy*, Camden History Society, 1980

Pocock, Tom (ed.), *Travels of a London Schoolboy 1826–1830: John Pocock's Diary of Life in London and Voyages to Cape Town and Australia*, Historical Publications, 1996

Porter, Stephen, *The Great Fire of London*, Bramley Books, 1996

—*The London Charterhouse*, Amberley, 2009

Priestley, J. B., *Angel Pavement*, 1930

Richardson, Ruth, *Dickens and the Workhouse*, Oxford University Press, 2012

Simms, George R., *How the Poor Live*, vol. III, 1889

—*Living London*, 1906

Stow, John, *A Survey of the Cities of London and Westminster*, 1598, revised by John Strype *c.* 1720, current revised edition 1980

Tames, Richard, *Clerkenwell and Finsbury Past*, Historical Publications, 1999

Thornbury, Walter, *Old and New London: A Narrative of its History, its People and its Places*, vols I and II, 1871–73 [see also under Walford]

Thorne, Robert, *Liverpool Street Station*, Academy Editions, 1978

Truel, Madeleine and Lucha, *L'Enfant du Métro*, Paris, 1943

Tutton, Michael, *Paddington Station 1833–1854*, Railway and Canal Historical Society, 1999

Verne, Jules, *Voyage au Centre de la Terre*, Paris, 1863

Walford, Edward, *Old and New London: A Narrative of its History, its People and its Places*, vols IV and V, 1875–78 [see also under Thornbury]

Weinreb, Ben and Hibbert, Christopher (eds), *The London Encyclopaedia*, 1983

Wells, H. G., 'The Door in the Wall' (short story), 1910

—*The Time Machine*, 1895

—*Tono-Bungay*, 1912

—*The War of the Worlds*, 1898

Wilson, Derek, *Sweet Robin: Biography of Robert Dudley Earl of Leicester 1533–88*, 1997

Wise, Sarah, *The Italian Boy: Murder and Grave-robbery in 1830s London*, 2004

Wolmar, Christian, *The Subterranean Railway*, 2004

Woodeforde, the Revd James, *The Diary of a Country Parson, 1759–81*, reprinted by the Folio Society, 1992

Woodward, C. Douglas, *The Vanished Coaching Inns of the City of London*, 2009

Articles, academic papers; manuscript sources in addition to those mentioned in the Acknowledgements

Anon., 'Domesday Book', actually 'Liber Domus Dei', manuscript register compiled in 1624 of those who contributed to the rebuilding of St Giles-in-the-Fields: for several centuries in the possession of the parish but recently lodged in the London Metropolitan Archives

Anthony, Sian, 'Medieval Settlement to 18th–19th-Century Rookery: Excavations at Central St Giles 2006–8', *MOLA Study Series no. 23*, 2011

Bird, Samantha L., *Stepney: Profile of a London Borough from the Outbreak of the First World War to the Festival of Britain 1914–1951*, Cambridge thesis, 2011

Boreman, Robert, *A Mirrour of Christianity, and a miracle of charity* . . . etc., pamphlet printed 1669 on the death of Alice, Duchess Dudley, a copy in the possession of Camden Local Archives

Carrier, Dan, 'Lauderdale House and Magna Carta', *Camden New Journal*, 9 April 2015

Dennis, Richard, 'Gower Street to Euston Square: A Local History of the Underground', annotated version of a UCL lunchtime lecture given 15 January 2013

Dennis, Richard, 'Letting off Steam: The Perils and Possibilities of Underground Travel in Victorian and Edwardian London', paper delivered at the Institute of Historical Research, UCL, 17 January 2013

Gage, John, 'The Rise and Fall of the St Giles Rookery', article published in *Camden History Review*, vol. 12, 1984

Gliddon, Marchant Alexander, *History of Stepney 1819–1869*, manuscript in possession of Tower Hamlets Archive Library

Green, David, *People of the Rookery: A Pauper Community in Victorian London*, occasional paper from the Department of Geography, King's College London, 1986

Hebbert, Michael, 'Megaproject as Keyhole Surgery: London Crossrail', from *Built Environment*, vol. 37, No. 1, 2012

Hill, G. W. and Frere, W. H., *Memorials of Stepney Parish* [in fact the transcribed Stepney Vestry minutes from 1579 to 1662], 1891, held in Tower Hamlets Archive Library

Richardson, Nick, 'Heathrow to Canary Wharf', *London Review of Books*, 11 October 2012

Robinson, Simon, *Liverpool Street Underground*, manuscript paper written for PTS Consulting, 2012

Role, Raymond, 'Sir Robert Dudley Duke of Northumberland', *History Today*, vol. 53, March 2003

Sankey, David, *Worcester House, Stepney: Medieval Moated Manor House to Stepney City Farm*, MOLA publication for Crossrail Archaeology, 2015

Schofield, Nicholas, *Holborn, London's Via Sacra*, pamphlet published by the church of St Anselm and St Caecilia with Stephen Osborne, 2012

Acknowledgements

Many friends and acquaintances have offered incidental help in the course of this book, especially by suggesting the names of people to whom it might be useful to talk, or books or articles that might be relevant to my researches, or by mentioning street features that I might not have noticed. I shall not try to list them all here for fear of leaving someone out, but I am grateful to all – and you know who you are. I am similarly beholden to the three or four people who have helped me with the book's overall construction, by suggestions beforehand or by reading the completed typescript for me with a critical eye, and, as ever, to my supportive literary agent and my editor.

More specifically, a book such as this is heavily dependent on original records, and cannot be written without the existence of archive collections and the active help and interest offered by their custodians. I am particularly grateful to Camden Local Studies and Archives, which has in its charge, as well as other recondite materials, the manuscript Vestry minutes of St Giles-in-the-Fields from 1616 to 1890; and I thank particularly the archivist, Tudor Allen, for his long-standing interest in my work. I am also very grateful to the Ven. William Jacob, Archdeacon of Charing Cross and then-priest in charge of St Giles, who, along with his then-verger Mark Hodkin, delayed sending their 'Domesday Book', the church registers and various other records, to the London Metropolitan Archives in order that I might study them more conveniently in their original form in the church's Vestry room, where many of the people mentioned in Chapter VIII of this book sat disputing local matters some two and three centuries before.

Grateful thanks also to Mark Aston, Librarian of the Islington Local History Centre, especially for his store of newspaper cuttings. Thanks, too, to Colin S. Gale, the archivist of the Bethlem Royal Hospital; and also and especially to Malcolm Barr-Hamilton, the archivist of Tower Hamlets Local History Library and Archives, for his helpful suggestions and his impressive collection of property deeds. I have also made use of the extensive collections of the London Metropolitan Archive, and of those of the Bishopsgate Institute, which is particularly rich in material relating to the evolution of the Liverpool Street district. Especial thanks also to Simon Robinson, who recommended the institute's resources to me and has generously shared with me the results of his own researches.

In addition, I have benefited from the expertise of various speakers over several years at the annual local history conferences of the London and Middlesex Archaeological Society, especially Christine Steer of Royal Holloway, University of London; Harvey Sheldon of the Rose Theatre Trust; Jelena Bekvalac, curator at the Museum of London; and Nick Elsden, Chris Thomas, Sadie Watson and Alison Telfer, all of the Mususem of London archaeology department, known as MOLA.

From the start of the active construction of Crossrail, c. 2009, and continually over subsequent years, I have received kindness from a number of its employees and associates, who have been ready to talk to me, to explain things and to provide sets of maps. Among them have been Tony Bryan (Project Manager), Peter MacLennan and Simon Bennett. But I must especially mention Jay Carver of MOLA, Crossrail's Lead Archaeologist, who has been extremely supportive of my researches throughout. Gratitude, too, to his colleague David Sankey, who spared the time to walk round the Stepney Green site with me for hours discussing the layout of the successive buildings on that much-churned acre of London earth.

The plentiful maps necessary for a book about London journeys have been provided by David Wenk, for whose interest and energy and readiness to discuss each one with me I have been extremely grateful.

The prints illustrating various moments and places in London's evolution I have largely sourced from nineteenth-century editions of the *Illustrated London News*, from the similarly ancient volumes of *Old and New London* (Walford and Thornbury), from the late-eighteenth-century Lysons's *Environs of London*, from *The Gentleman's Magazine*, and from a few other books long in my possession including *Trix in Town* and the album containing the story 'South Kentish Town'. (In the 1970s, the late John Betjeman very kindly gave me verbal permission to use any material of his relating to that district.)

The photograph entitled *Gloomy Sunday*, which shows the waste-lands caused in the 1960s East End by doctrinaire redevelopment, was taken by the photographer John Claridge, who has generously allowed me to use it in this book. Seven other photographs, all recent, including one of the tomb-effigy of Lady Dudley's daughter and one of a steam train arriving in Farringdon a hundred and fifty years after the line first opened, were taken for me by my husband, Richard Lansdown, who has been consistently useful and supportive, as ever, during my assorted expeditions into Crossrail-land and in the preparation of pictorial material.

Index